PROFESSIONAL COMMUNICATIONS IN THE PUBLIC SECTOR

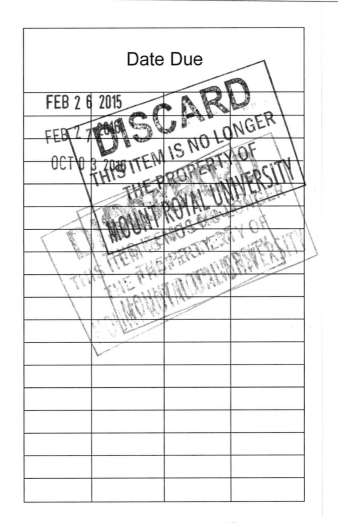

PROFESSIONAL COMMUNICATIONS IN THE PUBLIC SECTOR

A PRACTICAL GUIDE

Ted Glenn

Canadian Scholars' Press
Toronto

Professional Communications in the Public Sector
by Ted Glenn

First published in 2014 by
Canadian Scholars' Press Inc.
425 Adelaide Street West, Suite 200
Toronto, Ontario
M5V 3C1

www.cspi.org

Canadian Scholars' Press Inc. gratefully acknowledges financial support for our publishing activities from the Government of Canada through the Canada Book Fund (CBF).

Library and Archives Canada Cataloguing in Publication

Glenn, Ted, 1960-, author   Professional communications in the public sector : a practical guide / Ted Glenn.

Includes bibliographical references and index. Issued in print and electronic formats. ISBN 978-1-55130-631-5 (pbk.).--ISBN 978-1-55130-632-2 (pdf).-- ISBN 978-1-55130-633-9 (epub)

1. Communication in public administration--Canada.   2. Communication in politics--Canada. I. Title.

JF1525.C59G54 2014   352.3'840971   C2014-9049455   C2014-904946-3

Text design by Aldo Fierro
Cover design by Em Dash Design

12   13   14   15   16   5   4   3   2   1

Printed and bound in Canada by Webcom

Canada

MIX
Paper from
responsible sources
FSC
www.fsc.org   FSC® C004071

CONTENTS

PREFACE

This book addresses an important gap in Canadian post-secondary education and training related to professional public sector communications. Few Canadian colleges and universities offer courses at either the undergraduate or graduate level that help students prepare specifically for careers in professional communications in the public sector. Most programs in advertising, government relations, public relations, public administration, public policy, or public management offer at most a class or two on government communications or communicating with government.

In my view, this gap in education and training can be partially attributed to the academic community's general lack of interest in and understanding of the communications function in Canada's public sector. This is reflected in the fact that very little research has been done on the subject to date, and that which has been done has focused on the federal government in general and advertising in particular. Leading journals, such as the *Canadian Journal of Political Science, Canadian Public Administration,* and *Canadian Public Policy,* have not published on the topic in at least a decade, while Canadian public administration textbooks do not cover the subject at all and Canadian public policy texts do so in only a rudimentary fashion.

This book aims to address the current gap in professional public sector communications education and training by providing a practical, hands-on examination of how the communications function is exercised in Canada's public sector. It does not attempt or pretend to provide a systematic or theoretically contextualized treatment of the topic; rather, I have tried as much as possible to document the professional communications best practices of organizations across Canada's public sector and select non-profit organizations that have a strong public service orientation to demonstrate what new and soon-to-be professionals need to know to build successful careers in the field.

ACKNOWLEDGEMENTS

The discussion of the public sector communications function provided in chapter 1 is based on the results of a pilot project on professional communications in the federal, Ontario, and City of Toronto governments originally reported in my March 2014 article for *Canadian Public Administration*, "The Management and Administration of Government Communications in Canada." Research for this project was funded in part by the Humber College Staff Initiated Research Fund (SIRF). Thanks to Joan Arsenault for such excellent research assistance on this project. I also need to acknowledge funding provided by Humber College for the research assistance on best practices in public sector communications tactics reported in chapter 5. Thanks to Peter Armstrong for such refined judgment and exemplary research skills pulling this chapter together.

Thanks also to Daniella Balabuk and the rest of the team at Canadian Scholars' Press for taking this project on to begin with. As a post-secondary teacher first and foremost, I am heartened to have found a publisher with such dedication to providing quality teaching materials to Canadian students and their teachers.

Finally, thanks to Sara (and the rest of my family) for putting up with me while I finished writing this book. There. It's done.

INTRODUCTION

CONTENTS OF THIS BOOK

This book adopts a strategic perspective on professional public sector communications. It defines the main areas of responsibility in a new professional's communications job according to the key activities involved in strategic public sector communications, and is organized around these areas accordingly. From a strategic perspective, the main activities involved in the conduct of professional public sector communications are

- describing the strategic environment that defines and within which public sector communications takes place;
- identifying the individuals and groups that have a stake in how public sector organizations achieve their strategic goals;
- defining the objectives that communications initiatives are designed to achieve;
- crafting the key messages that organizations use to communicate with targeted audiences;
- developing a set of core tactics used to transmit key messages to targeted audiences, namely press releases, backgrounders, FAQs, letters to the editor, speeches, public events, and various Web 2.0 technologies; and
- evaluating whether and how communications activities achieve stated objectives.

Chapter Overview

Chapter 1 provides an introduction, defining the professional communications function in Canada's public sector and explaining how and for what purposes professional public sector communications is used. Using the strategic perspective mentioned above as a framework, chapters 2 through 4 of this book attempt to explain the broad environment in which professional communications takes place in Canada's public sector. Chapter 2 begins by explaining how political executives set strategic goals for public sector organizations and choose the means of achieving those goals. It concludes by showing how public sector organizations identify and assess the individuals and groups that have a stake in the goods and/or services that public sector organizations use to achieve their strategic goals. Chapter 3 focuses on explaining how public sector organizations establish clear, precise, specific communications objectives to support their broader strategic or policy goals. The chapter also explains the role that indicators and baselines play in helping organizations evaluate whether or not communications objectives are being achieved. Chapter 4 explains how public sector organizations develop key messages, which are the main points or ideas that organizations want to communicate to members of a target audience about a particular product, service, initiative, or proposal. This chapter begins with a short primer on clear writing—a cornerstone of effective message composition—focusing particularly on choice of language, organization of material, and presentation of material.

Chapters 5 through 7 describe the main tactics that public sector organizations use to achieve strategic communications objectives, with a particular focus on those tactics with which new professionals are expected to be proficient at the start of their careers. Chapter 5 showcases the suite of tactics used during almost every professional public sector communications campaign—press releases, backgrounders, FAQs/Q&As, op-eds/letters to the editor, and speeches. Chapter 6 introduces a four-step method developed by the Canada School of Public Service for managing public events such as news conferences, ministerial tours, fairs and exhibits, conferences, and open houses. Chapter 7 examines the briefing note, the most ubiquitous internal communications tool found in Canada's public sector today, with a focus on its four main variants: the information note, the meeting note, the decision note, and the issue note.

Chapter 8 showcases some of the key research tools that public sector organizations use in communications evaluation to establish baselines and populate indicators at the outtake and outcome levels, namely structured and unstructured interviews, questionnaires, focus groups, and content analysis.

Chapter 9 attempts to define what public sector communications professionals need to know about Web 2.0 technologies in order to research, analyze, communicate, and evaluate effectively in the Web 2.0 environment.

Chapter 10 provides a detailed capstone exercise that learners can use to hone their professional public sector communications skills.

Support for Teaching and Learning

This book is designed to support teaching and learning about professional public sector communications in five ways. First, each chapter begins with an overview of the content to be covered and includes specific learning outcomes that describe what learners can expect to achieve by the end of each chapter. Second, the chapters conclude with specially designed activities that learners and their teachers can use to apply the skills and knowledge covered in the chapter. Third, the chapters include annotated guides to important readings and online resources for learners who wish to access more information on covered topics. Fourth, each chapter identifies and defines key concepts that are covered; key terms are highlighted in bold in the text, and are listed at the end of the chapter. Each chapter also provides questions for critical reflection. Both are excellent resources for learners who want to ensure that they've achieved the learning outcomes set out at the beginning of each chapter. Fifth, chapter 10 concludes the book with a capstone exercise that requires learners to apply the skills and knowledge covered throughout the book in a single, integrated activity.

CHAPTER 1

AN INTRODUCTION TO PUBLIC SECTOR COMMUNICATIONS[1]

CHAPTER OVERVIEW

This chapter uses the results of a pilot study on communications in the governments of Canada, Ontario, and the City of Toronto to lay the foundation for understanding the professional communications function in Canada's public sector. It begins by defining the professional communications function in the public sector, and then draws on Howlett's policy instrumentation typology to explain how and for what purposes it is used. Next, it provides a high-level overview of how professional communications within the federal, Ontario, and City of Toronto governments is managed and administered, focusing specifically on the roles and responsibilities of key actors and institutions within those governments and the human and financial resources that are employed. The chapter concludes with a new professional's perspective on professional public sector communications.

LEARNING OBJECTIVES

By the end of this chapter, you will be able to

- define the professional communications function in Canada's public sector;
- use Howlett's policy instrumentation typology to explain how and for what purposes professional public sector communications is used;
- describe how communications within the federal, Ontario, and City of Toronto governments is managed and administered; and
- explain what professional communications looks like from a new professional's perspective.

INTRODUCTION

Each year, Canadian public sector organizations spend hundreds of millions of dollars trying to understand and communicate with a broad range of domestic and international audiences. They employ thousands of specially trained communications professionals; use a variety of short-, medium-, and long-term strategies and processes to establish communications objectives; apply a vast array of tactics (websites, news releases, advertising, public events, etc.) to achieve those objectives; and operate highly complex monitoring systems in all media (print, broadcast, and electronic) to evaluate whether those objectives are being achieved. The modern communications enterprise, in fact, pervades every aspect of public sector activity today, from decision and policy-making to service delivery, to the point that "the management of the state's communication may even rival in importance the management of the state itself" (O'Shaughnessy 2004, 172). This phenomenon is not limited to Canada: the modern public sector communications enterprise is "ubiquitous around the world, and technological advancements are spurring more sophisticated practices of monitoring, communicating with, and responding to the electorate" (Giasson, Lees-Marshment, and Marland 2012b, 241).

This book is designed to provide a practical, hands-on account of how professional communications is conducted in Canada's public sector in order to help new and soon-to-be professionals build successful careers in this important and growing field. It draws upon the best practices of organizations throughout Canada's public and non-profit sectors to illustrate what exactly new and soon-to-be professionals need to know about professional communications and how best to put that knowledge into practice.

This chapter sets the foundation for the book by addressing some key gaps that exist in current knowledge about the public sector communications function in Canada using the results of a pilot study on communications in the governments of Canada, Ontario, and the City of Toronto (first published in Glenn 2014). It begins by defining what the government communications function is and then uses Howlett's policy instrumentation typology to explain how and for what purposes it is used. Next, it provides a high-level overview of how communications within the federal, Ontario, and City of Toronto governments is managed and administered, focusing specifically on the roles and responsibilities of key actors and institutions within those governments and the human and financial resources that are employed. The chapter concludes by illustrating what the practice of professional public sector communications is like from a new professional's perspective using a fictional day-in-the-life vignette. Appendix 1.1 provides an overview of Canada's public sector for those readers who do not have a strong background in Canadian government.

1.1 WHAT IS PUBLIC SECTOR COMMUNICATIONS?

Communications is a core management function that both public and private organizations use to control the flow of information between the organization and its various internal and external audiences to help achieve strategic organizational goals. As an early textbook on the subject put it, communications is "the management function that identifies, establishes, and maintains mutually beneficial relationships between an organization and the various publics on whom its success or failure depends" (quoted in Cutlip and Broom 2012, 4).

In the public sector, Howlett (2009, 2011) suggests that communications constitutes a distinct class of instrumentation that organizations use to help achieve policy goals (see also Aday, Brown, and Livingston 2008; Pasquier and Villeneuve 2012). Building on Hood's classic governing instrument typology, Howlett argues that **public sector communications** is best understood as an information- or knowledge-based resource that is provided or withheld from societal actors to "influence and direct policy actions" (2009, 24). The Government of Canada's corporate communications policy defines the function similarly:

> As a function of good management, open and proactive communication ensures that the public receives government information, and that the views and concerns of the public are taken into account in the planning, management and evaluation of policies, programs, services and initiatives. Government communications represent a vital public service that involves both providing information and listening to the public. To develop policies, programs and services that meet the needs of a diverse public, the government must understand the environment within which it operates and respond to the concerns of the public in relevant and useful ways. (Treasury Board of Canada Secretariat 2012)

A recent study identified the following activities as the core elements of the public sector communications function in Canada today (Glenn 2014):

TABLE 1.1: CORE PUBLIC SECTOR COMMUNICATIONS ACTIVITIES

Activity	Description
Advertising	Any message planned for or purchased by a government organization for placement in newspapers, television, radio, Internet, cinema, etc.
Consultation and engagement	The use of websites, media notices, advertising, "town hall" meetings, advertising, and other vehicles to communicate and consult with an internal or external audience about a proposed or existing government initiative.
Corporate identity	The identification and maintenance of a recognizable and unified visible corporate identity throughout government buildings, facilities, programs, services, and activities.
Correspondence	The management of mail, emails, faxes, and telephone calls that a government organization receives (Thomas 2010).[2]
Crisis and emergency communications	The plans, tools, and methods that government officials use to communicate with internal and external audiences during an emergency or a crisis.
Electronic communications	The use of Internet-based tools to give internal and external audiences 24-hour access to information about government programs, services, and initiatives.
Environmental assessment	The identification and tracking of current and emerging issues affecting or likely to affect the government, as well as trends reported in the various media.
Evaluation	The efforts used to measure how and whether a specific communication activity helps a government policy or program achieve its goals or objectives and comply with internal policies and audits.
Issues management	The process of anticipating, identifying, evaluating, and responding to issues that affect an organization's relationships with key audiences (Cutlip and Broom 2012).
Marketing	The promotion of an organization's policies, programs, services, and initiatives to the public in support of its communications goals.
Media production	The production, distribution, and evaluation of motion picture films, videotapes, television programs, and interactive audiovisual and multimedia productions in support of a government organization's communications goals.
Media relations	The cultivation and management of relations with specific members of the media to promote public awareness and understanding of government policies, programs, services, and initiatives. Specific media relations tactics include key informant interviews, news conferences, op-ed writing, technical briefings, and news releases.
Partnerships and collaboration	Joint activities or initiatives that involve another company, organization, group, or individual where the partnering entities have shared or compatible objectives, contribute resources (financial or in-kind), share in the benefits, and agree to a fair allocation of risk taking.
Public events	Opportunities to inform the public about significant government initiatives or programs.
Public opinion research	The gathering of opinions, attitudes, perceptions, judgments, feelings, ideas, reactions, or views that are intended to be used to inform a government initiative, program, or service, whether that information is collected from persons (including employees of government institutions), businesses, institutions, or other entities, through quantitative or qualitative methods, irrespective of size or cost.
Publishing	All information materials—regardless of publishing medium—produced for mass distribution to internal or external audiences.
Risk communications	The plans and tactics that government officials use to anticipate and assess potential risks to public health and safety, the environment, and policy and program administration.
Spokesmanship	The presentation and explanation of government policies, priorities, and decisions to the public by ministers or designated communications personnel.
Sponsorship	An arrangement by which a government organization provides another government, company, organization, group, or individual with financial resources or in-kind assistance to support a project or activity of mutual interest and benefit.
Strategic communications planning	A medium- to high-level activity used to elaborate how all parts of an organization should interact with its external and internal environments in an integrated, intentional, and informed way.

Source: Author.

1.2 HOW IS PUBLIC SECTOR COMMUNICATIONS USED?

According to Howlett, public sector organizations use communications as an information- or knowledge-based resource to "influence and direct policy actions" (2009, 24) in two separate domains. In the **substantive domain**, public sector organizations use communications to affect change in "the type, quantity, price or other characteristics of goods and services being produced in society, either by the public or private sector" (Howlett, Ramesh, and Perl 2009, 116). Consumer product labelling requirements and exhortations to unions to manage wage increase expectations are examples of communications tools that are used at the "front end" of the substantive domain to affect how goods and services are produced. Healthy eating advertising campaigns, tourism advertising, and anti–drinking and driving campaigns illustrate how communications are used at the "back end" to change how goods and services are consumed.

In the **procedural domain**, public sector organizations use communications to affect change in how individuals and groups behave in policy processes (Howlett 2009; Howlett, Ramesh, and Perl 2009). At the front end of the domain, specific communications activities are used to affect the behaviour of actors in the agenda-setting and formulation stages of the policy process and, at the back end, during the implementation and evaluation stages. Examples at the front end of policy-making include access-to-information laws, public opinion research, and stakeholder consultations, all of which "provide policy network actors with the knowledge required to effectively filter and focus their demands on government for new policy measures or reforms to older ones" (Howlett 2009, 24). Examples at the back end include government websites, issues management, media relations, and spokesmanship, which can be used to "provide additional information to policy network members in specific sectoral or issue areas [in order to] legitimize government actions and pre-empt criticism and dissent" (ibid.).

In practice, public sector organizations use communications to achieve a blend of substantive and procedural goals, with the specific kind and exact mix of instrumentation used by any one organization determined by that organization's mandate and overall role in the public sector (see appendix 1.1 for more information on Canada's public sector). For example, at one end of the communications continuum are organizations, such as the federal **Privy Council Office** (PCO) and the Ontario Cabinet Office (CO), that have procedurally oriented mandates designed to help **first ministers** (the leader of a government cabinet) and their cabinets set the government's overall strategic directions and legitimize government actions once determined.[3] Consistent with these mandates, Glenn (2014) suggests that communications personnel in the PCO and CO work almost exclusively in areas dedicated to achieving procedural goals. PCO's Strategic Communications staff use activities such as strategic communications planning and public opinion research to influence the behaviour of actors in the agenda-setting and design stages of the policy cycle. Personnel in the PCO's Media Centre and CO's Digital Communications and Strategic New Media divisions use activities such as issues management, media relations, and spokesmanship to legitimize government action in the implementation and evaluation stages of the policy process.

At the other end of the communications continuum are organizations, such as Statistics Canada and the Toronto Transit Commission (TTC), with substantive mandates focused primarily on the production and delivery of public goods and services. According to Glenn (2014), almost all communications personnel at Statistics Canada, working in divisions such as Census Communications, Official Release and Publications, and Translation, focus on producing and disseminating all manner of statistics and analysis for Canadian and international audiences. At the TTC, all seven communications staff use communications instruments such as advertising, crisis management, and user bulletins to modify and influence transit service consumer behaviour (the back end of the procedural domain). Public Works and Government Services Canada and the Ontario Ministry of Government Services provide internal new media communications platforms such as GCpedia and OPSpedia and other internal communications services geared to disseminating information about their programs and services.

Organizations like Health Canada fall somewhere in between. Glenn (2014) reports that roughly half of Health Canada communications staff members are engaged with procedural instrumentation. Staff in the Public Opinion Research and Evaluation and the Stakeholder Information and Reporting divisions, for example, are primarily engaged at the front end of the procedural domain, using communications tools to influence the behaviour of actors in the agenda-setting and formulation stages of policy processes. Staff in the Regulatory Communications division, by contrast, are primarily engaged at the back end of the procedural domain, using communications tools to influence the behaviour of actors in the implementation and evaluation stages. The other half of communications staff at Health Canada engages with substantive instrumentation. Staff in the Food and Drugs Act Liaison Office, for example, engage at the front end of the domain using communications activities to affect change in the behaviour of producers of goods and services, while Consumer Information Bureau staff use communications to target the behaviour of consumers at the back end. This distribution of resources across the substantive and procedural continuum reflects Health Canada's role as industry regulator, fiduciary of public health, and policy-maker and executor.

1.3 THE MANAGEMENT AND ADMINISTRATION OF PUBLIC SECTOR COMMUNICATIONS

In Canada's federal, provincial/territorial, and (to a lesser degree) municipal governments, both political and permanent executives share responsibility for managing the communications function (Brown 2012; Glenn 2001, 2005; Kiss 2014; Thomas 2010, 2011). Members of the federal and provincial/territorial political executives (i.e., first ministers and their cabinet ministers) are generally considered to be the **principal spokespersons** for their departments and have responsibility for their government's overall communication priorities, objectives, and requirements. This involves working with non-partisan public servants. As principal spokespersons, members of the political executive also have ultimate responsibility for "presenting and explaining government policies, priorities and decisions to the public" (Treasury Board of Canada Secretariat 2012). **Non-partisan communications personnel**, on the other hand, are responsible for handling communication activities related to "issues and matters pertaining to the policies, programs, services and initiatives they administer" and are to carry these out "in an accountable, non-partisan fashion consistent with the principles of Canadian parliamentary democracy and ministerial responsibility" (ibid.). All "political matters" are to be left to "the exclusive domain of ministers and their offices" (ibid.).

In theory, the division between non-partisan communications activities and "political matters" resembles other core functional areas of Canadian government—especially policy and finance—in which both political and permanent executives play complementary, symbiotic roles in management and administration. In practice, the communications function is rather different. As Brown describes, it is a "rare area that is found organizationally in both the public service and political spheres, [reflecting] its position on the cusp between politics and administration, nurturing both but belonging fully to neither" (2012). The unique status of communications is illustrated by how the governments of Canada, Ontario, and the City of Toronto manage and administer the function.

The Government of Canada

Key elements of the machinery currently used by the Government of Canada to manage and administer its communications activities were first put in place in the early 1970s. During Prime Minister Trudeau's first term, communications activities were streamlined, consolidated, and standardized across the federal government (see Brown 2012 for a detailed account). Under Trudeau's reforms, for example, heads of communications at the director-general level were put in each line department and given overall responsibility for delivering communications supports for that department's policies, programs, and services. These positions remain central features of the federal communications model today: according to the federal communications policy, **communications heads** are currently responsible for "managing corporate identity, advertising, publishing, marketing, environment analysis, public opinion research, media relations, event participation, and other communication activities" including Web content (Treasury Board of Canada Secretariat 2012). Heads of communications continue to report directly to their deputy ministers.

Another key surviving feature of the Trudeau reforms is the centralizing influence of cabinet and central agencies on the federal communications enterprise. The **Cabinet Committee on Operations** is responsible for overseeing the government's communications agenda and managing the day-to-day issues management process. Cabinet as a whole receives communications support primarily from the Office of the **Assistant Secretary to the Cabinet (Communications and Consultation)** in the PCO. Thomas (2011) observes that

> the assistant secretary provides advice on strategic issues and leads government-wide initiatives on communications. Her advice is non-partisan, but her role is to support the prime minister and the priorities of the government of the day. She is responsible for coordinating and ensuring consistency in the messaging of 36 cabinet ministers, 27 parliamentary secretaries and the heads of over 100 departments and agencies. She is also responsible for the coordi-

nation across government of the politically sensitive activities of public opinion research, public consultations, the adoption of new communications technologies, media monitoring, advertising and crisis communications. To perform these daunting responsibilities in a global, turbulent 24/7 media environment, she has the support of approximately 100 employees, including strategic communications analysts, media analysts, web and social media experts.

The PCO also plays a centralizing role in managing the federal government's advertising process, arguably one of the most visible and controversial communications activities in any government. The PCO chairs the **Government Advertising Committee** (which is composed of communications heads from various line departments) and is responsible for reviewing and approving all major ad campaigns proposed by departments. Working with the Treasury Board Secretariat (TBS), the PCO is also responsible for determining funding allocations for those campaigns. The non-partisan communications support provided by the PCO is supplemented by partisan advice from "exempt" staff in the Prime Minister's Office (PMO). Thomas describes this role as "a listening post and gatekeeper, determining which 'political' matters are to be brought to the attention of the prime minister and ensuring that the prime minister's political and policy directions for government are translated into action by the permanent bureaucracy" (2010, 95).

Two other central agencies, the **Treasury Board Secretariat** and **Public Works and Government Services Canada** (PWGS), make important contributions to the centralized character of the federal communications enterprise. Generally, the TBS has responsibility for developing and monitoring how individual departments apply the federal government's communications policy and assessing performance and results. The TBS also helps manage the federal government's Identity Program, an initiative to shape and manage the government's public image as seen on signs, logos, and other items. PWGS operates a single-window service point for contracting "advertising and public opinion research, for publishing and electronic media monitoring, for film, video, audiovisual and multimedia productions, and for fairs and exhibitions" across the federal government (Treasury Board of Canada Secretariat 2012). PWGS manages the vendor-of-record processes for all procurement of advertising and polling services and makes annual reports on advertising and polling activities across the federal government (ibid.).

The Government of Ontario

The Government of Ontario's current communications machinery was instituted in the late 1990s. Similar to the Trudeau reforms, Premier Mike Harris and his advisors sought to enhance the capacity of central agencies (especially the Premier's Office and Cabinet Office) to provide strategic communications direction across the entire government (Glenn 2001). Like the PMO, the **Premier's Office** was given responsibility for providing political advice to the premier and cabinet on all major communications plans and activities, including the day-to-day issues management process. A new **Priorities and Planning Committee of Cabinet** (a subcommittee of the cabinet) was created to establish, monitor, and approve the government's strategic communications priorities and oversee how ministries achieve those priorities.

On the non-partisan side, "a new **deputy minister of communications** position [was created] within Cabinet Office (together with three new assistant deputy ministers) and each ministry's communications resources [were reorganized] into single communications branches" (ibid., 194). Cabinet Office Communications was responsible for helping to establish the government's communications priorities, key policies, and programs, communicating them to ministries, and guiding and supporting communications plans and products at the ministry level. In each ministry, communications responsibilities were consolidated in one branch under the direction of one director with a dual reporting relationship—to the departmental deputy minister and to the deputy minister of communications in Cabinet Office, who is the senior official in charge of the office's communications. This structure "gave the Office of the Premier and Cabinet Office the power to approve all communications initiatives, including news releases, advertising campaigns, and market research, and to coordinate all communications roll-outs" (ibid.). This model remains largely in place today.

The City of Toronto

In Toronto's municipal government, almost all responsibility for managing and administering the communications function resides with non-partisan communications officials in the central City Manager's Office. Here, the **Strategic Communications Division** is one of six divisions responsible for ensuring that "messages to the public are clear and consistent, and support civic participation and understanding of Council priorities, emerging issues and City programs and services."[4] Some of the larger agencies, boards, and commissions within the city's government structure, such as the Toronto

Transit Commission (seven staff) and Toronto Community Housing (eight staff), also have their own communications departments.

The absence of a formal political role in the management and administration of City communications is also evident in key management processes. In terms of advertising, for example, the Strategic Communications Division reviews all major advertising initiatives proposed by individual divisions, including those related to public meetings or consultations, major capital projects, large-purchase campaigns worth $10,000 or more, and those campaigns "designed to encourage changes in behaviour (social marketing campaigns)" (City of Toronto 2008).

Three factors help to explain the absence of a formal political role in the management and administration of communications in Toronto. First is the enduring legacy of the century-old urban reform movement that sought to "introduce technocratic expertise and professional detachment from politics" into the management and administration of Canadian municipal government in general (Graham and Phillips, with Maslove 1998; see also Tindal and Tindal 2004). Second, the fusion of executive and legislative functions in Toronto's municipal council system means that there is no identifiable executive structure capable of asserting the kind of political control over City communications activities; executives in the federal and provincial systems assert control via cabinet and central agencies. Third, the City of Toronto does not operate in the kind of hyper-partisan environment that drives a lot of political involvement in federal and Ontario government communications activities due to the absence of a formalized, disciplined party system. This does not mean that City communications activities are completely immune from charges of partisanship (Dale 2013).

Communications Administration

Personnel in communications divisions make up a surprisingly small proportion of Canada's public servants (Glenn 2014). Based on staff directory entries consulted in June 2012, 2,799 out of a total of 216,045 full-time federal public servants (1.3 percent), 1,030 out of a total 65,245 Ontario public servants (1.6 percent), and 45 out of a total 30,698 City of Toronto public servants (0.2 percent) work in communications.[5] In the federal public service, the six largest communications divisions are found in Health Canada (270 personnel), Employment and Social Development Canada (217 personnel), Statistics Canada (194 personnel), Public Works and Government

Services Canada (190 personnel), Transport Canada (171 personnel), and Aboriginal Affairs and Northern Development Canada (171 personnel).

FIGURE 1.1: COMMUNICATIONS PERSONNEL BY GOVERNMENT OF CANADA DEPARTMENT

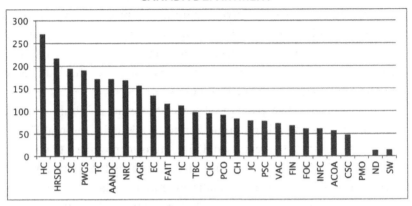

AANDC Aboriginal Affairs and Northern Development Canada
AGR   Agriculture and Agri-Food Canada
ACOA   Atlantic Canada Opportunities Agency
CH   Canadian Heritage
CIC   Citizenship and Immigration Canada
CSC   Correctional Service of Canada
EC   Environment Canada
FIN   Finance Canada, Department of
FOC   Fisheries and Oceans Canada
FAIT   Foreign Affairs and International Trade Canada
HC   Health Canada
HRSDC Human Resources and Skills Development Canada
IC   Industry Canada
INFC   Infrastructure Canada
JC   Justice Canada, Department of
ND   National Defence and the Canadian Forces
NRC   Natural Resources Canada
PMO   Prime Minister of Canada
PCO   Privy Council Office
PSC   Public Safety Canada
PWGS   Public Works and Government Services Canada
SC   Statistics Canada
SW   Status of Women
TC   Transport Canada
TBC   Treasury Board of Canada Secretariat
VAC   Veterans Affairs Canada

Large departments use communications for substantive and procedural purposes, with the exact mix of instrumentation determined by each department's mandate and overall role in government. For example, Employment and Social Development Canada (ESDC), like Health Canada, fuses communications for both substantive and procedural purposes, reflective of its role as industry regulator, fiduciary of public health, and policy-maker and executor. Almost half of ESDC's 217 communications staff work in the procedurally focused Strategic Communications and Stakeholder Relations division, and one-third work in the substantively oriented Program Communications division. By contrast, almost all communications personnel at Transport Canada, and three-quarters at Aboriginal Affairs and Northern Development Canada, work in divisions influencing the behaviour of actors in their respective policy processes.

In Ontario, the five largest communications divisions are in the ministries of Health and Long-Term Care (94 staff), Cabinet Office (89 staff), Education (69 staff), Environment, and Agriculture, Food, and Rural Affairs (59 staff).

FIGURE 1.2: COMMUNICATIONS PERSONNEL BY GOVERNMENT OF ONTARIO MINISTRY

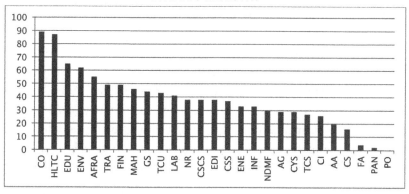

AA	Aboriginal Affairs
AFRA	Agriculture, Food, and Rural Affairs
AG	Attorney General
CO	Cabinet Office
CYS	Children and Youth Services
CI	Citizenship and Immigration
CSS	Community and Social Services
CSCS	Community Safety and Correctional Services
CS	Consumer Services
EDI	Economic Development and Innovation
EDU	Education
ENE	Energy
ENV	Environment
FIN	Finance
FA	Francophone Affairs
GS	Government Services
HLTC	Health and Long-Term Care
INF	Infrastructure
LAB	Labour
MAH	Municipal Affairs and Housing
NR	Natural Resources
NDMF	Northern Development, Mines and Forestry
PO	Office of the Premier
PAN	Pan Am and Parapan Am Games
TCS	Tourism, Culture, and Sport
TCU	Training, Colleges, and Universities
TRA	Transportation

Ontario ministries on the whole dedicate more resources to procedural ends: Cabinet Office, for example, has the largest communications division of any ministry within the Ontario government (89 personnel), while the federal Privy Council Office ranks 14th (91 personnel) among federal departments. This proceduralist orientation is also evident in the mix of communications personnel in large ministries like Education and Environment, where two-thirds of communications staff work in divisions such as Issues and Media Relations in Education and Strategic Communications in Environment. Even at Agriculture and Rural Affairs, a ministry with a strong substantive mandate similar to Statistics Canada and Transport Canada, one-third of communications staff work in a procedurally oriented division like Strategic Communications. Despite this procedural orientation, the Ontario government has received nowhere near the criticism the federal government has received for operating in an overly partisan manner over the past decade.

In Toronto, in the City Manager's Office, one-third of the 45 communications staff conduct procedural work, such as media relations and issues management, while the rest provide substantive supports to line departments. In agencies such as the Toronto Transit Commission and Toronto Community Housing, all communications staff focus on substantive activities, especially those designed to influence consumer behaviour (crisis management, service interruptions, user advice and information, etc.).

Partisan versus Non-partisan Personnel

Non-partisan staff are not the only human resources used to administer the communications function in Canadian governments. (On the role of political staff in Canadian government in general, see Benoit 2005; Thomas 2011; Brodie 2012). In addition to the 3,874 non-partisan communications staff working for the governments of Canada, Ontario, and the City of Toronto, another 200 work within ministerial offices providing explicitly partisan advice to executive decision-makers. **Partisan staff** are appointed to work for ministers and elected members of the legislature and council to provide explicitly partisan or political advice and support. In the Government of Canada, 104 staff work in partisan communications positions out of a total 478 partisan positions (21 percent), with the largest numbers residing in the PMO (37 out of 89 positions in the PMO), the Minister of Industry's office (7 out of 19 positions), and the Minister of International Trade's office (6 out of 26 positions). In Ontario, 92 of 299 staff in partisan positions work in communications (31 percent), with the largest numbers working in the Premier's Office (21 out of 68 positions), the Minister of Health and Long-Term Care's office (7 out of 23), and the offices of the Ministers of Education (4 out of 17) and the Environment (4 out of 11). Three staff work in communications within the Mayor of Toronto's office out of a total partisan staff complement of 16.

The relatively high proportion of political staff assigned responsibility for communications activities in the federal and Ontario governments should not be surprising. A key part of a federal or Ontario cabinet minister's job is to act as "principal spokesperson" for his or her individual department and government as a whole. This responsibility includes working with other ministers and non-partisan personnel to help to establish departmental and whole-of-government communication priorities, objectives, and requirements in the context of the government's overall strategic direction. This is a major component of most Canadian cabinet ministers' jobs and, in terms of support, ministers require "something more than the expert, but non-partisan, advice of the public service to meet the demands on them. To make wise policy [and communications] decisions, ministers need 'a combination of sound technical and political advice'" (Brodie 2012, 33; see also Benoit 2005). While it would be difficult to determine exactly what proportion of a minister's staff should be dedicated to communications activities, the 25 percent dedicated to this federally and in Ontario combined does not seem inconsistent with the significance of the ministerial spokesperson responsibility and its unique support requirements.

1.4 THE ABUSE OF PUBLIC SECTOR COMMUNICATIONS

The unique and symbiotic relationship that exists between political and permanent executives in the management and administration of communications in Canada's public sector has at times resulted in the function being dragged into "the **swampy zone**" that exists between "information and propaganda and between public and partisan interests" (Brown 2012, emphasis added). It is necessary and quite acceptable for public sector organizations to advocate proposals to educate and engage citizens in policy development processes. A World Bank report noted that communications in the public sector "is not just about efficient and effective information dissemination.... The willingness and ability to speak with citizens must be coupled with a willingness and ability to listen to them, incorporate their needs and preferences into the policy process, and engage local patterns of influence and trusted sources of information" (Aday, Brown, and Livingston 2008, 1).

In Canada, there has been vigorous debate as to whether communications used to advocate policy positions has "an educational informative value or whether [it is] of a persuasive agenda-setting nature" (Giasson, Lees-Marshment, and Marland, 2012a, 17; see also Rose and Roberts, 1995; Rose, 1993, 2000, 2001). The debate has intensified in the last few years with the advent of political marketing, the 24/7 media cycle, and the information and communications technology (ICT) revolution. Thomas argues that these developments have caused Canadian political executives to become "extremely preoccupied with generating favorable publicity and avoiding negative news spills" and that this preoccupation has "spilled over from the political centre of government into the administrative culture of the senior ranks of the public service" (2011). The result is that quite legitimate communications activities—especially those used to achieve procedural goals—have at times been subject to overly partisan administration, dragging government communications as a consequence deep into Brown's swampy zone.

For many observers, the case of the federal government's promotion of the 2009 Economic Action Plan illustrates how deeply public sector communications can be dragged into this zone. Rather than adhering to a purely non-partisan marketing strategy that promoted the economic virtues of capital expenditures in a recession, the federal Conservative Party was accused of using the government's advertising dollars to explicitly promote its leader and electoral program. Critics pointed to the use of a "Tory blue" colour scheme for the Action Plan website and signage, the term "Harper government" as opposed to Government of Canada, and cheque props that had the Conservative Party logo on them instead of the Government of Canada logo as evidence of undue partisan administration (Kozolanka 2006, 2012). For many, these overtly partisan activities pushed the government's advertising campaign from public information and policy advocacy to party propaganda (see Rose and Mellon 2010).

The Economic Action Plan incident also underscores one of the most important ethical principles involved in the practice of public sector communications in Canada—the imperative of political neutrality or non-partisanship. Ontario's auditor general defines partisanship as any activity "that may be viewed as promoting the governing party's political interests by fostering a positive impression of the government or a negative impression of any group or person critical of the government" (Office of the Auditor General 2011, 412). All non-partisan communications personnel (i.e., those who work outside of ministers' offices) are expected to communicate with the public "about policies, programs, services and initiatives in an accountable, non-partisan fashion consistent with the principles of Canadian parliamentary democracy and ministerial responsibility" and in a manner that ensures that the "public trust and confidence in the impartiality and integrity of the Public Service of Canada are upheld" (Treasury Board of Canada Secretariat 2012). Chapter 3 examines the significance of non-partisanship in professional public sector communications in Canada in more detail.

1.5 PUBLIC SECTOR COMMUNICATIONS: A NEW PROFESSIONAL'S PERSPECTIVE

This book is designed to help new professionals prepare to work as communicators in Canada's public sector. To that end, this section attempts to provide a new professional's perspective on what the job of a professional public sector communicator looks like by profiling a day in the life of Lakshmi, a fictional communications professional who works in a fictional provincial public service agency.

A Day in the Life

Like most communications professionals working in Canada's public sector today, Lakshmi starts her day early by playing catch-up with the 24/7 news cycle. Her alarm buzzes her awake at 6:00 a.m., but her RSS and Twitter feeds have already produced a virtual pile of media stories related to the work of her high profile provincial agency. She needs to review these over breakfast and during her commute to be prepared for the barrage of requests for updates and insights that will come not only from media outlets, but also her boss, agency president, and the Premier's Office. It doesn't help that the host of a popular morning radio show is interviewing the leader of the opposition about her plans for agency reform.

In the office by 8:00 a.m., Lakshmi scans her inbox for internal emails in preparation for the daily public affairs meeting that starts at 8:15 a.m. One email stands out: someone in media monitoring has sent her a story from a small rural newspaper (that her RSS feed missed!) about an important stakeholder group that has criticized the agency's services to rural communities. The story is a bit of a surprise as the issue has been relatively quiet for the past six months, since the new agency head launched a major service reform initiative. In fact, Lakshmi remembers meeting with a colleague, a senior policy advisor named Ken, just last week who said he had met with the stakeholder group very recently and thought that its members were relatively satisfied with the progress of reforms. What could have changed so quickly? With no time to answer this question before the 8:15 a.m. meeting, Lakshmi assigns the task of investigating to Melissa, an intern working with the agency for the summer.

Lakshmi is the last one to arrive at the public affairs meeting and sneaks in just before the door closes. Her director, Rob, dispenses with formalities and turns directly to Lakshmi to ask about the stakeholder group's recent change of heart. Lakshmi tells the director the news caught her off guard as well, especially given the outcomes of her meeting with the senior policy advisor last week, and lets him know that she will join Melissa after the meeting and get to the bottom of the issue.

For the balance of the meeting, Lakshmi is glued to her tablet. Melissa has sent a note saying that she's found a blog—six days old—posted by someone claiming to have overheard an agency official making derisive comments about the service issue at a local restaurant. The blog was vague and had only been viewed by 75 people, but the blogger was clear that he overheard an agency official making light of the community and its service needs.

When the meeting ends, Lakshmi follows Ken, the policy advisor, back to his office and asks if he knows anything about the issue. Ken turns very pale and looks slightly horrified. He says that he met an old friend for dinner after the stakeholder meeting and recalls making a casual joke about why he was visiting the rural community, but assures Lakshmi that he did not make any negative comments about the group, the community, or the agency.

Lakshmi heads straight for her director's office. Rob is relieved that Lakshmi has found the root of the issue. The two agree that the issue is manageable at this point and that making a formal response to it with a news release or at a press conference might simply escalate the problem. Rob and Lakshmi decide to reach out informally to the leadership of the stakeholder group and assure them that the agency's reform plans are still on track. To be on the safe side, Rob asks Lakshmi to draft a news release and issue note for the president and minister responsible in case the issue escalates and a public response is required.

Back in her office, Lakshmi asks Melissa to take an initial cut at the news release and issue note and then returns a call from a journalist who will be travelling with her team on an agency "road show" next week. Three months in the making—Lakshmi's current pet project—the road show is designed to publicize the very service reforms at the root of the stakeholder's comments and will feature public speeches by both the agency president and minister responsible in a number of small- to medium-sized rural towns throughout the province. The journalist wants to know why the stakeholder group has reacted so negatively to the agency's reform initiative after having publicly supported it. She also asks if she should expect any other surprises once the road show starts. Lakshmi has been cultivating a good, professional rapport with this journalist since she joined the agency two years ago. Because of this rapport, she is able to assure the journalist that the article was the product of a simple misunderstanding that she and her director are trying to resolve with stakeholder leadership and that she would personally reach out to the journalist if there were any developments on the issue before or during the road show.

After lunch, Lakshmi reviews Melissa's first draft of the news release and issue note and revises some of the wording in the key messages to better align with the wording the president used in his radio interview this morning. She then sends it to Ken to ensure that the content summarizing the agency service reforms is still correct and up to date. She also sends a copy to the president's office to ensure that the president approves of the revised wording of the key message. While she waits for a response, Lakshmi joins Melissa in scanning newspaper websites, blogs, and social media to see if the stakeholder group's comments have been picked up or referenced elsewhere. So far, nothing has been published in the traditional media, although a handful of references have shown up on Twitter and Facebook.

With comments from Ken and the president's office, Lakshmi finalizes the content of the news release and issue note and sends it off to Rob for review. She stops by Rob's office to see if he needs anything else before she leaves for the night. Rob says he has scheduled a call with stakeholder leadership first thing in the morning and then plans to meet with the president's chief of staff right after. He asks Lakshmi if she can sit in on the call and help him develop a recommendation on whether to issue the press release. Lakshmi writes it into her calendar and tells Rob that she will also keep an eye out for any significant developments on the story that arise overnight.

LEARNING ACTIVITY

Activity 1.1: Core Mandate

For this activity, work with a partner to identify a core government department at the federal, provincial, or territorial level not examined in this chapter and whose work is of interest to you. In a report of 1,500 words/four pages maximum,

- identify and describe the mandate of your chosen department in terms of its procedural and/or substantive policy orientation;
- use your department's website to identify four or five communications tools (e.g., press releases, backgrounders, FAQs/Q&As, speeches) recently used by your department; and
- assess whether and how these tools support your department's mandate.

FURTHER READING

Despite the prominence of government communications in Canada today, most Canadians do not have a comprehensive picture of what the communications function in government is, nor do they understand how and for what purposes it is used, or have detailed knowledge of how communications activities are managed and administered. Neither Canadian public administration textbooks nor leading journals, such as the *Canadian Journal of Political Science*, *Canadian Public Administration*, and *Canadian Public Policy*, cover communications, at least those published on the topic since 2000.

The literature that does exist on the topic, while limited in volume, is nonetheless very useful when trying to understand the nature of the communications function in Canada's public sector. On the public sector communications function in general, see Michael Howlett's 2009 article, "Government Communication as a Policy Tool: A Framework for Analysis." On the evolution of the federal government's communication function, see David C. G. Brown's very comprehensive 2012 conference paper, "The Administrative Dilemmas of Government Communications" (available on the Canadian Political Science Association's website). On the current state of the communications function within the federal government, see Paul G. Thomas's 2010 contribution to the Oliphant Commission, "Who Is Getting the Message? Communications at the Centre of Government." Simon Kiss provides an account of how the communications function has evolved in the Alberta government in his 2014 article, "Responding to the 'New Public': The Arrival of Strategic Communications and Managed Participation in Alberta."

ONLINE RESOURCES

The Government of Canada hosts two key websites on the topic of public sector communications. The first is home to the Communications Policy of the Government of Canada (www.tbs-sct.gc.ca/pol/doc-eng. aspx?id=12316&section=text), the most comprehensive statement on the nature and scope of the government communications function of any Canadian government. The second is home to the annual reports on Government of Canada advertising activities (www.tpsgc-pwgsc.gc.ca/pub-adv/annuel-annual-eng.html). Each annual report provides critical information on major campaigns and government expenditures on advertising for the fiscal year.

For those students with little background in Canadian government, two sites are worth visiting. The first is the Library of Parliament's multimedia, interactive version of the late Senator Eugene Forsey's classic *How Canadians Govern Themselves* (www.parl.gc.ca/About/Parliament/ SenatorEugeneForsey/Home/Index-e.html). The second site contains the document "Accountable Government: A Guide for Ministers and Ministers of State" (pm.gc.ca/grfx/docs/guidemin_e.pdf), which provides guidance and advice on how the federal government is organized and operates.

QUESTIONS FOR CRITICAL REFLECTION

1. What exactly is the purpose and function of communications in any organization—public, private, or non-profit?
2. Based on your knowledge and experience, is the communications function different in public sector organizations than in private sector or non-profit organizations? If so, how is it different?
3. Using government personnel directories and/or social media sites like LinkedIn, identify two or three communications professionals working in public sector organizations near where you live. If possible, arrange informal information interviews with these individuals in order to help you identify the knowledge and skills that new professionals need to succeed in communications careers in Canada's public sector. (Ryerson University

provides a good introduction to information interviews at www.ryerson.
ca/career/students/searchforajob/identifyjobleads/informationinterview/.)

KEY TERMS

Assistant Secretary to the Cabinet (Communications and Consultation):
A senior non-partisan communications office within the federal Privy
Council Office who provides advice on strategic issues and leads government-wide initiatives on communications. While this person's advice is
non-partisan, his/her role is to support the prime minister and the priorities of the government of the day.

Cabinet Committee on Operations: A federal cabinet committee responsible for overseeing the government's communications agenda and managing the day-to-day issues management process.

Cabinet Office Communications: A division within Ontario's Cabinet
Office that is responsible for helping to establish the government's communications priorities, key policies, and programs, communicating them
to ministries, and guiding and supporting communications plans and
products at the ministry level.

City of Toronto Strategic Communications Division: One of six divisions in
the City Manager's Office responsible for ensuring "that messages to the public are clear and consistent, and support civic participation and understanding of Council priorities, emerging issues and City programs and services."[6]

communications: A core management function that both public and
private organizations use to control the flow of information between
the organization and its various internal and external audiences to help
achieve strategic organizational goals.

communications heads: Non-partisan communications officials who are
responsible for "managing corporate identity, advertising, publishing,
marketing, environment analysis, public opinion research, media relations, event participation, and other communication activities," (Treasury Board of Canada Secretariat 2012) including Web content. Heads of
communications typically report directly to a deputy minister.

deputy minister of communications, Cabinet Office: The senior official
in charge of Ontario's Cabinet Office communications.

first minister: The first minister is the leader of a government cabinet. In
Canada, the first minister in the federal government is the prime minister;
in provincial/territorial governments, the first minister is the premier.

Government Advertising Committee: A federal government committee composed of communications heads from various line departments that is responsible for reviewing and approving all major ad campaigns proposed by departments.

non-partisan communications personnel: Members of the permanent executive who are responsible for handling communications activities related to issues and matters pertaining to the policies, programs, services, and initiatives they administer in an accountable, non-partisan fashion.

partisan staff: Individuals appointed to work for ministers and elected members of the legislature to provide explicitly partisan or political advice and support.

Premier's Office: A central agency within the Ontario government with responsibility for providing political advice to the premier and cabinet on all major communications plans and activities, including the day-to-day issues management process.

principal spokesperson: The role that ministers assume for their departments and government that gives them responsibility for establishing, presenting, and explaining overall communications priorities, objectives, and requirements.

Priorities and Planning Committee of Cabinet: A subcommittee of the Ontario cabinet created to establish, monitor, and approve the government's strategic communications priorities and oversee how ministries achieve those priorities.

Privy Council Office: A central agency within the federal government responsible for overseeing and managing the government's communications processes, including advertising.

procedural domain: An area in which public sector organizations use communications to affect change in how individuals and groups behave in policy processes.

public sector communications: An information- or knowledge-based resource that is provided or withheld from societal actors "to influence and direct policy actions" (Howlett 2009, 24).

Public Works and Government Services Canada (PWGS): A federal government department that operates a single-window service point for contracting "advertising and public opinion research; for publishing and electronic media monitoring; for film, video, audiovisual, and multimedia productions; and for fairs and exhibitions across the government"

(Public Works and Government Services Canada 2012). PWGS also manages the vendor-of-record processes for all procurement of advertising and polling services and makes annual reports on advertising and polling activities across the federal government.

substantive domain: An area in which public sector organizations use communications to affect change in "the type, quantity, price, or other characteristics of goods and services being produced in society, either by the public or private sector" (Howlett, Ramesh, and Perl 2009, 116).

"swampy zone": A term used by David Brown (2012) to describe the area between "information and propaganda and between public and partisan interests" that reflects that unique and symbiotic relationship that exists between political and permanent executives in the management and administration of communications in Canada's public sector.

Treasury Board Secretariat (TBS): A federal government department responsible for developing and monitoring how individual departments apply the federal government's communications policy, and assess performance and results. TBS also helps manage the federal government's Identity Program.

NOTES

1 This chapter is based on Ted Glenn, "The Management and Administration of Government Communications in Canada," *Canadian Public Administration* (Spring, 2014, 3–25).

2 Thomas (2010) provides interesting insight into the scope and magnitude of government correspondence today. With reference to correspondence to the prime minister:

> Over the preceding five years the volume of communications of all kinds ranged from a high of approximately 2.15 million contacts of all kinds to a low of approximately 1.2 million contacts. After first being established in November 1997, the email address for the prime minister has become by far the most popular communications channel, with just over one million incoming emails in 2006–07 and just over 80,000 outgoing email replies in the same year. It is interesting that old-fashioned "snail mail" still accounted for more than 600,000 contacts in 2006–07 and over one million in the preceding year. The variance between messages received and replies sent reflect mainly the fact that write-in campaigns, petitions, thank you letters, and other correspondence do not require a response. (100)

3 Mandates for the federal government organizations described in this project were derived from individual departmental performance reports (www.tbs-sct.gc.ca/dpr-rmr/index-eng.asp), reports on plans and priorities (www.tbs-sct.gc.ca/rpp/index-eng.asp), departmental websites, and the Government Electronic Directory Service (sage-geds.tpsgc-pwgsc. gc.ca). Mandates for the Ontario government organizations reported in this project were derived from individual departmental results-based plans (www.fin.gov.on.ca/en/about/rbplanning), departmental websites, and InfoGO (infogo.gov.on.ca), the Ontario government's electronic directory. Mandates for the City of Toronto organizations reported in this project were derived from internal documentation available through the City's online corporate directory (www.toronto.ca/city_directory).

4 Information retrieved from www.toronto.ca/city_directory/corporate-directory.htm#1 (accessed September 14, 2012).

5 The following directories were consulted in May and June 2012 to come up with the personnel counts presented in this section: the federal Government Electronic Directory Service (sage-geds.tpsgc-pwgsc.gc.ca); the Ontario InfoGO (infogo.gov.on.ca); and the City of Toronto's online corporate directory (www.toronto.ca/city_directory).

6 See note 4.

WORKS CITED

Aday, S., R. Brown, and S. Livingston. 2008. "The George Washington University/ University of Leeds Government Communications Audit Project." Washington, DC: Communication for Governance and Accountability Program, World Bank.

Bennett, Gavin, and Nasreen Jessani, eds., 2011. *The Knowledge Transition Toolkit: Bridging the "Know-Do" Gap: A Resource for Researchers.* Ottawa: IRDC.

Benoit, Liane. 2005. "Ministerial Staff: The Life and Times of Parliament's Statutory Orphans." In *Commission of Inquiry into the Sponsorship Program and Advertising Activities. Restoring Accountability: Research Studies, Vol. 1; Parliament, Ministers and Deputy Ministers.* Ottawa: Public Works and Government Services Canada.

Brodie, Ian. 2012. "In Defence of Political Staff." *Canadian Parliamentary Review.* Autumn.

Brown, David C. G. 2012. "The Administrative Dilemmas of Government Communications." Paper presented at the Canadian Political Science Association Annual Conference, Edmonton, Alberta.

City of Toronto. 2008. *Advertising Policy.* Toronto: Strategic Communications Division.

Cutlip, Scott, and Glenn Broom. 2012. *Effective Public Relations.* 8th ed. Englewood Cliffs, NJ: Prentice Hall.

Dale, Daniel. 2013. "Toronto Press Releases Will No Longer Echo Mayor Rob Ford." *Toronto Star,* January 23. www.thestar.com/news/city_hall/2013/01/23/toronto_press_releases_will_no_longer_echo_mayor_rob_ford.html

Giasson, Thierry, Jennifer Lees-Marshment, and Alex Marland. 2012a. "Introducing Political Marketing." In *Political Marketing in Canada*, edited by Alex Marland, Thierry Giasson, and Jennifer Lees-Marshment, 3–21. Vancouver: UBC Press.

———. 2012b. "Challenges for Democracy." In *Political Marketing in Canada*, edited by Alex Marland, Thierry Giasson, and Jennifer Lees-Marshment, 241–254. Vancouver: UBC Press.

Glenn, Ted. 2001. "Politics, Leadership, and Experience in Designing Ontario's Cabinet." *Canadian Public Administration* 44 (2): 188–203.

———. 2005. "Politics, Personality and History in Ontario's Administrative Style." In *Executive Styles in Canada: Cabinet Decision-Making Structures and Practices at the Federal and Provincial Levels*, edited by Luc Bernier, Keith Brownsey, and Michael Howlett, 155–170. Toronto: University of Toronto Press.

———. 2014. "The Management and Administration of Government Communications in Canada." *Canadian Public Administration* (March).

Graham, Katherine, and Susan Phillips, with Allan Maslove. 1998. *Urban Governance in Canada: Representation, Resources, and Restructuring.* Toronto: Harcourt Canada.

Howlett, Michael. 2009. "Government Communication as a Policy Tool: A Framework for Analysis." *Canadian Political Science Review* 3 (2): 23–37.

———. 2011. *Designing Public Policies: Principles and Instruments.* New York: Routledge.

Howlett, Michael, M. Ramesh, and Anthony Perl. 2009. *Studying Public Policy: Policy Cycles & Policy Systems.* Don Mills, ON: Oxford University Press.

Kiss, Simon. 2014. "Responding to the 'New Public': The Arrival of Strategic Communications and Managed Participation in Alberta." *Canadian Public Administration* (March).

Kozolanka, Kirsten. 2006. "The Sponsorship Scandal as Communication: The Rise of Politicized and Strategic Communications in the Federal Government." *Canadian Journal of Communication* 31 (2): 343–66.

———. 2012. "'Buyer' Beware: Pushing the Boundaries of Marketing Communications in Government." In *Political Marketing in Canada*, edited by Alex Marland, Thierry Giasson, and Jennifer Lees-Marshment, 107–122. Vancouver: UBC Press.

Office of the Auditor General of Ontario. 2011. *2011 Annual Report.* Toronto: Queen's Printer.

O'Shaughnessy, Nicholas. 2004. *Politics and Propaganda: Weapons of Mass Seduction.* Ann Arbor, MI: University of Michigan Press.

Pasquier, Martial, and Jean-Patrick Villeneuve. 2012. *Marketing Management and Communications in the Public Sector.* New York: Routledge.

Public Works and Government Services Canada. 2012. *2010–2011 Annual Report on Government of Canada Advertising Activities.* Ottawa: Public Works and Government Services Canada. www.tpsgc-pwgsc.gc.ca/pub-adv/rapports-reports/2010-2011/tdm-toc-eng.html

Rose, Jonathan. 1993. "Government Advertising During a Political Crisis: The Case of the Quebec Referendum." *Canadian Journal of Communication* (Spring).

———. 2000. *Making Pictures in Our Heads: Government Advertising in Canada.* Westport: Praeger.

———. 2001. "The Advertising of Politics and the Politics of Advertising." In *Communications in Canadian Society* (5th ed.), edited by Craig McKie and Benjamin Singer, 151–164. Toronto: Thompson Educational Publishing.

Rose, Jonathan, and Hugh Mellon. 2010. "When the Message Is the Meaning: Government Advertising and the Branding of States." In *Mediating Canadian Politics,* edited by Linda Trimble and Shannon Sampert, 75–91. Scarborough: Pearson.

Rose, Jonathan, and Alasdair Roberts. 1995. "Selling the Goods and Services Tax: Government Advertising and Public Discourse in Canada." *Canadian Journal of Political Science* 28 (2): 221–30.

Thomas, Paul G. 2010. "Who Is Getting the Message? Communications at the Centre of Government." *Public Policy Issues and the Oliphant Commission: Independent Research Studies,* prepared for Commission of Inquiry into Certain Allegations Respecting Business and Financial Dealings Between Karlheinz Schreiber and the Right Honourable Brian Mulroney, edited by Craig Forcese, 77–136. Ottawa: Minister of Public Works and Government Services Canada.

———. 2011. "Communications and Prime Ministerial Power." Paper presented at a conference in honour of Donald J. Savoie, Bouctouche, New Brunswick, June 8–10.

Tindal, Richard, and Susan Nobes Tindal. 2004. *Local Government in Canada.* 6th ed. Toronto: Nelson.

Treasury Board of Canada Secretariat. 2012. *Communications Policy of the Government of Canada.* www.tbs-sct.gc.ca/pol/doc-eng.aspx?id=12316&section=text

CHAPTER 2

THE STRATEGIC CONTEXT FOR PUBLIC SECTOR COMMUNICATIONS

CHAPTER OVERVIEW

This chapter describes the strategic context in which professional public sector communications is conducted. It begins by explaining how public sector organizations identify and describe the strategic direction and goals that executives set for their governments, first in electoral platforms and subsequently in cabinet mandate letters, throne speeches, budgets, and the various annual reports of individual public sector organizations. The chapter then shows how public sector organizations use stakeholder analysis to identify and describe the individuals and groups that have specific interests or stakes in the success or failure of the goods and services that governments use to achieve their strategic goals.

LEARNING OBJECTIVES

By the end of this chapter, you will be able to

- identify and describe the strategic goals and directions that have been established for public sector organizations using five main sources: electoral platforms, cabinet mandate letters, throne speeches, budgets, and the annual reports issued by individual public sector organizations;
- identify the individuals and organizations that have an interest or stake in a public sector organization's strategic direction using publicly available sources (public hearings, reports, websites, etc.) and/or content analysis of print/social media;

- assess the relative power and influence that stakeholders have over the organization's ability to achieve its strategic communications goals using a power-interest assessment tool; and
- develop a basic plan for communicating with stakeholders using a prescribed template.

INTRODUCTION

In Canada's system of government, first ministers (the prime minister at the federal level, premiers in the provinces) are responsible for establishing the strategic direction of government and establishing that position before elected representatives in the legislature. First ministers exercise this responsibility in four ways: (1) by proposing the general direction for government policy during general elections; (2) once elected to office, by preparing the speech from the throne to outline the government's broad policy agenda for each new legislative session; (3) by approving the annual budget presented by the Minister of Finance; and (4) by giving final approval to the content of government legislation approved by the cabinet prior to introduction in the legislature.

Canadian first ministers use two special powers to help discharge their responsibility for establishing the strategic direction of government. First is the power to appoint individuals to cabinet, the central decision-making body in government that has responsibility for helping first ministers set government policy and manage the key issues of government on a day-to-day basis. Individual cabinet ministers are responsible for ensuring that the specific departments they are assigned responsibility for achieve the goals and objectives set out by cabinet. Second is the power to determine the broad organization and structure of government. To this end, first ministers allocate ministers' portfolios, establish their mandates, clarify the relationships among them, and identify the priorities for their portfolios through mandate letters. First ministers' approval is required to create new institutions and eliminate existing organizations, some of which may also be subject to parliamentary decisions. Any proposals made by ministers for significant organizational change or to alter their own mandates or those of other ministers must receive initial approval from the first minister.

This chapter begins by explaining how public sector organizations identify and describe the strategic direction and goals that first ministers establish for their governments, first in electoral platforms and subsequently in cabinet mandate letters, throne speeches, budgets, and the various annual reports of individual public sector organizations. It shows how public sector organizations use stakeholder analysis to identify and describe the individuals and groups that have specific interests or stakes in the success or failure of the goods and services that governments use to achieve their strategic goals.

2.1 THE STRATEGIC DIRECTION OF GOVERNMENT

This section illustrates how a first minister establishes the strategic direction and goals for a government using the case of Premier Brad Wall's Saskatchewan Party and its election to office in 2007.[1] The section begins by describing some of the more prominent **electoral commitments** (the promises made by a political party during a general election) made by the Saskatchewan Party during the 2007 election, and showing how these were refined in 2007 ministerial mandate letters, the 2007 speech from the throne, the 2008 budget, and the 2008 annual reports of the Department of Advanced Education, Employment, and Labour and the Saskatchewan Liquor and Gaming Authority.

Electoral Commitments

In 2007, future premier Brad Wall's Saskatchewan Party released *Securing the Future*, a 45-page campaign document that set out 63 specific commitments organized around nine basic objectives. Table 2.1 outlines some of the prominent commitments made by the party during the election campaign.

Mandate Letters

Mandate letters are documents in which first ministers set out performance expectations for cabinet appointees, including the specific activities or initiatives that the first minister expects the minister to achieve or undertake to support delivery of the government's electoral mandate. Below is an excerpt from the mandate letter given to Rob Norris, appointed Minister of Advanced Education, Employment, and Labour on November 21, 2007 (Saskatchewan 2007a).[2] In the letter, note the mix of both specific direction ("Establish a Saskatchewan scholarship fund, to be matched by scholarship funding raised by post-secondary institutions") and general direction ("Ensure post-secondary institutions contribute to the goals of building an innovative economy, increasing training and educational seats and keeping tuition affordable for students").

TABLE 2.1: *SECURING THE FUTURE* **COMMITMENTS**

Objective	Promise
New ideas to keep young people in Saskatchewan	• provide rebates of up to $20,000 in post-secondary tuition for graduates who stay in Saskatchewan for seven years; • provide a $10,000 tax-free exemption each year for five years for young entrepreneurs and self-employed young people under the age of 30; • increase post-secondary funding by $125 million or 28 percent; and • create a $3 million Saskatchewan scholarship fund.
Writing a prescription for better health care	• hire 800 new registered nurses and train 100 new doctors; • provide a $15 cap on the cost of prescription drugs for children aged 14 and under; • provide a $15 cap on the cost of prescription drugs for seniors with incomes under $64,043; • spend an additional $40 million over four years on cancer care and prevention; • spend an additional $4 million to promote healthy living and wellness; • develop a long-term care strategy for seniors, health care equipment, and infrastructure; • create a health care ombudsman; and • undertake a "patient first review" of the health care system.
New ideas for families	• double education property tax rebates; • eliminate the PST on used cars and trucks; • provide an annual $150 per child Active Families Benefit to help parents with the cost of sports and cultural activities for children aged 6 to 14; • maintain funding levels for child care, early learning, and early childhood development; • double the Caregivers Amount Tax Credit from $4,019 to $8,038; • increase K–12 education operating funding by $118 million or 20 percent over four years; • spend an additional $2 million over four years on school lunch and anti-hunger programs in schools; and • support community-based organizations, including spending an additional $20 million over four years on food banks and other community-based organizations.
New ideas for jobs and economic growth	• invest $1.8 billion over four years in highways and transportation infrastructure; • create Enterprise Saskatchewan to develop long-term provincial labour force development strategy; • reinstate the Saskatchewan Mineral Exploration Tax Credit; • create the Saskatchewan Infrastructure Growth Initiative for Municipalities that provides $300 million in five-year, interest-free loans to municipalities; • fully fund the provincial share of the Canadian Agricultural Income Stabilization Program; • double property tax rebates on agricultural land over four years; • create Innovation Saskatchewan within Enterprise Saskatchewan to coordinate government support for research, development, and commercialization of innovation; and • establish a fair and balanced labour environment that respects the rights of workers and employers.
Building pride in Saskatchewan	• strengthen relations with First Nations; • double funding for tourism programming by $32 million; and • spend an additional $20 million on provincial and regional parks;

	• maintain funding levels for arts organizations; and • create a provincial capital commission.
Publicly owned Crowns that work for Saskatchewan	• retain public ownership of Crown corporations; • provide low-interest loans of up to $25,000 to homeowners and businesses for green initiatives; • provide a 20 percent discount on hybrid and high fuel efficiency vehicles; • increase investment in innovative communications infrastructure; and • reduce SaskPower greenhouse gas emissions.
Making our communities safer	• hire 120 new police officers; • provide an additional $4 million to combat organized crime and gangs; • provide an additional $4 million (a 25 percent increase) in funding for transition houses and sexual assault centres; • provide $100,000 in new funding for a sexual assault umbrella association; • provide $2 million for free home security devices for low-income seniors; • increase the Victim Impact Surcharge by 5 percent; • provide $16 million in new funding for 100 new long-term addiction treatment beds; • double existing funding for protecting children from sexual exploitation over the Internet; and • empower police to seize the vehicles of repeat drunk drivers.
New ideas to help Saskatchewan go green	• provide an additional $40 million over four years for the Green Initiatives Fund; • meet the province's greenhouse gas emission reduction targets; • provide, through SaskPower and SaskEnergy, low-interest loans to install geothermal heating and renewable power in homes, businesses, and institutions; and • lower the cost to register and insure a 2006 or later model hybrid or high fuel efficiency vehicle.
More accountable government	• establish fixed election dates; • restrict the amount and type of pre-election advertising by government; • pass balanced budget legislation, with surpluses dedicated to debt reduction; • pay down $250 million in debt immediately; • limit increases in the size of the civil service to the rate of population growth; • provide $1 million over four years to the Johnson-Shoyama Graduate School of Public Policy; and • establish a provincial public integrity commissioner.

Source: Saskatchewan. Ministry of Advanced Education, Employment and Labour. 2008. Ministry of Advanced Education, Employment and Labour Annual Report 07–08. www.finance.gov.sk.ca/annreport/ AEELAnnualReport200708.pdf

Feature 2.1

Premier of Saskatchewan
Legislative Building
Regina Canada S4S 0B3

November 21, 2007

Hon. Rob Norris
Minister of Advanced Education, Employment and Labour
Minister Responsible for Immigration
Minister Responsible for the Saskatchewan Workers' Compensation
    Board

Dear Minister:

I want to congratulate you on your appointment as Minister of Advanced Education, Employment and Labour, Minister Responsible for Immigration and Minister Responsible for the Saskatchewan Workers' Compensation Board, and thank you for accepting responsibility for delivering on our Government's plan for Securing the Future.

Throughout our proud history as a province, Saskatchewan people have embraced the future with hope and determination. Strengthened by the belief that hope beats fear, generation after generation of Saskatchewan people have worked hard to build a better future for themselves and their children.

On November 7th, 2007, the people of Saskatchewan voted for change and entrusted a new government with responsibility for delivering on the promise of Saskatchewan and serving the people of our great province. Our Government accepts this responsibility with humility and the belief that we must accomplish our goals in a manner which ensures accountability to those who have placed their trust in us. Integrity and accountability will be at the forefront of our dealings as a government, and in your work as a Minister of the Crown.

These thoughts must be in your mind as you take up your duties as Member of the Executive Council and deliver on the priorities of our Government. The purpose of this letter is to outline my expectations of you in your role as Minister.

We will be working together as a team to meet our Government's commitments, and I encourage you to collaborate with your colleagues and fellow members of Cabinet as you undertake your responsibilities. However there are clear priorities which are to be addressed by you and your Ministries:

In your capacity as Minister of Advanced Education:

- Ensure post-secondary institutions contribute to the goals of building an innovative economy, increasing training and educational seats and keeping tuition affordable for students.
- Establish a Saskatchewan scholarship fund, to be matched by scholarship funding raised by post-secondary institutions.
- Work with post-secondary institutions to create more co-op and applied learning opportunities.
- Develop a long-term provincial initiative between First Nations, post-secondary institutions and industry to increase the number of First Nations workers in the labour force.
- Increase training and employment opportunities for apprentices and review the current journeyman to apprentice ratio in consultation with industry and labour.
- Ensure Saskatchewan is an active participant in inter-provincial Western Canadian partnerships related to labour market development and post-secondary education.

This is an exciting time for our province. Through our Government's hard work and your accomplishment of the above-noted objectives, we will deliver on our plan for Securing the Future and making Saskatchewan a leader in the New West, Canada and the World.

Yours sincerely,
Brad Wall
Premier

Source: Brad Wall, Premier of Saskatchewan. Ministry of Finance. 2007. Rob Norris Mandate Letter. http://www.finance.gov.sk.ca/performance-planning/HonRobNorris-AEELImmirgration.pdf

The Speech from the Throne

Once cabinet is assembled and ministers have received their mandate letters, the next task of a newly elected government is to inform the legislature and the public of its plans for implementing the party's electoral commitments. This is the primary purpose of the **speech from the throne**. In many ways, the throne speech is the "'strategic lynchpin'" in Canadian governance as it marks the transition point between the promises a party makes during an electoral campaign, the broad commitments it makes as a government once in office (and that members of the legislature hold executives to account for), and specific funding that it allocates to achieving those commitments during the annual budget.

Although it is delivered in the legislature by the governor general or lieutenant-governor, the first minister and his office prepare this seminal speech outlining the government's priorities for the new legislative session. After its delivery, members of the legislature debate and ultimately vote on its content. By convention, the speech is considered to be a matter of confidence.

On December 10, 2007, the Lieutenant-Governor of Saskatchewan, Dr. Gordon Barnhart, delivered the speech from the throne to open the first session of the 26th legislature (Saskatchewan 2007b). Entitled "Securing the Future," the speech included 34 specific commitments organized around 18 core themes (described in table 2.2). Note that not all of the government's 2007 electoral promises and mandate letter commitments (for example, the promise to establish a Saskatchewan scholarship fund) made it into the speech. The failure to include a commitment in a throne speech does not mean that the government has abandoned that commitment. Logistically, all governments have to prioritize which items they want to highlight in the throne speech as legislatures provide only a limited amount of time (typically less than one hour) for the delivery of the speech. Operationally, governments also have to prioritize which commitments they want to act on over the course of their mandates based on factors such as perceived political priority and implementation complexity. This can mean that some electoral commitments are left off of a government's immediate strategic agenda in favour of including them in a second throne speech. The event horizon for most Canadian throne speeches is typically 18 to 24 months.

TABLE 2.2: THRONE SPEECH COMMITMENTS

Objective	Promise
New ideas to keep young people in Saskatchewan	• provide rebates of up to $20,000 in post-secondary tuition for graduates who stay in Saskatchewan for seven years; • provide a $10,000 tax-free exemption each year for five years for young entrepreneurs and self-employed young people under the age of 30; • increase post-secondary funding by $125 million or 28 percent; and • create a $3 million Saskatchewan scholarship fund.
Writing a prescription for better health care	• hire 800 new registered nurses and train 100 new doctors; • provide a $15 cap on the cost of prescription drugs for children aged 14 and under; • provide a $15 cap on the cost of prescription drugs for seniors with incomes under $64,043; • spend an additional $40 million over four years on cancer care and prevention; • spend an additional $4 million to promote healthy living and wellness; • develop a long-term care strategy for seniors, health care equipment, and infrastructure; • create a health care ombudsman; and • undertake a "patient first review" of the health care system.
New ideas for families	• double education property tax rebates; • eliminate the PST on used cars and trucks; • provide an annual $150 per child Active Families Benefit to help parents with the cost of sports and cultural activities for children aged 6 to 14; • maintain funding levels for child care, early learning, and early childhood development; • double the Caregivers Amount Tax Credit from $4,019 to $8,038; • increase K–12 education operating funding by $118 million or 20 percent over four years; • spend an additional $2 million over four years on school lunch and anti-hunger programs in schools; and • support community-based organizations, including spending an additional $20 million over four years on food banks and other community-based organizations.
New ideas for jobs and economic growth	• invest $1.8 billion over four years in highways and transportation infrastructure; • create Enterprise Saskatchewan to develop long-term provincial labour force development strategy; • reinstate the Saskatchewan Mineral Exploration Tax Credit; • create the Saskatchewan Infrastructure Growth Initiative for Municipalities that provides $300 million in five-year, interest-free loans to municipalities; • fully fund the provincial share of the Canadian Agricultural Income Stabilization Program; • double property tax rebates on agricultural land over four years; • create Innovation Saskatchewan within Enterprise Saskatchewan to coordinate government support for research, development, and commercialization of innovation; and • establish a fair and balanced labour environment that respects the rights of workers and employers.
Building pride in Saskatchewan	• strengthen relations with First Nations; • double funding for tourism programming by $32 million; and • spend an additional $20 million on provincial and regional parks;

The environment	• meet existing greenhouse gas emission target of reducing levels by 32 percent by 2020; • insist that carbon offsets or penalties imposed on heavy greenhouse gas emitters stay in Saskatchewan; • maintain public ownership of provincial Crown corporations; • provide assistance for the cost of installing geothermal and solar heating; • ensure that new government vehicles are either hybrid or high fuel efficiency vehicles; and • help drivers purchase a hybrid or high efficiency vehicle by lowering the cost of registration.
Education	• increase operating funding for K–12 education by 20 percent over four years • fund education from general revenue
Quality of life for First Nations and Métis	• make instruction in history and content of treaties mandatory in the K–12 curriculum; and • work with First Nations and Métis to develop a protocol for protecting their rights and interests by honouring the government's duty to consult and accommodate.
Keeping our word	• introduce legislation to establish a fixed election date every four years
Accountability	• introduce a Saskatchewan Growth and Financial Security Act to: require a balanced provincial budget each and every year; set out a formula for allocating budgetary surpluses (half to paying down debt and half to economic growth initiatives); and restrict the rate of public service growth to the rate of growth in the general provincial population

The Budget Speech

The **budget speech** formally kicks off the annual financial cycle in Canadian government. After spending months putting together detailed spending plans and revenue projections for the coming year, the Minister of Finance delivers an hour-long (or so) speech in the legislature, usually in late winter, outlining the government's fiscal, social, and economic policies and priorities for the coming fiscal year. The speech is followed by the submission of the main estimates, which set out in detail the government's projected expenditures for the upcoming fiscal year.

On March 19, 2008, Saskatchewan Finance Minister Rod Gantefoer delivered the Saskatchewan Party's first budget (Saskatchewan 2008b).[3] Similar to the Securing the Future electoral platform, the budget was organized into nine core themes and included numerous specific commitments (the most significant are included in table 2.3).

When reviewing these commitments, it is important to remember that Canadian government budgets in general are by law limited in scope and application to one calendar year. As a result, if a government has committed to spend a designated amount over the course of its four-year term, it might commit to spending only a portion of those monies in any one given year and not abrogate its overall commitment. In this case, for example, in the 2007 election the Saskatchewan government committed to spending $2 million on school lunch and anti-hunger programs over the course of its mandate, but committed to spending only $500,000 on such programming in 2008–2009. The government fulfilled its commitment to spend $2 million on these programs in subsequent budgets.

TABLE 2.3: BUDGET COMMITMENTS

Area	Commitment
Education and training	• $12 million in 2008–09 for a Graduate Retention Program to provide post-secondary graduates with tuition rebates of up to $20,000 over the seven years following graduation; • an additional $25.5 million (an 8.4 percent increase) to cover the costs of freezing university tuition levels; • $48.7 million for education property tax relief; • create an Active Saskatchewan Families Benefit worth $150 per year beginning in 2009–10; • a $34.6 million (or 20 percent) increase in school operating funding; • maintenance of existing funding levels for child care, early learning, and early childhood development; • doubling the Caregiver Tax Credit from $4,095 to $8,190; • $500,000 in new funding for school lunch and anti-hunger programs; and • $5 million to provide increased support to food banks and community-based organizations to provide life skills, development, and employment training to under-skilled individuals.
Health care	• announced an agreement with the Saskatchewan Union of Nurses to hire 800 new nurses by 2011; • $5 million to expand medical student seats to 100 and physician residency seats to 120 by 2010–11, and an additional $1.1 million on physician recruitment and retention; • $700,000 for a $15 cap on prescription costs to children under 14 and "income-tested" seniors; • $10.7 million for the Saskatchewan Cancer Agency for cancer care and prevention; • $1 million to develop a 10-year health sector human resource plan, a 10-year capital plan, and a Seniors' Health Care Strategy; • announced development of legislation to establish the health care ombudsman; and • $1.5 million for a "patient first" review of the health care system.
Economic growth	• $1 million in new funding and $7.4 million in reallocated funding to support the newly created Enterprise Saskatchewan; • announced the reinstatement of the Mineral Exploration Tax Credit; • $510 million for highways and transportation infrastructure; • $75 million in interest-free loans ($300 million over four years) to municipalities for lot development as part of the Saskatchewan Infrastructure Growth Initiative; • $91.5 million to fully fund the Canadian Agricultural Income Stabilization (CAIS) Program; • $8 million to double funding for tourism programming; • $5 million increase in the parks budget, including $700,000 to establish a Capital City Commission; and • maintenance of existing funding levels for provincial arts organizations.

Public safety	• $3 million in 2008–09 for 30 additional police officers and other enhancements to substance abuse treatment and supportive employment programs for offenders; • "an increase" in the Victim Surcharge; • $5.1 million for an additional 88 addictions treatment beds; • $8.7 million in new funding to combat organized crime and Internet child exploitation; and • $1.1 million for transition houses and sexual assault centres.
Government accountability	• announced the government's decision to fix election dates every four years and introduce changes to the province's balanced budget legislation; • announced a $250 million debt payment in 2008–09; and • announced $250,000 in funding to the Johnson-Shoyama School of Public Policy for 2008–09.
Miscellaneous	• $10 million for the Green Initiatives Fund; • $11.3 million for upgrades to the Provincial Radio Telecommunications System; • an additional $1 million for a First Nations and Métis consultation capacity fund; and • $200,000 to host a Round Table on Aboriginal Consultation.

Table 2.4 provides a more comprehensive picture of promises and commitments made over the course of the 2007 election campaign, and in the 2007 throne speech and 2008 budget. Note how some core strategic commitments, such as tuition rebates to encourage graduate retention, transition directly from the 2007 election platform to the throne speech to the budget, while other initiatives, such as the $2 million for free home security devices for low-income seniors promised during the election, do not get mentioned elsewhere but are implemented eventually (Saskatchewan 2012).

TABLE 2.4: STRATEGIC COMMITMENTS

Strategic commitment	Election campaign November 2007	Throne speech December 2007	Budget March 2008
Education and training	• provide $20,000 post-secondary tuition rebates for graduates who stay in Saskatchewan for seven years • provide a $10,000 tax-free exemption for young entrepreneurs and self-employed young people under 30 • increase post-secondary funding by $125 million or 28 percent • create a $3 million Saskatchewan scholarship fund	• provide $20,000 post-secondary tuition rebates for graduates who stay in Saskatchewan for seven years • allow young entrepreneurs under 30 to earn $10,000 per year tax-free for five years • increase post-secondary funding by $125 million over four years	• $12 million in 2008–09 to rebate $20,000 in post-secondary tuition for graduates who stay in Saskatchewan for seven years • $25.5 million (an 84 percent increase) to cover the costs of freezing university tuition levels

	• increase entrepreneurial and business education in schools		
Health care	• hire 800 new registered nurses • train 100 new doctors • provide a $15 cap on prescription drug costs for children under 14, seniors with incomes under $64,000 • focus more health care expenditures on front-line care • $40 million over four years for cancer care and prevention • $4 million to promote healthy living and wellness • develop a long-term care strategy for seniors • develop a 10-year plan for health care equipment/ infrastructure • create a health care ombudsman • undertake a "patient first" review of the health care system	• work with the Saskatchewan Union of Nurses and others to hire 800 registered nurses by 2011 • commit to creating more training seats and more residency positions for doctors • establish a prescription drug program that covers most seniors and children • commit to conduct a "patient first" review of health care system	• announced agreement with the Saskatchewan Union of Nurses to hire 800 new nurses by 2011 • $5 million to expand medical student seats to 100 and physician residency seats to 120 by 2010–11; $1.1 million for physician recruitment and retention • $700,000 to expand the $15 cap on prescription costs to children under 14 and "income-tested" seniors • $10.7 million to strengthen support for cancer care and prevention • $1 million to develop a 10-year health sector human resource plan, a 10-year capital plan, and a Seniors' Health Care Strategy • confirmed development of legislation for a health care ombudsman • $1.5 million for a "patient first" review of the health care system
Economic development	• create Enterprise Saskatchewan • reinstate the Saskatchewan Mineral Exploration Tax Credit • invest $1.8 billion over four years on transportation infrastructure • double property tax rebates on agricultural land • create Innovation Saskatchewan to coordinate government support for research, development, and commercialization • establish a fair and balanced labour environment	• create Enterprise Saskatchewan • introduce legislation to achieve balance in labour laws • no new direct government investment in forestry companies	• $8.4 million in funding for Enterprise Saskatchewan • reinstatement of the Mineral Exploration Tax Credit • $510 million for highways and transportation infrastructure • $5 million increase in the parks budget, including $700,000 to establish a Capital City Commission • maintain existing funding for provincial arts organizations • $11.3 million for the Provincial Radio Telecommunications System to replace the FleetNet system

	• maintain funding for provincial arts organizations • new investment in communications infrastructure		
Families	• double education property tax rebates • eliminate the PST on used cars and trucks • provide an annual $150 per child Active Families Benefit • maintain funding levels for child care, early learning, and early childhood development • double the Caregivers Amount Tax Credit • increase K–12 education funding by $118 million or 20 percent • $2 million over four years on school lunch and anti-hunger programs • $20 million over four years on food banks	• double education property tax rebates over four years • remove the PST on purchase of a used car or light truck • introduce a $150 per child Active Families Benefit • increase K–12 education funding by 20 percent over four years • commit to funding education from general revenue • more funds for school lunch and anti-hunger programs • $20 million over four years to community-based organizations that provide employment skills training	• $48.7 million for education property tax relief in 2008–09 • confirmed elimination of PST on used cars and trucks • created an Active Saskatchewan Families Benefit worth $150 per year beginning in 2009–10 • maintenance of existing funding levels for child care, early learning, and early childhood development • doubled the Caregiver Tax Credit from $4,095 to $8,190 • a $34.6 million (or 20 percent) increase in school operating funding • $500,000 in new funding for school lunch and anti-hunger programs • $5 million to food banks and community-based organizations to provide life/employment skills training
Public safety	• hire 120 new police officers • hire more corrections workers • $4 million or 25 percent increase in funding for transition houses and sexual assault centres • $100,000 for a sexual assault umbrella association • $2 million for free home security devices for low-income seniors • increase the Victim Impact Surcharge by 5 percent • $16 million for 100 new long-term addictions treatment beds • $4 million to combat organized crime and gangs	• hire 120 new police officers over four years • will begin work on funding 100 new long-term addictions treatment beds • will work to crack down on drugs and gangs in prisons	• $3 million for 30 additional police officers and enhancements to substance abuse treatment and supportive employment programs for offenders • $1.1 million for transition houses and sexual assault centres • $500,000 for a summit of community-based organizations (CBOs) to develop a new social policy direction for Saskatchewan • "an increase" in the Victim Surcharge • $5.1 million for an additional 88 addictions treatment beds • $8.7 million in new funding to combat

	• double existing funding to protect children from sexual exploitation over the Internet • allow police to seize the vehicles of repeat drunk drivers		organized crime and Internet child exploitation
Green initiatives	• meet provincial greenhouse gas emission reduction targets • provide low-interest loans to install geothermal heating and renewable power • provide low-interest loans up to $25,000 for green initiatives • reduce SaskPower greenhouse gas emissions • $40 million over four years for the Green Initiatives Fund • provide a 20 percent discount on price of hybrid and high fuel efficiency vehicles • reduce costs to register/insure a 2006 or later model hybrid or high fuel efficiency vehicle	• commit to meeting existing greenhouse gas emission reduction targets • provide assistance for the cost of installing geothermal and solar heating • help drivers purchase a hybrid or high fuel efficiency vehicle by lowering the cost of registering these vehicles • commit to ensuring that new purchase government vehicles are either hybrid or high fuel efficiency	• $10 million for the Green Initiatives Fund
Intergovernmental affairs First Nations Municipalities Federal government	• make instruction in history and content of the treaties mandatory in K–12 curriculum • work with First Nations and Métis peoples to develop a protocol to honour the government's duty to consult and accommodate • commit to increasing funding for municipal revenue sharing by 7 percent annually • commit to negotiating a new revenue-sharing deal with municipalities • create the Saskatchewan Infrastructure Growth Initiative to provide $300 million in interest-free loans to municipalities • fully fund provincial share of the Canadian Agricultural Income Stabilization Program	• commit to make instruction in history and content of the treaties mandatory in K–12 curriculum • work with First Nations and Métis peoples to develop a protocol to honour the government's duty to consult and accommodate • increase revenue sharing to provide immediate assistance to municipalities • will negotiate a new revenue-sharing agreement with municipalities • assist municipalities in meeting demand for commercial and residential lots • fully fund provincial share of the Canadian Agricultural Income Stabilization Program	• $1 million for a First Nations and Métis consultation fund; $200,000 for Round Table on Aboriginal Consultation • increase municipal revenue sharing by 7 percent for 2008–09 • $75 million in interest-free loans ($300 million over four years) to municipalities for commercial/residential lot development • $91.5 million to fully fund the Canadian Agricultural Income Stabilization Program

Saskatchewan pride	• double funding for tourism programming by $32 million • $20 million for provincial/regional parks • maintain funding levels for arts organizations • create a provincial capital commission	• double tourism funding • invest in new electrified campsites and new park infrastructure	• $8 million to double funding for tourism programming • $5 million for provincial/regional parks, including $1.2 million to electrify 274 campsites • $4.2 million to maintain funding levels for arts organizations • $700,000 to establish the Capital City Commission
Government accountability	• retain public ownership of Crown corporations • establish fixed election dates • restrict amount/type of pre-election advertising by gov't • pass balanced budget legislation, with surpluses dedicated to debt reduction • pay down $250 million in debt immediately • limit rate of civil service growth to rate of population growth • $1 million over 4 years to the Johnson-Shoyama Graduate School of Public Policy • establish a provincial Public Integrity Commissioner	• maintain public ownership of Crown corporations • will introduce legislation to establish fixed election dates • will introduce balanced budget legislation, with surpluses dedicated to debt reduction • will introduce legislation to restrict rate of public service growth to the rate of general population growth	• confirmed the government's decision to fix election dates • confirmed introduction of changes to balanced budget law • $250 million debt payment • $250,000 in funding to the Johnson-Shoyama School of Public Policy

Annual Reports

Most government departments and organizations in the broader public sector are required to present an **annual report** on their operations and activities for the previous year to the legislature. These reports vary in content and title, ranging from the federal government's department performance reports,[4] to Ontario's results-based plans,[5] to Saskatchewan's annual reports,[6] but all share the common objective of providing a yearly account of major activities and operations undertaken. In its 2007–2008 annual report, Saskatchewan's Department of Advanced Education, Employment, and Labour states that the report was "prepared during a time of transition to a new government's agenda" and was designed to "provide results from key actions and performance measures published in 2007/08, as well as the new government's strategic priorities since November presented in the Minister's Mandate letter and the 2007 Throne Speech" (Saskatchewan 2008a). To that end, the report identifies the specific commitments made in the throne speech and the minister's mandate letter, and then reports on progress the department has made to date:

TABLE 2.5: DEPARTMENT OF ADVANCED EDUCATION, EMPLOYMENT, AND LABOUR 2007–2008 ANNUAL REPORT COMMITMENTS

Commitment	Reported progress to date
Mandate letter, November 2007	
Ensure post-secondary institutions contribute to the goals of building an innovative economy, increase training and educational seats, and keep tuition affordable for students.	"The Ministry is working with the post-secondary education and training system to deliver responsive education and training to meet the needs of the economy, maximize the productivity of Saskatchewan people in the labour market, enhance labour force participation, and increase engagement in public-private partnerships."
Establish a Saskatchewan scholarship fund, to be matched by scholarship funding raised by post-secondary institutions.	"The Ministry has conducted preliminary work to establish this scholarship fund. Further research and consultations with stakeholders will continue in the 2008/09 fiscal year."
Work with post-secondary institutions to create more co-op and applied learning opportunities.	"Initial work to increase co-op and applied learning opportunities began in 2007/08 and will continue with the province's post-secondary education institutions in the 2008/09 fiscal year."
Develop a long-term provincial initiative between First Nations, post-secondary institutions, and industry to increase the number of First Nations workers in the labour force.	"Additional funding provided to Saskatchewan Indian Institute of Technologies (SIIT) to increase seats in both Adult Basic Education (ABE) and skill-training programs prepares First Nations people for active participation in the labour force. Initiatives will continue in the next fiscal year."
Throne speech, December 2007	
Tuition rebates of up to $20,000 over seven years for those students who stay in the province after graduation to start their careers.	"The Ministry introduced the Graduate Retention Program (GRP), a refundable income tax credit to rebate up to $20,000 for actual tuition fees paid by Saskatchewan post-secondary graduates who stay in the province for seven years after graduation, in a new bill titled The Graduate Retention Program Act."
Establish a fair and balanced labour environment in Saskatchewan that respects the rights of workers and employers.	"Removing legislated limits on the length of collective bargaining agreements. Introduced amendments to The Trade Union Act that remove the three-year limit on collective agreements."
Work with the province's public sector unions to ensure essential services are in place in the event of a strike or labour action.	"The Ministry introduced The Public Services Essential Services Act to: define essential public services and balance the rights of workers with the need to ensure public safely; and safeguard the public from potential problems that may arise due to a work stoppage, where there is a reasonable apprehension of danger to life, health or safety, destruction of equipment or premises, serious environmental damage, or disruption of the courts."
Ensuring democratic workplaces.	"Introducing amendments that require secret ballots on any vote to certify a union in a workplace and a 50 per cent plus one result for successful certification; and ensuring freedom of information in the workplace during any unionization drive, by allowing unions and management the opportunity to communicate fairly with employees."

Source: Saskatchewan. Ministry of Advanced Education, Employment and Labour. 2008a. *Ministry of Advanced Education, Employment and Labour Annual Report 07–08.* www.finance.gov.sk.ca/annreport/AEELAnnualReport200708.pdf

Similarly, the Saskatchewan Liquor and Gaming Authority's (SLGA) annual reports illustrate how a government's strategic commitments inform the priorities and operations of organizations within the broader public sector. SLGA's 2008 annual report begins by stating that "a significant number of commitments have already been made to Saskatchewan people in 2007–08 in the election platform, the Speech from the Throne and in the public Minister's Mandate letters" (Saskatchewan Liquor and Gaming Authority [SLGA] 2008, 2) regarding the SLGA's mandate and mission, specifically in the areas of social responsibility, environmental stewardship, and its promotion of a stronger business climate through the liquor regulatory system. To deliver on its commitments, the SLGA launched a series of stakeholder consultations in the wake of the 2007 election to "ensure that the regulatory environment is flexible and supportive of the needs of business and their customers" (ibid., 6). The product of those consultations was a series of actions to deliver on the government's strategic commitments.

TABLE 2.6: SASKATCHEWAN LIQUOR AND GAMING AUTHORITY 2007–2008 ANNUAL REPORT COMMITMENTS

Commitment	Reported progress to date
Enhance social responsibility	• extend prohibitions on the sale and consumption of alcoholic beverages for special occasion permits; • enhance prohibitions against the use of false identification by minors to gain access to or remain in a permitted premise; and • enhance prohibitions against individuals bringing their own alcoholic beverages into permitted premises for consumption.
Create an efficient regulator system to promote a stronger business climate	• permit eligible businesses to offer supplies, space, equipment, and expertise to customers who want to make their own wine or beer on-site rather than at home in order to allow existing businesses to expand and diversify their operations and create an opportunity for new entrants into the market; • allow more flexible hours of operation for liquor permit holders; • modify the capacity limits on businesses licensed to sell liquor; • replace arbitrary maximum capacity limits with limits based on fire code requirements; • permit eligible businesses to offer "off-sale" liquor services such as home delivery; and • allow gift shops to include alcohol in gift baskets.
Environmental stewardship	Report commits to "bring forward recommendations on how SLGA can conduct its operations in a more environmentally friendly manner. All relevant policies will be revised to reflect SLGA's commitment to this goal and the decision-making process will incorporate environmental impact considerations. Plans have been put in place to conduct energy efficiency audits on all existing store locations."

Source: Saskatchewan Liquor and Gaming Authority. 2008. *Saskatchewan Liquor and Gaming Authority Annual Report 07–08.* Regina: SLGA. www.slga.gov.sk.ca/Prebuilt/Public/SLGA Annual 2008.pdf

2.2 STAKEHOLDER ANALYSIS

Once the strategic goals that a political executive wants to achieve and the specific methods by which they will be achieved have been described, the next step in the strategic communications planning process is **stakeholder analysis.** This is a three-step process that involves (1) identifying the individuals, groups, and organizations that have an interest or stake in the organization's strategic goals and methods of achievement; (2) assessing the power and influence of stakeholders to impact the organization's capacity to achieve its strategic goals; and (3) developing a plan for communicating with stakeholders based on their power-interest assessment results (see Schmeer 1999; Wimmer, de Soysa, and Wagner 2002; Thesenvitz 2003).

Stakeholder Identification

The stakeholder analysis process begins by identifying **stakeholders,** defined as the people, groups, and organizations that have some interest in the activity or initiative that the strategic communications plan is designed to support. A number of potential sources of information can be used to identify stakeholders, including departmental correspondence records (correspondence records maintained by the minister's office); lists of people, groups, and organizations that may have participated in public hearings held by the department in the past; and content analysis of print and/or social media (content analysis is described in more detail in chapters 8 and 9). To illustrate, table 2.7 identifies some of the stakeholders for Saskatchewan's Graduate Retention Program.

TABLE 2.7: STAKEHOLDERS FOR SASKATCHEWAN'S GRADUATE RETENTION PROGRAM

Stakeholder type	Stakeholders
Students	Students: • 32,000 in degree programs • 5,500 in certificate/diplomas programs • 6,800 apprentices • 5,200 in adult basic education Student representative bodies: • Individual college and technical institute student unions (e.g., Dumont Technical Institute Campus Students, First Nations University Students' Association, Saskatchewan Indian Institute of Technologies [SIIT] Saskatoon Campus Students, SIAST Adult Basic Education Students)

	• University of Saskatchewan Students' Union • University of Saskatchewan Graduate Students' Association • Canadian Federation of Students–Saskatchewan
Post-secondary institutions	Publicly funded post-secondary education and training providers: • 8 regional colleges that provide adult basic education and skills training • Saskatchewan Institute of Applied Science and Technology (SIAST), with 4 campuses • 2 universities (University of Regina and University of Saskatchewan), along with their federated and affiliated colleges • 4 Aboriginal institutions (Gabriel Dumont Institute of Native Studies and Applied Research, and its subsidiary, the Dumont Technical Institute; the Saskatchewan Indian Institute of Technology; and the First Nations University of Canada) • Campus Saskatchewan (a partnership between post-secondary institutions and government to use technology-based learning to increase access to post-secondary studies) • Saskatchewan Apprenticeship and Trades Certification Commission (training is provided by SIAST, SIIT, regional colleges, private vocational schools, SaskPower, etc.) Privately funded post-secondary education and training providers: • 32 private vocational schools registered under the Private Vocational Schools Regulation Act Apprenticeship
Employers	• employers who would benefit from having access to an increased pool of post-secondary education graduates created by the initiative • industries in which apprenticeship is regulated (50 trades and 4 sub-trades, including 37 Red Seal trades)
Others	• high schools • parents of prospective and existing post-secondary students • Saskatchewan New Democratic Party • general public • other political parties (Progressive Conservative Party, Liberal Party)

Stakeholder Assessment

Once stakeholders have been identified, the next task in stakeholder analysis involves describing and categorizing each stakeholder in terms of its interest in the activity or initiative at hand and the power it has to support or oppose the activity or initiative (Ackermann and Eden 2011). **Interest** can be defined as the nature of the stake that a stakeholder has in the activity or initiative at hand, which can range from simple curiosity to investment, i.e., a special claim on or to the production or consumption of the public good or service in question by virtue of a legal contract, commitment, tradition, or ownership stake. **Power,** by contrast, is a slightly more complicated variable that refers to the ability of a stakeholder to affect positively or negatively the outcome of an activity or initiative. A stakeholder's power is the product of four different elements:

- access to key decision-making processes related to the approval and/or implementation of an activity or initiative
- resources, or the human, financial, technological, or logistical assets that a stakeholder has or can easily mobilize in support of or in opposition to an activity or initiative
- alliances, or the ability to collaborate with other like-minded organizations to support or oppose an activity or initiative
- leadership, or the willingness to initiate, convene, or lead an action for or against an activity or initiative

Ideally, stakeholders should be contacted directly using tools such as surveys, interviews, and focus groups to gather the data needed to describe and assess the nature of a stakeholder's interest in an activity or initiative (see Schmeer 1999; Wimmer, de Soysa, and Wagner 2002; Thesenvitz 2003). In most workplaces, however, public sector communications professionals do not have the time, resources, or opportunity to consult stakeholders directly and are left to conduct their assessments using existing data or sources that are readily and easily available within their organization and media reports. These more basic assessments are typically conducted in two steps. First, stakeholders are assessed in each dimension of interest on a scale of 1 to 5, where 1 = weakest and 5 = strongest. In terms of their expected position dimension, stakeholders are assigned one of the following: *S* for support, *O* for oppose, and *N* for neutral.

As table 2.9 suggests, stakeholders can be placed in one of four categories depending on their interest and power scores:

1. **Key Players** are those individuals and groups that have high power and interest to affect the overall success or failure of a communications initiative. As such, these stakeholders should form the primary audience for the communications initiative, either to maintain their support or to persuade them at least not to oppose the activity or initiative.
2. **Context Setters** have the potential to be highly influential stakeholders due to their high power scores, but at present show little interest in affecting the outcome of the activity or initiative. Context Setters should be monitored in case their interests or perceived interests change and they become Key Players, or if there appears to be the possibility of "converting" them to be Key Players in support of the activity or initiative.

3. **Subjects** are those stakeholders that have high interest in an activity or initiative but lack the power (resources, leadership, access to decision making, etc.) needed to convert that interest into any real influence over outcomes. Subjects need to be monitored, as they can become Key Players by forming alliances with stakeholders who have power.

4. **The Crowd** is stakeholders who have little interest or power to affect the outcome of an activity or initiative. Unless the environmental context changes radically, little to no effort should be made to communicate with them.

TABLE 2.8: GRADUATE RETENTION PROGRAM STAKEHOLDER ASSESSMENT RESULTS

Stakeholder	Expected position	Interest	Power				Power total
			Access	Resources	Leadership	Alliances	
Students							
8 regional colleges	S	4	3	2	4	4	3
SIAST	S	4	3	2	4	4	3
2 universities	S	4	3	4	5	5	4
4 Aboriginal institutions	S	4	3	3	4	4	3.5
Campus Saskatchewan	S	4	3	3	4	4	3.5
32 vocational schools	S	2	3	2	2	2	2
Post-secondary institutions							
adult basic education students	S	3	2	1	1	1	1
regional college students	S	5	2	2	2	2	2
SIAST students	S	5	2	2	2	2	2
undergraduate students	S	5	2	3	5	5	4
Aboriginal students	S	5	2	2	4	4	3
graduate students	O	5	2	3	4	4	3
Employers/Others							
employers/associations	S	5	4	4	4	5	4
industries	S	4	3	4	4	4	4
high schools	S	4	2	2	2	3	2
parents	S	4	2	3	2	2	2
Saskatchewan New Democratic Party	O	5	4	2	5	5	4
general public	A	3	1	3	3	1	2
other political parties	O	3	2	2	4	3	3

Source: Author.

Stakeholder assessment results can be plotted on a power-interest grid as a first step in developing a plan for communicating for specific stakeholders (Ackermann and Eden 2011):

TABLE 2.9: ACKERMANN AND EDEN'S POWER-INTEREST GRID

	SUBJECTS (LOW POWER/HIGH INTEREST)	PLAYERS (HIGH POWER/HIGH INTEREST)
Interest	*Management strategy*: encourage coalitions to increase power and convert to Players; or neutralize interest and convert to Crowd	*Management strategy*: significant stakeholders who deserve sustained attention
	THE CROWD (LOW POWER/LOW INTEREST)	CONTEXT SETTERS (LOW INTEREST/HIGH POWER)
	Management strategy: could raise interest/power to create allies, but might not be worth time/effort	*Management strategy*: seek to raise awareness level to develop interest and convert to Players
	Power	

Source: Fran Ackermann and Colin Eden. 2011. "Strategic Management of Stakeholders: Theory and Practice." *Long Range Planning* 44: 183.

According to the scores attributed above, the stakeholders for Saskatchewan's Graduate Retention Program could be placed on the power-interest grid as shown below:

FIGURE 2.1: GRADUATE RETENTION PROGRAM STAKEHOLDERS

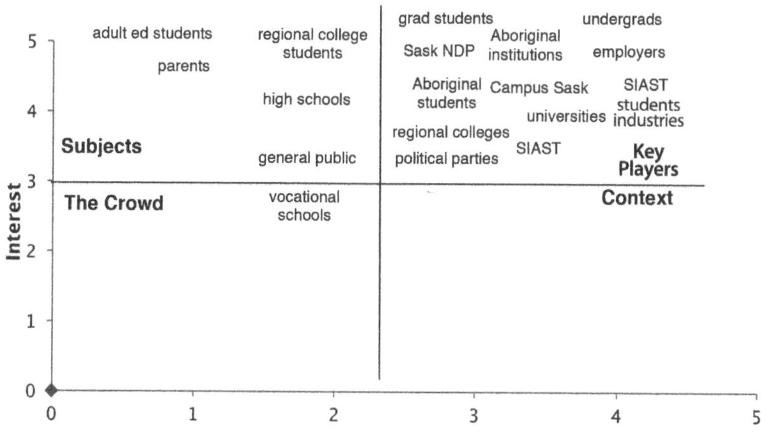

Source: Author.

Communicating with Stakeholders

The last step in stakeholder analysis involves developing a basic plan for communicating with stakeholders based on their location on the power-interest grid.

TABLE 2.10: BASIC STAKEHOLDER COMMUNICATIONS PLAN

Stakeholder/ group	Anticipated reaction	Stakeholders' key issues	Proposed strategy	Government's key message(s)
Undergraduate students	• On record as supporting	• Some might view the policy as diminishing the value of post-secondary education • Is the policy retroactive? • Limit on program options?	• Key student union endorsements • Broad-based advertising	• We believe that young people are the future of our country. • Making Saskatchewan the province of choice for post-secondary graduates is key to meeting our province's talent challenge.
Post-secondary institutions	• On record as supporting	• Is the policy retroactive? • Effect on enrollment—will schools restrict numbers to compensate? • Limit on program options?	• Key post-secondary education endorsements • Minister announcements at select campuses	• Provides a strong incentive for students to enroll in Saskatchewan post-secondary institutions, complete their education, and remain in the province. • Keeping skilled and educated young people in Saskatchewan is essential to maintaining the momentum of the growing economy and to support the continuing shift to a knowledge-based economy.
Employers	• On record as supporting	• Challenges with recruitment and retention in tight labour market	• Key employer endorsements • Minister announcements at/with key employers	• Provides employers with a valuable recruitment and retention tool. • One more way that government is helping employers find and attract the qualified, skilled workers our province needs.
Graduate students	• On record as opposed	• Program applies only to undergraduate students	• News releases, FAQs	• This government is focused on retaining as many graduates as possible, as quickly as possible. We will review expanding the program to include graduate students when the current initiative is rolled out.

Chapter 4 provides more details on message development.

LEARNING ACTIVITIES

Activity 2.1: Federal/Provincial/Territorial Strategic Direction and Goals

Identify and describe the strategic direction and goals that have been established for public sector organizations in one jurisdiction (federal, provincial, or territorial) in one particular sector (e.g., post-secondary education, economic development, health care, environment). Be sure the context for these goals and directions is described as extensively as possible, including electoral platforms, cabinet mandate letters (if publicly available), throne speeches, budgets, and annual reports from at least three public sector organizations that operate within your chosen sector.

Activity 2.2: Municipal Strategic Direction and Goals

Identify and describe the strategic direction and goals that have been established for public sector organizations within a particular sector (e.g., recreation, economic development, health care, environment) in one municipality. Be sure the context for these goals and directions is described as extensively as possible, including electoral platforms, major speeches by the mayor, strategic planning documents released by council, budgets, and annual reports from at least three public sector organizations that operate within your chosen sector.

Activity 2.3: Stakeholder Analysis

Conduct an analysis of stakeholders that have an interest in one strategic goal or initiative identified in activities 2.1 or 2.2, following these steps: (1) identify the individuals, groups, and organizations that have an interest or stake in the organization's strategic goals and methods of achievement using lists from publicly available sources (public hearings, reports, websites, etc.) and/or content analysis of print/social media; (2) assess the relative power and influence that stakeholders have over the organization's ability to achieve its strategic goals using the power-interest assessment tool described in this chapter; and (3) develop a plan for communicating with stakeholders, using the communications plan described in this chapter as a guide.

FURTHER READING

Like communications, little has been written about strategy in Canada's public sector in general or the strategic context for public sector communications specifically. Jenny Stewart provides a good overview introduction to strategy in the public sector in her 2004 article, "The Meaning of Strategy in the Public Sector."

Two excellent sources for understanding how public and non-profit organizations conduct and manage and strategic communications processes are Kathy Bonk, Emily Tynes, Henry Griggs, and Phil Sparks' 2008 book *Strategic Communications for Nonprofits* (2nd ed.), and the chapter "Communication Strategy" from Gavin Bennett and Nasreen Jessani's 2011 book *The Knowledge Translation Toolkit: Bridging the "Know-Do" Gap; A Resource for Researchers.*

ONLINE RESOURCES

As shown in this chapter, the case of Saskatchewan during the Saskatchewan Party's first term in office offers particularly good insight into on what a strategic framework for government looks like. Other jurisdictions that are useful in this regard include British Columbia and Nova Scotia.

For British Columbia, visit www.bcliberals.com/news/in-the-news/ourPlan and read the BC Liberals' 2013 electoral commitments in the "Strong Economy, Secure Tomorrow" platform. Then visit www.leg.bc.ca/documents/4-1-0.htm to assess how these electoral commitments informed subsequent throne speech and budget commitments.

For Nova Scotia, visit www.liberal.ns.ca/wp-content/uploads/2013/09/2013-Liberal-Platform.pdf and read the provincial Liberals' 2013 electoral commitments in the "Nova Scotia First" platform. Then visit nslegislative.ca/index.php/proceedings/throne-speech-podcasts/ and www.novascotia.ca/finance/en/home/budget/budgetspeeches.aspx to assess how these electoral commitments informed subsequent throne speech and budget commitments.

QUESTIONS FOR CRITICAL REFLECTION

1. What does "strategy" mean for a public sector organization? What is the "strategic context" for public sector communications?
2. Is the strategic context of communications different in the public and private sectors?
3. In strategic communications planning, what separates an interested member of the public from a stakeholder?

KEY TERMS

annual report: A formal statement by a public sector organization that summarizes its major operations and activities for the previous year.

budget speech: An hour-long (or so) speech delivered by the Minister of Finance in the legislature that outlines the government's fiscal, social, and economic policies and priorities for the coming fiscal year. The speech is followed by the submission of the main estimates, which set out the government's projected expenditures for the upcoming fiscal year.

Context Setters: Stakeholders that at present show little interest in affecting the outcome of an activity or initiative, but have the potential to be highly influential due to high levels of power.

The Crowd: Stakeholders who have little interest or power to affect the outcome of an activity or initiative.

electoral commitments: Promises made by a political party during a general election. Also referred to as an electoral platform.

interest: The nature of the stake that a stakeholder has in the activity or initiative at hand, which can range from simple curiosity to investiture, i.e., a special claim on or to the production or consumption of the public good or service in question by virtue of a legal contract, commitment, tradition, or ownership stake.

Key Players: Stakeholders that have the power and interest to affect the overall success or failure of a communications initiative.

mandate letters: Documents in which first ministers set out performance expectations for cabinet appointees, including the specific activities or initiatives that the first minister expects the minister to achieve or undertake to support delivery of the government's electoral mandate.

power: The ability of a stakeholder to affect positively or negatively the outcome of an activity or initiative.

speech from the throne: A formal address by the governor general or lieutenant-governor used to articulate the strategic direction of government and establish that position before elected representatives in the legislature.

stakeholder: An individual, group, or organization that has an interest or stake in an organization's strategic goals and/or methods of achievement.

stakeholder analysis: A three-step process that involves (1) identifying the individuals, groups, and organizations that have an interest or stake in the organization's strategic goals and methods of achievement, (2) assessing the power and influence of stakeholders to impact the organization's capacity to achieve its strategic goals, and (3) developing a plan for communicating with stakeholders based on their power-interest assessment results.

Subjects: Stakeholders that have high interest in an activity or initiative, but lack the power (resources, leadership, access to decision making, etc.) needed to convert that interest into any real influence over outcomes.

NOTES

1 Saskatchewan is used for illustration purposes here because of the unusually high degree of transparency that Premier Brad Wall enforced upon his government's strategic direction in its first term. Transparency is evidenced by the fact that his government published the ministerial mandate letters (a first in Canada) and enforced a relatively strict alignment between the government's strategic objectives and its operational priorities.

2 Mandate letters are typically private documents that only the first minister, minister, cabinet secretary, and deputy minister have access to. Saskatchewan Premier Brad Wall made the content of his 2007 mandate letters available to the public.

3 The timing of budget speeches in Canada varies greatly, usually from late February to April, although most jurisdictions attempt to deliver prior to the end of the March 31st fiscal year.

4 See www.tbs-sct.gc.ca/dpr-rmr/index-eng.asp

5 See www.fin.gov.on.ca/en/about/rbplanning/

6 See www.finance.gov.sk.ca/PlanningAndReporting

WORKS CITED

Ackermann, Fran, and Colin Eden. 2011. "Strategic Management of Stakeholders: Theory and Practice." *Long Range Planning* 44: 179–96.

Bennett, Gavin, and Nasreen Jessani, eds. 2011. "Chapter Six: Communication Strategy." In *The Knowledge Translation Toolkit: Bridging the "Know-Do" Gap; A Resource for Researchers,* 103–28. Ottawa: IDRC.

Bonk, Kathy, Emily Tynes, Henry Griggs, and Phil Sparks. 2008. *Strategic Communications for Nonprofits: A Step-by-Step Guide to Working with the Media.* 2nd ed. San Francisco: Jossey-Bass.

Saskatchewan. Ministry of Finance. 2007a. *Rob Norris Mandate Letter.* www.finance.gov.sk.ca/performance-planning/HonRobNorris-AEELImmirgration.pdf

———. Office of the Lieutenant Governor. 2007b. *Securing the Future: Speech from the Throne 2007.* Regina: Queen's Printer. www.gov.sk.ca/adx/aspx/adxGetMedia.aspx?DocID=1619,617,534,206,Docume

————. Ministry of Advanced Education, Employment and Labour. 2008a. *Ministry of Advanced Education, Employment and Labour Annual Report 07–08.* www.finance.gov.sk.ca/annreport/AEELAnnualReport200708.pdf

————. Ministry of Finance. 2008b. *Budget 2008–09: Ready for Growth.* Regina: Queen's Printer. www.gov.sk.ca/news?newsId=0c824b99-4a5f-4e48-8689-56ecf7328700

————. 2012. *Government Launches Seniors Home Security Program.* www.gov.sk.ca/news?newsId=e645b68a-7f09-4949-8e15-62e0f8158053.

Saskatchewan Liquor and Gaming Authority. 2008. *Saskatchewan Liquor and Gaming Authority Annual Report 07–08.* Regina: Saskatchewan Liquor and Gaming Authority. www.slga.gov.sk.ca/Prebuilt/Public/SLGA Annual 2008.pdf

Saskatchewan Party. 2007. Securing the Future. www.saskparty.com/Downloads/2007 Election Platform.pdf

Schmeer, Kammi. 1999. *Guidelines for Conducting a Stakeholder Analysis.* Bethesda, MD: Partnerships for Health Reform, Abt Associates Inc. www.who.int/management/partnerships/overall/GuidelinesConductingStakeholderAnalysis.pdf

Stewart, Jenny. 2004. "The Meaning of Strategy in the Public Sector." *Australian Journal of Public Administration* 63 (4): 16–21.

Thesenvitz, Jodi. 2003. *Workplace Health Promotion Stakeholder Analysis.* Toronto: Health Communication Unit, Centre for Health Promotion, University of Toronto.

Wimmer, Andreas, Indra de Soysa, and Christian Wagner. 2002. *Political Science Tools for Assessing Feasibility and Sustainability of Reforms.* Bonn: Independent Evaluation Office of the International Monetary Fund. www.ieo-imf.org/ieo/files/completedevaluations/052902.pdf

CHAPTER 3

PLANNING TO COMMUNICATE

CHAPTER OVERVIEW

This chapter explains how public sector organizations plan to communicate with their intended audiences. It begins by explaining how organizations define communications objectives in a manner consistent with and in support of policy or program objectives at three different levels: output, outtake, and outcome. It then describes the role that indicators play in helping organizations evaluate whether or not communications objectives are being achieved. The chapter concludes with a discussion of baselines, metrics that provide snapshots of current conditions against which any future changes introduced by a communications activity can be measured.

LEARNING OBJECTIVES

By the end of this chapter, you will be able to understand and develop

- an overall communications objective that defines what a public sector organization wants to accomplish when communicating with identified audiences about an initiative being used to achieve a strategic goal;
- output objectives that define the tangible goods or services that are to be produced by specific communications activities;
- outtake objectives that define what a public sector organization wants target audience members to take away from specific communications activities; and
- outcome objectives that define how the organization would like members of a target audience to change as a result of the core themes or messages of specific communications activities.

INTRODUCTION

For Asibey, Parras, and van Fleet (2008), the most critical question to ask about any communications activity is, what contribution toward our strategic goals do we expect to gain from this communication effort and how can we tell whether we are making progress? The first step that public sector organizations take to answer this question is to establish clear, precise, specific communications objectives. In communications, objectives do three things: (1) define exactly what organizations want to achieve when communicating with identified audiences about specific proposals or initiatives, (2) directly inform the choice of tactics used to implement the communications strategy that supports a proposal or initiative, and (3) establish the standards against which the success of the communications strategy can be judged. This chapter begins by explaining how public sector organizations define communications objectives in a manner consistent with and in support of policy or program objectives at three different levels: output, outtake, and outcome. It then describes the role that indicators play in helping organizations evaluate whether or not communications objectives are being achieved. The chapter concludes with a discussion of baselines, metrics that provide snapshots of current conditions against which any future changes introduced by a communications activity can be measured. Chapter 8 continues this discussion by showcasing the most common research tools public sector organizations use to generate data for indicators and baselines as part of the communications evaluation process.

3.1 OBJECTIVES

Recall from chapter 1 that communications is defined as a core management function that public sector organizations use to control the flow of information between the organization and its various internal and external audiences to help achieve strategic organizational goals. **Communications objectives** are an essential component of the communications function because they define what an organization wants to achieve when communicating with identified audiences about a specific program, service, proposal, or initiative. Communications objectives must be aligned with the objectives of the program, service, proposal, or initiative they are designed to support. The UK Government Communication Network (GCN) provides the following examples of communications objectives that align with policy and program objectives (United Kingdom 2012):

TABLE 3.1: COMMUNICATIONS OBJECTIVES

Objective	Description
Example 1	
Policy objective	To ensure that compliance with a new tax regulation is above 80 percent
Communications objective	To ensure that the majority of the general public understands the reasons why complying with the regulation benefits the economy
Sub-objective 1	To ensure that the public is given a fair and balanced view of the policy, via the media
Example 2	
Policy objective	To get 10,000 more people working as community service volunteers in your area
Communications objective	To get 40,000 people in the area to register as potential volunteers on a community website
Sub-objective 1	To increase the proportion of the public that recognizes the value of volunteering from 20 percent to 40 percent
Sub-objective 2	To get 80,000 people to visit the website and find out more about how to volunteer
Sub-objective 3	To secure 40,000 incremental registrations
Example 3	
Program objective	To ensure that unauthorized staff absences fall by 50 percent
Communications objective	To ensure that all staff are able to follow the correct processes for reporting absences from work
Sub-objective 1	To ensure that all staff recognize that there is a policy for reporting absences from work and that it must be followed
Sub-objective 2	To ensure that all staff understand how to access the guidance on how to report absences

Source: Adapted from United Kingdom. Government Communication Network. 2012. *Evaluating Government Communication Activity: Standards and Guidance*, p. 9. London: Cabinet Office.

Communications objectives are typically defined in three dimensions—output, outtake, and outcome. **Output objectives** attempt to define the tangible goods or services produced by a specific communications activity. **Outtake objectives** are designed to define exactly what organizations want target audience members to take away from a specific communications activity. **Outcome objectives** are designed to define the extent to which an organization would like members of a target audience to change (feelings, opinions, attitudes, and/or behaviour) as a result of the core themes or messages included in a communications activity.

Output Objectives

Output objectives define the tangible goods or services that an organization intends to produce via a specific communications activity. Output objectives can have either an intermediary audience or an end audience. **Intermediary audiences** include the individuals, groups, organizations, or institutions that are targeted to deliver an organization's key message to an end audience (e.g., media, stakeholders, delivery partners, non-governmental organizations). **End audiences** include the groups and individuals that are the ultimate targets of a policy, program, or initiative. To craft output objectives for both intermediary and end audiences, the GCN provides the following examples of measures that can be adapted to suit most communications strategies:

TABLE 3.2: COMMUNICATIONS OUTPUTS

Output type	Description
Press	• Intended number of coverage pieces achieved • Intended frequency of exposure to coverage by end audience
Marketing	• Proportion of the target audience to be reached by media activity • Intended number of impressions (one page view) on the web page • Intended number of stakeholders contacted and number of contacts actually made
Internal	• Intended number of staff attending events and training sessions • Intended number of impressions on a website or social media space

Source: Adapted from United Kingdom. Government Communication Network. 2012. *Evaluating Government Communication Activity: Standards and Guidance,* p. 12. London: Cabinet Office.

Outtake Objectives

Outtake objectives define what public sector organizations want target audience members to take away from a specific communications activity, typically in terms of key message awareness/retention, comprehension, and motivation. Examples of outtake objectives include: achieving a 5 percent increase in public awareness of policy X; having 85 percent of the population of region Y understand the behavioural implications of a new hunting regulation; and getting 95 percent of a province's population to understand new municipal voting procedures one year after their introduction. The GCN provides the following examples of outtake metrics that can be adapted to suit most communications strategies:

TABLE 3.3: COMMUNICATIONS OUTTAKES

Outtake type	Description
Awareness/retention	What is the intended number of people who will become aware of the communications activity and/or key message(s)?
Comprehension	How many people will understand the key messages in the communications activity?
Motivation	What is the intended effect of the communications activity on end users' feelings and attitudes? On behaviour?

Source: Adapted from United Kingdom. Government Communication Network. 2012. *Evaluating Government Communication Activity: Standards and Guidance,* p. 14. London: Cabinet Office.

Outcome Objectives

Outcome objectives define the changes in the behaviour of target audience members that result from exposure to the core themes or messages of a specific communications activity. Examples of outcome objectives include: increasing voter turnout rates in a given municipality by 10 percent as a result of increased awareness of the importance of voting; and decreasing the number of driving regulation violations by 5 percent in a 12-month period as a result of increased understanding of changes to the regulations. The GCN provides the following examples of outcome metrics that can be adapted to suit most communications strategies:

TABLE 3.4: COMMUNICATIONS OUTCOMES

Outcome type	Description
Talk	• How many people will discuss the activity or its message with peers, friends and families? • How many partners or stakeholders will discuss it?
Direct response	• How many people will respond to or otherwise interact with the organization as a result of the activity? This could include visiting a website, attending training, ringing a phone line or having a face-to-face discussion.
Indirect response	• How many people will respond to or otherwise interact with third parties as a result of your activity? This could include people interacting with stakeholders or partners or other local and national services.
Other actions	• How many people will take (or will claim to take) any other action as a result of your activity? For example, in a stop-smoking campaign this might include people buying books, patches or other similar products.

Source: Adapted from United Kingdom. Government Communication Network. 2012. *Evaluating Government Communication Activity: Standards and Guidance*, p. 14. London: Cabinet Office.

3.2 INDICATORS

In communications, objectives define what organizations want to achieve when communicating with identified audiences about a specific program, service, proposal, or initiative. In contrast, **indicators** are metrics that allow organizations to assess whether or not objectives are being achieved. Indicators need to be set for each objective at the output, outtake, and outcome levels (Lindenmann 2002).

Output Indicators

Output indicators are variables that report on the quantity of goods or services produced by a specific communications activity and the associated levels of consumption. An indicator of output production might be the number of materials (websites, social media broadcasts, media interviews, pamphlets, advertisements, etc.) produced by a specific communications campaign. The GCN provides the following examples of output production indicators that can be adapted to suit most communications strategies:

TABLE 3.5: OUTPUT PRODUCTION INDICATORS

Activity type	Metric
Purchased media	Audience reach and frequency of exposure, which could include: • estimated reach, coverage, and frequency (TV, press, radio, outdoor ads, etc.) • the number of impressions served (digital advertising) • the number of planned clicks (paid-for search) • the number of inserts produced/leaflets planned to be distributed (direct marketing)
Media activity Proactive publicity Media reactions Media briefings and handling	The number of: • media briefing activities; materials issued to the media • corrections, reactive statements, and rebuttals issued; the number of interviews arranged • media briefings and media handling sessions organized for ministers and officials
Social media	The website, social media, or other digital space and related content created to meet communication objectives
Public/stakeholder engagement	Depending on nature of engagement activity, could include the number of: • invitations to events sent • requests to provide feedback issued • specific activities undertaken to publicize engagement activity • visits to a website created to gather feedback • nature of contacts made with specific stakeholders
Internal communications	The number of internal communication activities, including: • invitations to events or training sessions sent • emails or other written communication sent • content posted on the intranet • informal events (without prior invitation)
Expenditures	Any costs incurred in running activities; time and internal resources used

Source: Adapted from United Kingdom. Government Communication Network. 2012. *Evaluating Government Communication Activity: Standards and Guidance,* pp. 30–48. London: Cabinet Office.

An indicator of output consumption (a metric that reports on end audience usage) might be how many households receive a particular pamphlet, or how many readers receive a newspaper that carries a specific paid advertisement. In table 3.6, the GCN provides examples of output consumption indicators that can be adapted to suit most communications strategies.

Outtake Indicators

Recall that outtake objectives define how and what an organization wants target audience members to take away from a particular communications activity. **Outtake indicators** report on how successfully these objectives were reached; they are usually arranged along a continuum that ranges from awareness and comprehension of core themes and messages at one end, to retention and recall at the other. In table 3.7, the GCN provides examples of outtake indicators that can be adapted to suit most communications strategies.

TABLE 3.6: OUTPUT CONSUMPTION INDICATORS

Output type	Metric
Purchased media	The number or percentage of end audience reached by media activity and how often they will see it
Media activity Proactive publicity Media reactions Media briefings and handling	The number of: • media contacts reached; the number of times each was contacted • media contacts reached with corrections, reactive statements, and rebuttals; the number of interviews that take place • briefings and training sessions organized, the information and skills passed on
Social media	The number of end audience members who visit the site or digital space at least once during the evaluation period (unique users)
Public/stakeholder engagement	Depending on the nature of engagement activity, these might include the number of people who: • are reached via publicity, invitations and requests • attend the event • visit the website or digital space The number of conversations with specific stakeholders as a result of contacts generated
Internal communications	The number of employees who: • receive invitations to events or training sessions, emails, or other written communication • view content on the intranet • attend events and training

Source: Adapted from United Kingdom. Government Communication Network. 2012. *Evaluating Government Communication Activity: Standards and Guidance,* pp. 30–48. London: Cabinet Office.

Outcome Indicators

Outcome indicators report on how target audience members change as a result of the core themes or messages included in a communications activity. Communications outcomes range from opinions, attitudes, and preferences to behaviour. An **opinion** is a verbal expression, or spoken or written point of view. An **attitude** is a deeper and more complex concept, reflecting not only what people say, but also what they know and think and how they are inclined to act. **Preferences** can be thought of as opinions and attitudes "in action," or an individual's use of opinions and attitudes to choose one alternative over another. In table 3.8, the GCN provides examples of outcome indicators that can be adapted to suit most communications strategies.

TABLE 3.7: OUTTAKE INDICATORS

Outtake type	Metric
Awareness	The number of users (both intermediary and end audience members) who: • recognize specific communications products/activities (ads, leaflets, letters, event invitations, etc.) • gain awareness of key/supporting messages • view advertising, communication or publicity about the key/supporting messages
Recall	The number of users (both intermediary and end audience members) who: • recall viewing key/supporting messages • recall the places where they saw the key/supporting messages • accurately describe specific communications products and/or activities (ads, leaflets, letters, event invitations, etc.) they have seen
Retention/comprehension	The number of users (both intermediary and end audience members) who • understand the key messages • like the activity/message • think the message was relevant to them • think the activity/message was clear and engaging • understand the key/supporting message(s) that the activity was promoting

Source: Adapted from United Kingdom. Government Communication Network. 2012. *Evaluating Government Communication Activity: Standards and Guidance*, pp. 30–48. London: Cabinet Office.

Behaviour is the identifiable collection of actions and inactions that an individual displays in a given environment, and serves as the ultimate product of processing information contained in a key message or theme. The GCN recommends using the metrics in table 3.9 as a starting point for developing indicators of desired behavioural outcomes.

TABLE 3.8: OUTCOME INDICATORS

Outcome type	Metric
Purchased media	
Opinion	The number of users (both intermediary and end audience members) who: • like the activity/messages • think the message was relevant to them • think the activity/message was clear and engaging • understand the key/supporting message that the activity was promoting
Attitude/preference	The number of users (both intermediary and end audience members) who feel that the activity/message had an impact on their: • views/attitudes/feelings in general • views/attitudes/feelings about the organization
Media activity	
Proactive publicity	The attitude of the media (and key media contacts where applicable) toward the activity/message
Media reactions	The attitude of the media toward key issues
Media briefings and handling	What ministers and senior officials think about the briefing and training provided, i.e., do they find it useful? Do they intend to put it into practice?

Source: Adapted from United Kingdom. Government Communication Network. 2012. *Evaluating Government Communication Activity: Standards and Guidance*, pp. 30–48. London: Cabinet Office.

TABLE 3.9: BEHAVIOURAL OUTCOMES

Desired behavioural outcome	Metric
User to seek information via call centre	The number of people who will call and why
User to seek information via digital advertising	The reasons that motivated people to call (ads, media coverage, word of mouth, etc.) The number of people who will: • click on digital advertising or text links • visit a website or social media space as a result of advertising
User to seek information via social media	The average length of time spent on a website or social media space The number of: • visit sources (i.e., where people came to the site from) • pages visited within site • videos/embedded content viewed on a website or social media space • people who seek additional information • "likes" on Facebook; "retweets" on Twitter • "bounces" (i.e., number of people who visit one page of a website and then leave)

User to seek information via correspondence	The number of emails received (positive/negative); the number of letters received (positive/negative)
User to register for a service, product, or information	The number of people who: • request to register for product/service/information • complete registration • actually receive the product/service/information • use the product/service/information • sign up to receive information in the future • complete the registration process • make an appointment with organization representative • attend made appointments
User to start, stop, or continue a particular behaviour	The number of people who: • take the relevant steps to change their behaviour as a result of the communications activity and/or key messages • engage in the promoted behaviour • continue with the changed behaviour over time
User to interact with organization and/or others	The number of people who: • forward key/supporting message on to others (i.e., retweet) • claim to have discussed key/supporting message with others (online and offline) • pass on or sharing content digitally (e.g., Twitter, Facebook, Reddit) • interact with organization online (i.e., number of Facebook fans or friends, the number "liking" content) The amount of "talk" on digital forums, blogs, websites, etc; the planned-for amount of "talk" that is positive (and accurate)

User to attend engagement event	
Attend event	The number of people/percentage of target audience who attend event The number of event attendees who interact with staff during the event
Acquire new skill/modify behaviour	The number of attendees who undertake specific actions/behaviours consistent with key/supporting messages The number of attendees who put promoted skills/information into practice
Pass message on to others	The number of attendees who pass key message on/discuss event message with others; number of key stakeholder representatives who do same The number of stakeholders or members of the public who claim to have discussed key messages with others (online and offline), including: • the number passing on or sharing content digitally (e.g.,tweets, retweets, sharing link on Facebook) • amount of digital talk on forums, blogs, websites, etc. (tracked via buzz monitoring) • amount of positive (and accurate) digital talk
Provide usable feedback	The number of people who respond to the engagement activity in any way, including: • comments or feedback received on website, in writing, by phone, or face-to-face • the quality of feedback and comments received • the number of people attending additional/future public meetings or hearings

Source: United Kingdom. Government Communication Network. 2012. *Evaluating Government Communication Activity: Standards and Guidance*, pp. 30–48. London: Cabinet Office.

3.3 BASELINES

Clear, precise, specific objectives at the output, outtake, and outcome levels define what public sector organizations want to achieve when communicating with identified audiences about specific proposals or initiatives. Public sector organizations use **baselines**, defined as starting reference points or snapshots of current conditions against which any changes initiated by a communications activity can be measured, to determine what has been achieved. For example, if an objective for a particular communications strategy is to achieve a 5 percent increase in public awareness of policy X, the current level of public awareness of policy X would need to be established in order to successfully evaluate whether or not the strategy achieved the objective. For the measurement and evaluation of any communications activity to be meaningful, baselines need to be established for each indicator attached to an objective prior to the launch of any communications activity.

Chapter 9 examines the most common research tools that public sector organizations use to generate data for both indicators and baselines as part of the communications evaluation process.

LEARNING ACTIVITIES

Activity 3.1: Assess an Existing Communications Initiative

Identify an initiative that is currently being used by a public sector organization to achieve an established strategic goal. The initiative must be old enough and of sufficient priority to have generated a critical mass of related, publicly available communications materials (e.g., press releases, backgrounders, FAQs, speeches, letters to the editor). Using these materials, try to identify and describe the following:

- overall communications objective(s)
- output objectives
- outtake objectives
- outcome objectives

Activity 3.2: Develop the Strategic Framework for a New Initiative

Choose an initiative that is being used to achieve one of the strategic goals established for a public sector organization you described in activity 2.1 or 2.2. For this initiative, develop the following:

- an overall communications objective that defines what the responsible organization should try to achieve when communicating with identified audiences about the initiative. Make sure the overall communications objective is aligned with the objectives of the initiative it is designed to support
- output objectives that define the tangible goods or services that should be produced by specific communications activities
- outtake objectives that define exactly what the organization should want target audience members to take away from the communications activities
- outcome objectives that define how the organization would like members of a target audience to change (feelings, opinions, attitudes, and/or behaviour) as a result of the core themes or messages included in a communications activities

FURTHER READING

Robinson and colleagues provide an excellent account of how one public sector organization developed and executed a communications plan for an HIV clinical trial in the *Communications Handbook for Clinical Trials: Strategies, Tips, and Tools to Manage Controversy, Convey Your Message, and Disseminate Results* (2014). Chapter 3 in particular provides good treatment—with specific examples—of strategic communications plan development in a public health context. A second excellent source that provides insight into the communications planning process, including many examples, is the UK Government Communication Network's *Evaluating Government Communication Activity: Standards and Guidance* (2012).

ONLINE RESOURCES

The following websites provide links to other sites that offer a wealth of tips, tools, and resources for creating communications strategies in public and non-profit organizations: (1) KnowHow NonProfit (www. knowhownonprofit.org/campaigns/communications/effective-communications-1/communications-strategy) and (2) Communicate and Howe! (www.communicateandhowe.com/what-we-do/strategy/create-nonprofit-communications-strategy/). In addition, WikiHow's overview "How to Write a Communications Strategy" provides specific examples of actual communications strategies (www.wikihow.com/Write-a-Communications-Strategy).

QUESTIONS FOR CRITICAL REFLECTION

1. Why is the task of establishing objectives so critical to the success of the communications function in public sector organizations in general?
2. On the surface, just by looking at any given tactic, can the quality of objectives for any communications initiative be assessed? How?

KEY TERMS

attitude: Reflects not only what people say, but also what they know and think and how they are inclined to act.

baseline: A starting reference point or snapshot of current conditions against which changes initiated by a communications activity can be measured.

behaviour: The identifiable collection of actions and inactions that an individual displays in a given environment, which serves as the ultimate product of processing information contained in a key message or theme.

communications objectives: Define what an organization wants to achieve when communicating with identified audiences about a specific program, service, proposal, or initiative.

end audience: The groups and individuals that are the ultimate targets of a policy, program, or initiative.

indicator: A variable that allows organizations to assess whether or not objectives are being achieved. Indicators need to be set for each objective at the output, outtake, and outcome levels.

intermediary audience: The individuals, groups, organizations, or institutions that are targeted to deliver an organization's key message to an end audience (e.g., media, stakeholders, delivery partners, non-governmental organizations).

opinion: A verbal expression, or spoken or written point of view.

outcome indicator: A variable that reports on how target audience members change as a result of the core themes or messages included in a communications activity.

outcome objective: Defines the extent to which an organization would like members of a target audience to change (feelings, opinions, attitudes, and/or behaviour) as a result of the core themes or messages included in a communications activity.

output indicator: A variable that reports on the quantity of goods or services produced by a specific communications activity and the associated levels of consumption.

output objective: Defines the tangible goods or services that are produced by a specific communications activity.

outtake indicator: A variable that reports on how and what an organization wants target audience members to take away from a particular communications activity, usually arranged along a continuum that ranges from awareness and comprehension of core themes and messages at one end, to retention and recall at the other.

outtake objective: Defines exactly what organizations want target audience members to take away from a specific communications activity.

preferences: Opinions and attitudes "in action," or an individual's use of opinions and attitudes to choose one alternative over another.

WORKS CITED

Asibey, Edith, Toni Parras, and Justin van Fleet. 2008. *Are We There Yet? A Communications Evaluation Guide.* New York: The Communications Network.

Lindenmann, Walter K. 2002. *Guidelines for Measuring the Effectiveness of PR Programs and Activities.* Gainesville, FL: Institute for Public Relations.

Robinson, Elizabeth, Deborah Baron, Lori Heise, Jill Moffett, and Sarah Harlan. 2014. *Communications Handbook for Clinical Trials: Strategies, Tips, and Tools to Manage Controversy, Convey Your Message, and Disseminate Results.* Washington, DC: Family Health International.

United Kingdom. Government Communication Network. 2012. *Evaluating Government Communication Activity: Standards and Guidance.* London: Cabinet Office.

CHAPTER 4

CLEAR WRITING AND KEY MESSAGE DEVELOPMENT

CHAPTER OVERVIEW

This chapter focuses on the most important skill in the professional communicator's tool box—the ability to write clearly. It begins with a short primer on clear writing—choice of language, and organization and presentation of material—and then examines how clear writing is employed in the development of key messages, the heart and soul of all communications tactics.

LEARNING OBJECTIVES

By the end of this chapter, you will be able to

- define what clear writing is and explain why it is important to public sector communications;
- use basic principles of language, organization, and presentation in the development of various communications tactics;
- define what a key message is;
- identify key messages used in existing communications campaigns; and
- develop key messages for new initiatives that
    - identify a target audience;
    - explain the nature of the problem or issue that is causing the organization to act;
    - identify options for addressing the problem or issue;
    - articulate what specific actions the organizations is taking to deal with the problem or issue; and
    - evoke a sense of values that are likely to motivate target audience members to believe and ultimately act upon the message.

INTRODUCTION

The ability to write clearly is one of the most basic—and important—competencies that new professionals in public sector communications need to possess and develop. Clear writing is an essential component of all public sector communications activities—from drafting a communications strategy, to defining communications objectives, to writing a press release, to tweeting about an organization's latest initiative. Clear writing, however, is not merely a simplified form of writing. It involves more than replacing jargon and technically complex language with shorter sentences and familiar words. **Clear writing** is a way of presenting information so that everyone—young and old, technicians and lay people—can read and understand it. It is achieved by focusing on the whole message, and considering not only what the material says but also how it is organized and how it looks (Ontario 2011).

Clear writing is particularly important in the development of key messages, the main points or ideas that public sector organizations want to communicate with members of a target audience about a particular product, service, initiative, or proposal. Key messages must be written with particular clarity because they need to embody both communications and program objectives, engage key stakeholders in a way that supports the organization's strategic goals, and be sensitive to how the media has treated the nature of the public conversation that has taken place between the organization and its stakeholders.

This chapter begins with a short primer on clear writing—choice of language, and organization and presentation of material—and then turns to examine how clear writing is employed in the development of key messages.

4.1 CLEAR WRITING[1]

According to Ontario's Ministry of Agriculture, Food, and Rural Affairs (OMAFRA), clear writing is "a way of presenting information so that it is easy for everyone to read and understand ... [especially] people whose first language is not English, people who do not see well, and people who are too busy to read a large amount of text to gain a small amount of information" (Ontario 2011). Consider that

- 4 in 10 adult Canadians do not have the literacy skills they need to meet the ever-increasing demands of modern life;
- 14.6 percent of adult Canadians (3 million) do not have the skills to deal with the majority of writing materials that they are faced with in everyday life; and

- 27 percent of adult Canadians (5.8 million) have the skills to carry out reading tasks when the reading materials are simple and clearly laid out, but not the skills to cope with unfamiliar or complex reading material (ibid.).

The first thing communications professionals need to consider when setting out to write any communications product is the audience, specifically the following: Who is the main audience for the communications product? What are the needs and abilities of audience members? What message(s) does the organization want audience members to take away from the product?

Ideally, the main audience(s) for a specific communications activity will already have been identified and described in the stakeholder analysis performed as part of the environmental assessment illustrated in chapter 2. Potential audiences could include government employees; senior decision-makers within the organization; a supervisor; the general public; 13- to 19-year-olds who live in rural areas; highly trained professionals; members of a specific cultural group; people waiting in line for a public service; or people who are upset (which may be related to waiting in line). Whatever the audience, the best first step in preparing to write a communications product is to do some background research on the characteristics of main audience members. And remember that, most of the time, readers are less familiar with the subject than writers are.

In terms of message transmission, it is essential to focus on what the audience needs to know and not what is nice to know; in other words, don't say more than is needed. It is also important to think about how the audience is going to use the material: Will the document be a quick reference tool? Will it be displayed in a public area? Is the reader supposed to do something after reading the document? What information does the reader need to remember? Answers to these questions will affect how the material is organized and presented.

Language

The point of clear writing is to use the clearest words possible to describe actions, objects, and people. Often, writing clearly means choosing a two-syllable word over a three-syllable one, a familiar term instead of the latest bureaucratic expression, and, sometimes, several clearer words instead of one complicated word. Ultimately, the exact choice of wording needs to be based on what is clearest for the reader. If you are unsure, ask. Test draft documents with people who are likely to use them. Table 4.1 offers some tips on language choice:

TABLE 4.1: OMAFRA'S LANGUAGE CHOICE TIPS

Advice	Good example	Better example
Write directly to the reader.	All staff employees are asked to submit their reports by the end of the year.	Have your work reports in by December 31.
Don't change verbs into nouns.	Immunizing will be done twice a year.	We will immunize children each January and June.
Use the active voice—the subject does this action.	The coffee pot must be washed.	You must wash the coffee pot.
Use a positive tone.	Anyone not wearing a bathing cap will not be allowed in the pool.	You must wear a bathing cap while in the pool.
Avoid using jargon or acronyms.	The new OMAFRA office has a boardroom that rural stakeholders can use.	The new office of the Ontario Ministry of Agriculture, Food, and Rural Affairs (OMAFRA) has a boardroom that rural stakeholders can use.
Explain difficult words in their context.	Every season, your sprayer should be calibrated.	Every season, calibrate your sprayer by measuring the output of each nozzle to make sure that each one is putting out the same amount of spray.

Source: Ontario. Ministry of Agriculture, Food, and Rural Affairs (OMAFRA). 2011. *Clear Writing Factsheet.* www.omafra.gov.on.ca/english/rural/facts/07-049.htm

Organization

Clear, organized thinking produces clear, logical writing. Some communications problems may be solved by changing words or sentence structure, but others involve the way words or thoughts are arranged. The organization of any communications product is an essential part of clearly conveying the key message. To organize clearly, start by asking the following: What does the reader most need to know? What is your main message or theme? Decide what information needs to be included and what can be left out without detracting from the key message(s). This process should produce a prioritized list of main and secondary points.

The next step in the organization process involves developing a structure for the document that makes it easy to use and informative. For example, chronological order might be the most logical approach for describing procedures. If people already know something about the subject and the point of the document is to share new information, start with the old, then introduce the new. If the point is to describe something completely new, start with general information about the objectives or reasons for the new information, then deal with the specifics. Table 4.2 offers some general tips for organizing clearly:

TABLE 4.2: OMAFRA'S ORGANIZATION TIPS

Advice	Good example	Better example
Use headings that summarize the text.	Attention!	Information on New Government Grants
Write complete sentences only when it makes sense to do so. List critical points apart from the text.	The Annual Fall Clean-Up Day will be held on Saturday, October the 20th from 9:00 a.m. to 3:30 p.m. at the Anyplace Township Dump. Garbage must be brought in pickup trucks or cars. No hazardous materials will be accepted at this time. All garbage must be unloaded by hand. Organize your garbage with wood on top, then metal objects, then tires on the bottom. This dump is open to Anyplace Township residents only. Dumping charges will be $10 per vehicle.	ANNUAL FALL CLEAN-UP DAY ANYPLACE TOWNSHIP RESIDENTS ONLY Date: Saturday, October 20, 20XX Time: 9:00 a.m. to 3:30 p.m. Place: Anyplace Township Dump Cost: $10 per vehicle Load your vehicle in the following order from bottom to top: Tires Metal Objects Wood * No hazardous materials will be accepted!
Avoid long, complicated sentences.	A viable agricultural base strengthens the rural community and likewise, agriculture benefits from close ties to community, business, education, social, and recreation facilities.	A viable agricultural base strengthens the rural community. Agriculture benefits from close ties to community, business, education, social, and recreation facilities.
Use parallel construction in lists—phrase each item using the same grammatical form.	The volunteer survey had the following suggestions: planning meetings should be held in the spring. Do all recruiting through the newspaper. We should conduct two fundraisers every year.	The volunteer survey had the following suggestions: Hold planning meetings in the spring. Recruit through the newspaper. Hold fundraising events twice a year.

Source: Ontario. Ministry of Agriculture, Food, and Rural Affairs (OMAFRA). 2011. *Clear Writing Factsheet.* www.omafra.gov.on.ca/english/rural/facts/07-049.htm

Presentation

Clear writing is more than just language and organization—to be clear, writing also needs to be presented in a way that makes it stand out and easy to understand. Table 4.3 offers some basic tips for improving clarity in presentation:

TABLE 4.3: OMAFRA'S PRESENTATION TIPS

Advice	Rationale
Use serif type for text.	Serif type has "feet" on the ends of the letters that move the reader's eye along the line, making it the best choice for paragraphs of text. Garamond is an example of a serif typeface.
Use sans-serif type for short headings.	Sans-serif type is suitable for headings and signs. Franklin Gothic is an example of a sans-serif typeface.
Do not use all capital letters in body text.	Using all capital letters makes text look too dense. People identify words and letters by shape.
Use bold type for emphasis.	Italics are difficult to read.
Use a legible size of type for body text.	Some fonts are more difficult to read at small sizes than others. Choose a point size and font combination that makes your body text easy for everyone to read.
Use graphics that enhance text.	Graphics should help to break up the text; however, do not over-use graphics and clutter up your page.
Use a simple design.	Do not try to add too many different fonts and styles; do not over-design your material. Simple is best! It is easier to read and more effective.
Text justification	Left-justified text (with uneven right margins) gives the reader's eye a rest at the end of each line and a point of reference to begin reading the next line. Justified text (text with even left and right margins) can save room on the page and looks neater, but appears dense and is difficult to read.
Bullets and boxes	Graphic elements such as bullets (•) and boxes can be used to organize text and draw attention to certain areas. Be careful to be consistent in how you use these or else they can be more confusing than helpful to your reader.
White space	Too much text gives a dense appearance and sends two messages to the reader: This is going to be hard to understand, and this is going to be boring. Columns and wide page margins make your text easier to read.

Source: Ontario. Ministry of Agriculture, Food, and Rural Affairs (OMAFRA). 2011. *Clear Writing Factsheet.* www.omafra.gov.on.ca/english/rural/facts/07-049.htm

4.2 KEY MESSAGES

The heart of any communications strategy is the **key message**, the main point or idea that an organization wants to communicate to members of a target audience. While typically short and to the point, effective key messages need to

- clearly identify a target audience;
- explain the nature of the problem or issue that is causing the organization to act;
- identify credible options for addressing the problem or issue;
- articulate what specific actions the organizations is taking to deal with the problem or issue; and
- evoke a sense of values that are likely to motivate target audience members to believe and ultimately act upon the message (Bennett and Jessani 2011).

As a former senior Red Cross official summarized:

> To be successful, a [key] message must be received by the intended individual or audience. It must get the audience's attention. It must be understood. It must be believed. It must be remembered. And ultimately, in some fashion, it must be acted upon. Failure to accomplish any of these tasks means the entire message fails. (quoted in Wilcox and Cameron 2012, 178)

A report for the US-based National Cancer Institute (NCI) recommends a three-step process for developing effective messages (National Cancer Institute [NCI] 2008). First, review existing materials. Most of the time, the key message(s) for a specific communications campaign will not be new. Most likely, messages will already have been developed around a strategic commitment in an election document, a throne speech, or budget. These need to be considered and reviewed both to ensure consistency in messaging on the same issue and to ensure that the message is still accurate, current, and complete, and relevant and appropriate for the intended audience.

Second, develop the primary concepts that are central the message. According to NCI, **message concepts** are "messages in rough form [that] represent ways of presenting information to the intended audiences. These may include statements only or statements and visuals—but not the actual messages themselves" (NCI 2008, 54). The following illustrates how NCI used focus groups to develop cancer risk message concepts for a recent awareness campaign.

To provide cancer risk information to the public in ways that it could be readily understood and used, NCI conducted a series of focus groups to learn what the groups thought of different methods for communicating about risks. The following insights from the groups underscored the importance of considering both word usage and presentation methods when developing message concepts and materials:

- Participants said that they want cancer risk messages to give them hope for preventing cancer and that risk information is less threatening when written in optimistic terms.
- When faced with "bad news" about cancer risks, they said that they look for why it does not apply to them.
- They wanted risk messages to address key questions such as "How serious is the risk?" and "What can be done to reduce or avoid the risk?" as well as explain how and where to get additional information.
- Word choice also influences how information is perceived; "risk" raises alarm, while "chance" minimizes it.
- Use of vague or unfamiliar terms (including "fourfold," "relative risk," and "lifetime risk") gives people reason to discount the information.
- Combining brief text and visuals (such as charts and graphs) can increase attention and understanding.
- Statistical risk information was difficult for many participants to understand; percentages were more understandable than ratios, but in either case accompanying explanations of the seriousness of the risk were needed.
- Participants were interested in "the complete picture"—that is, what is known and what is not yet known about a risk, and what it means for "human beings."
- The source of risk information colors credibility, with participants saying that they are less likely to trust the media or a source with a business interest and more likely to trust risk information supplied by a physician or medical journal.

Source: National Cancer Institute (NCI). 2008. *Making Health Communications Work*, p. 62. Rockville, MD: National Cancer Institute.

Third, test message concepts to ensure resonance with the audience. Message concepts should be tested for cultural appropriateness, or "the values, norms, symbols, ways of living, traditions, history, and institutions shared by a group of people," which affect how people perceive and respond to messages (NCI 2008, 62). Effective messages need to demonstrate a firm understanding of the cultural norms of the intended audiences (e.g., community versus individual values). The following documents NCI's efforts to develop messages about mammography that resonate across cultures:

Feature 4.2: Identifying Messages that Resonate

As part of an effort to design messages that are meaningful and appealing to women in different ethnic groups and to older women, NCI's Office of Communications conducted separate focus groups with African-American, American-Indian, Asian, Caucasian, and Latina women.

The groups tested 10 motivational messages about mammography. Once participants had individually selected the motivational messages they found most and least persuasive, the moderator led them in a more detailed discussion of each message's strengths and weaknesses. Throughout the discussion, the moderator probed participants' knowledge, attitudes, and behaviors concerning breast cancer and mammography, sometimes exploring underlying motivations and barriers.

Across focus groups, the following message elements were viewed most positively:

- Breast cancer can develop at any time.
- All women are at risk—even those age 65 and older, or those without a family history.
- Mammograms can detect breast cancer early.
- Early detection can save lives.

The least persuasive messages made explicit reference to issues that were considered turnoffs, fear, and age. Participants were uncomfortable with messages that specified age and, in some cases, gender. Many said that cancer was a risk for all people (some pointed out that men can get breast cancer), stating that older women (those over 40) should not be singled out. The notion of a mammogram being able to "save your life" was persuasive not only because it was positive, but also because it did not distinguish between age groups. In general, messages that seemed to tell women what to think were deemed offensive, while messages that were phrased as explanation or encouragement were more effective.

Source: National Cancer Institute (NCI). 2008. *Making Health Communications Work,* pp. 59–60. Rockville, MD: National Cancer Institute.

Message concepts should also be tested to ensure the effectiveness of the chosen appeal type. According to NCI, "to capture the intended audience's attention, you can scare people, tug at their hearts, make them laugh, make them feel good, or give them straight facts. What will work best? The answer generally depends on the intended audience's preferences, what your program is asking people to do, and how you plan to use the appeal in asking them to do it" (NCI 2008, 61). For example, message concepts that offer audience members a benefit without discussion of potential drawbacks tend to work when intended audience members are already in favour of an idea or practice. By contrast, message concepts that offer a benefit and directly address potential drawbacks tend to work when intended audience members are not in favour of an idea or practice. Depending on time and resources, message concept testing can be done either informally within the office or more formally with the use of opinion polling and focus groups.

The following illustrates the three-step message development process used as part of an NCI cancer research awareness campaign:

Feature 4.3: From Message Concept to Final Message

In 1996, the NCI's Office of Communications (OC), then the Office of Cancer Communications, launched the Cancer Research Awareness Initiative to increase the public's understanding of the process of medical discoveries and the relevance of discoveries to people's lives. OC's concept development and message testing for this initiative included the following activities.

Three values of medical research were selected for concept development:

1. Progress (e.g., we are achieving breakthroughs)
2. Benefits (e.g., prevention, detection, and treatment research are benefiting all of us)

3. Hope (e.g., we are hopeful that today's research will yield tomorrow's breakthroughs)

Based on these values, the following message concepts were developed and explored in focus groups with intended audience members:

- Research has led to real progress in the detection, diagnosis, treatment, and prevention of cancer.
- Everyone benefits from cancer research in some fashion.
- Cancer research is conducted in universities and medical schools across the country.
- Cancer research gives hope.
- At the broadest level, research priorities are determined by societal problems and concerns; at the project level, research priorities are driven primarily by past research successes and current opportunities.

The following messages were crafted after listening to intended audience members' reactions and their language and ideas about the importance of medical research:

A: Cancer Research: Discovering Answers for All of Us
B: Cancer Research: Because Cancer Touches Us All
C: Cancer Research: Discovering More Answers Every Day
D: Cancer Research: Because Lives Depend on It
E: Cancer Research: Only Research Cures Cancer

Mall-intercept interviews were conducted to pretest them. Based on responses from the intended audience in these interviews, message D was selected as the program theme.

Source: National Cancer Institute (NCI). 2008. *Making Health Communications Work,* pp. 56–59. Rockville, MD: National Cancer Institute.

Non-partisanship and Key Message Development

In Canada's public sector, key messages must also be **non-partisan**, that is, free from promoting or appearing to promote "the governing party's political interests by fostering a positive impression of the government or a negative impression of any group or person critical of the government" (Office of the Auditor General 2011, 412). The principle of non-partisanship is embedded in both legislation and codes of conduct that govern Canadian public sector communications practice. In Ontario, for example, the Government Advertising Act, 2004, "prohibits government advertising that may be viewed as promoting the governing party's political interests by fostering a positive impression of the government or a negative impression of any group or person critical of the government" (ibid.). To this end, the act requires the auditor general to review and approve government ads prior to usage and to report annually on the results of the review. In Alberta, the provincial government's Social Media—Web 2.0 Policy states that "regardless of the media being used, GoA [Government of Alberta] employees must not do anything that could harm the reputation of the Government of Alberta. They must ensure that any comment on matters of government policy is appropriate to their employee role and must respect the need to maintain politically neutral GoA services" (Alberta 2010, 1).

The following excerpt from a 2013 Government of Saskatchewan press release on the status of the balanced budget, a key political priority of the governing Conservative Party, offers a good example of how a key message maintains political neutrality:

Feature 4.4: Non-partisan Press Release

Saskatchewan has maintained its enviable position through the first three-quarters of this fiscal year, remaining the only province in Canada on track for a balanced budget.[...]

"Given the current world economy, preserving a balanced budget is challenging," Finance Minister Ken Krawetz said. "While Saskatchewan's economy is strong, resource revenue is down because of falling prices. This decline is offset somewhat by record investment and revenue from a growing tax base, which has expanded thanks to higher employment and population growth."[...]

"Fiscal responsibility continues to be our foundation, a key part of our Plan For Growth to help keep Saskatchewan moving forward," Krawetz said. "Given the volatility of world markets and unforeseen circumstances, we are pleased to be able to maintain a balanced budget."

Source: Saskatchewan. Department of Finance. 2013. "Saskatchewan Remains on Track for Balanced Budget." News release, February 15. www.gov.sk.ca/news?newsId=38eb2bce-7081-4711-a161-607523070228

Note how the release uses the relatively generic term "Saskatchewan" to reference a collective entity that could as easily be "the Government of Saskatchewan" or "the Government of Saskatchewan as led by the Conservative Party of Saskatchewan." A more partisan term would have been "the Conservative Government of Saskatchewan" or "Conservative Premier Wall's Government of Saskatchewan."

Maintaining political neutrality in key message development in the public sector is not an easy task, especially given the symbiotic relationship between permanent and political executives in the management and administration of the communications function in general (Brown 2012). Recall from chapter 1 that public sector communications professionals are responsible for managing all communication activities related to "issues and matters pertaining to the policies, programs, services and initiatives" their organizations administer, and are to administer these responsibilities "in an accountable, non-partisan fashion consistent with the principles of Canadian parliamentary democracy and ministerial responsibility" (Treasury Board of Canada Secretariat 2012). On the other hand, political executives are responsible for their government's overall communication priorities, objectives, and requirements, which include working with non-partisan public servants to "present and explain government policies, priorities and decisions to the public" (ibid.). Under this division of responsibilities, all "political matters" are to be left to "the exclusive domain of ministers and their offices" (ibid.). As noted in chapter 1, though, the advent of political marketing, the 24/7 media cycle, and the information and communications technology (ICT) revolution in recent years has caused Canadian political executives to become "extremely preoccupied with generating favorable publicity and avoiding negative news spills," and this preoccupation has "spilled over from the political centre of government into the administrative culture of the senior ranks of the public service" (Thomas 2011). The result is that quite legitimate communications activities have at times been dragged deep into the "swampy zone" that exists between "information and propaganda and between public and partisan interests" (Brown 2012).

The following press release, issued by Alberta Premier Alison Redford's office in 2012, illustrates how key messages can be dragged into Brown's swampy zone:

Feature 4.5: Press Release with Partisan Message

Redford Government Delivers on Issues that Matter to Albertans

"In the spring, Albertans made a strong statement on the issues that matter to them and what their government should focus on. Albertans expect us to focus on their priorities and to build and invest in Alberta's future. I am proud to say that we have done just that," said Premier Redford.

The Alberta Legislature passed 10 pieces of legislation, focused on improving accountability, openness and transparency across government, ensuring our natural resources are managed in an even more responsible and efficient manner, protecting new home buyers, and improving Alberta's world-class education system.

While the opposition focused on an agenda of unprecedented personal attacks, Premier Redford and the government caucus remained focused on the issues that matter to Albertans. The next sitting of the legislature will continue to fulfill Premier Redford's promise to Alberta and will build on this year's extensive conversations with Albertans on health, social policy and finances.[...]

Source: Alberta. Office of the Premier. 2012. "Redford Government Delivers on Issues that Matter to Albertans." www.documentcloud.org/documents/541037-partisan-docs20121217-09214197.html

---

For critics, the press release's negative reference to the opposition was "definitely a transgression ... [It was] inappropriate for government resources and government staff to be including partisan attacks in public communications" (Rusnell 2012).

LEARNING ACTIVITIES

Activity 4.1: Clear Writing Development
The objective of this activity is to develop clear writing skills. Go to Human Resources and Development Canada's Plain Language Online Training (www.plainlanguagenetwork.org/plaintrain/) and complete the online training.

Activity 4.2: Editing for Clarity
This activity is intended to help you develop editing skills to improve the clarity of an existing piece of public sector writing. To begin, work with a partner

and choose any public sector communications product, such as a press release, backgrounder, FAQ, or letter to the editor, that interests you and is long enough to warrant detailed analysis. If you are stuck, you can use one of the following:

- *Guidelines for Food and Beverage Sales in BC Schools* (www. bced.gov.bc.ca/health/2010_food_guidelines.pdf)
- *Blue-Green Algae and Their Toxins* (www.hc-sc.gc.ca/ewh-semt/ pubs/water-eau/cyanobacter-eng.php)
- *Treatment of Student Loans Under Canadian Bankruptcy Laws* (www2.parl.gc.ca/Content/LOP/ResearchPublications/prb0126-e.pdf)
- *New Relationships with Aboriginal People and Communities in British Columbia* (www.newrelationship.gov.bc.ca/shared/downloads/annual_report_2009_10.pdf)

Next, work with your partner to assess the clarity of the writing in the piece, paying particular attention to audience identification and needs, language choice, organization, and presentation. Finally, summarize your findings in a two-page analysis. Keep in mind that the goal of this assignment is not to summarize the information presented in the product, but rather to respond critically to it.

Activity 4.3: Key Message Assessment

Identify an initiative that is currently being used by a public sector organization to achieve an established strategic goal. The initiative must be old enough and of sufficient priority to have generated a critical mass of related, publicly available communications materials (e.g., press releases, backgrounders, FAQs, speeches, letters to the editor). Use these communications materials to identify and describe the key messages that you think the responsible public sector organization is using for the communications campaign.

Activity 4.4: Key Message Development

Identify a new initiative that a public sector organization will use to achieve a strategic goal. The initiative should be new enough that few communications materials have been generated to date. Develop three key messages for this initiative, ensuring that they (1) clearly identify a target audience, (2) explain the nature of the problem or issue that is causing the organization to act, (3) identify options for addressing the problem or issue, (4) articulate what specific actions the organizations is taking to deal with the problem or issue, and (5) evoke a sense of values that are likely to motivate target audience members to believe and ultimately act upon the message.

FURTHER READING

The US-based National Cancer Institute provides a very informative account of a message development process used in a public sector context in their 2008 publication *Making Health Communications Work*. Rebecca Leet provides similarly insightful treatment of message development in a non-profit context in her 2007 book, *Message Matters: Succeeding at the Crossroads of Mission and Market*. Chapter 7 of Elizabeth Robinson and colleagues' *Communications Handbook for Clinical Trials* (2014) provides a variety of tools and tips for developing and using key messages in non-profit and public sector contexts. In a slightly different but related context, Gary Mason's 2013 *Globe and Mail* article "Anatomy of a Comeback: How Christy Clark Beat the Odds" provides interesting insight into the message development process used in a political campaign. Finally, Kirsten Kozolanka provides an authoritative account of one of the more infamous cases of communications abuse in her 2006 article "The Sponsorship Scandal as Communication: The Rise of Politicized and Strategic Communications in the Federal Government."

ONLINE RESOURCES

Numerous sites provide tips, tools, resources, and hands-on exercises to improve grammar and vocabulary usage. In addition to Plain Language Online Training, mentioned above, two very good sites in this regard are (1) Better English Lessons (www.Better-English.com) and (2) Guide to Grammar and Writing (grammar.ccc.commnet.edu/grammar/index.htm), both of which offer numerous grammar and vocabulary exercises to improve clear writing.

In addition, Susan Doyle provides an excellent overview of Canadian government writing skills and characteristics on her Writing for Government website (web.uvic.ca/~sdoyle/E302/Notes/index.html). The Ontario Ministry of Agriculture, Food, and Rural Affairs' *Clear Writing Factsheet* also provides support and direction for clear writing in government (www.omafra.gov.on.ca/english/rural/facts/07-049.htm).

QUESTIONS FOR CRITICAL REFLECTION

1. In any given communications product, what kinds of words or phrases might indicate an inappropriate use of professional (i.e., non-partisan) public sector communications resources for partisan purposes?

2. Is it unethical for governing parties to use professional (i.e., non-partisan) public sector communications resources for partisan purposes? Why or why not?

KEY TERMS

clear writing: A way of presenting information so that everyone—young and old, technicians and lay people—can read and understand it. It is achieved by focusing on the whole message and considering not only what the material says, but also how it is organized and looks.

key message(s): The main point(s) or idea(s) that public sector organizations want to communicate to members of a target audience about a particular product, service, initiative, or proposal.

message concepts: These are "messages in rough form [that] represent ways of presenting information to the intended audiences. These may include statements only or statements and visuals—but not the actual messages themselves" (NCI 2008).

non-partisan: Information that is "free from promoting or appearing to promote the governing party's political interests by fostering a positive impression of the government or a negative impression of any group or person critical of the government" (Office of the Auditor General 2011, 412).

NOTE

1 This section is based on the Ontario Ministry of Agriculture, Food, and Rural Affairs' (2011) *Clear Writing Factsheet*.

WORKS CITED

Alberta. Public Affairs Bureau. 2010. *Government of Alberta Social Media—Web 2.0 Policy.* www.publicaffairs.alberta.ca/pab_documents/GOASocialMediaPolicyPlusAppendix-approved.pdf

——. Office of the Premier. 2012. "Redford Government Delivers on Issues that Matter to Albertans." www.documentcloud.org/documents/541037-partisan-docs20121217-09214197.html

Bennett, Gavin, and Nasreen Jessani, eds. 2011. *The Knowledge Translation Toolkit: Bridging the "Know-Do" Gap; A Resource for Researchers*. Ottawa: IDRC.

Brown, David C. G. 2012. "The Administrative Dilemmas of Government Communications." Paper presented at the Canadian Political Science Association Annual Conference, Edmonton, Alberta.

Kozolanka, Kirsten. 2006. "The Sponsorship Scandal as Communication: The Rise of Politicized and Strategic Communications in the Federal Government." *Canadian Journal of Communication* 31 (2): 343–66.

Leet, Rebecca. 2007. *Message Matters: Succeeding at the Crossroads of Mission and Market.* St. Paul, MN: Fieldstone Alliance.

Mason, Gary. 2013. "Anatomy of a Comeback: How Christy Clark Beat the Odds." *Globe and Mail,* June 22. www.theglobeandmail.com/news/british-columbia/anatomy-of-a-comeback-how-christy-clark-beat-the-odds/article12754587/?page=all

National Cancer Institute (NCI). 2008. *Making Health Communications Work.* Rockville, MD: National Cancer Institute.

Office of the Auditor General of Ontario. 2011. *2011 Annual Report.* Toronto: Queen's Printer.

Ontario. Ministry of Agriculture, Food, and Rural Affairs (OMAFRA). 2011. *Clear Writing Factsheet.* www.omafra.gov.on.ca/english/rural/facts/07-049.htm

Robinson, Elizabeth, Deborah Baron, Lori Heise, Jill Moffett, and Sarah Harlan. 2014. *Communications Handbook for Clinical Trials: Strategies, Tips, and Tools to Manage Controversy, Convey Your Message, and Disseminate Results.* Washington, DC: Family Health International.

Rusnell, Charles. 2012. "Premier Issues Partisan News Release under Government of Alberta Letterhead." *CBC News,* December 18. www.cbc.ca/news/canada/edmonton/story/2012/12/17/edmonton-alberta-politics-news-release-partisan.html

Saskatchewan. Department of Finance. 2013. "Saskatchewan Remains on Track for Balanced Budget." News release, February 15. www.gov.sk.ca/news?newsId=38eb2bce-7081-4711-a161-607523070228

Thomas, Paul G. 2011. "Communications and Prime Ministerial Power." Paper presented at a conference in honour of Donald J. Savoie, Bouctouche, New Brunswick, June 8–10.

Treasury Board of Canada Secretariat. 2012. *Communications Policy of the Government of Canada.* www.tbs-sct.gc.ca/pol/doc-eng.aspx?id=12316&section=text

Wilcox, Dennis, and Glen Cameron. 2012. *Public Relations: Strategies and Tactics.* Toronto: Pearson Education.

CHAPTER 5
TACTICS

CHAPTER OVERVIEW

This chapter examines the most important tactics that new communications professionals need to master, namely the press release, the backgrounder, the FAQs, the letter to the editor, and the speech. This chapter defines and describes each of these tactics in detail and then provides examples of each based on good, better, and best practices.

LEARNING OBJECTIVES

By the end of this chapter, you will be able to

- describe the core tactics used in public sector communications in Canada today, namely the press release, the backgrounder, the FAQ, the letter to the editor, and the speech;
- distinguish different levels of quality in basic communications tactics using identifiable metrics; and
- develop core communications tactics (press release, backgrounder, FAQ, letter to the editor, and speech) to support a public sector communications strategy.

INTRODUCTION

Communications tactics are the specific activities that public sector organizations use to achieve the objectives set out in their communications strategies. As discussed in chapter 1, the most important tactics that new communications professionals need to master early in their careers are

- the **press release**, which is used to communicate key messages to the public through a media intermediary;

- the **backgrounder**, a relatively short but in-depth stand-alone document that provides additional information about a specific issue;
- **FAQs** (frequently asked questions), which is used to prepare spokespersons to engage with the media or general public about a product, service, or initiative;
- the **letter to the editor**, a method of clarifying an organization's position on a controversial issue of public importance, communicating the rationale for a upcoming or recent policy or program decision, or seeking public support for a new initiative that involves submitting an open letter to the editor to a newspaper or magazine for publication in a special letters section; and
- the **speech**, a prepared script that a spokesperson uses to address a targeted audience about specific topics.

This chapter examines each of these tactics in detail, first describing what each is and then providing a good, a better, and a best example of each.

5.1 PRESS RELEASES[1]

Press releases are used by public sector organizations to communicate key messages to their publics through some type of media intermediary. Press releases are popular because they allow organizations to create their own news stories and circulate them to the public through different media. If particularly well written, media outlets will often reprint the content of a release with few changes, thereby ensuring much wider—and free—distribution.

The Standard Release

Although there are about as many styles of press releases as there are organizations that use them, press releases generally include the following:

- letterhead or logo of the organization
- scheduled release time/date (either "For Immediate Release" or for release on a specific date)
- headline that highlights the message (e.g., New Children's Mental Health Plan First in Canada) in uppercase letters or boldface, or both

- location of release
- the body, which typically includes key messages and sometimes program or initiative details
- an end (denoted by a "–30–" centred at the bottom of the page)
- contact name and information

Writing a Press Release

A good way to start writing a press release is by developing a strong headline and then identifying the most important element of the issue or initiative (the part that readers most need to remember) and then trying to state it in 10 words or less. The next step involves crafting the all-important first paragraph of the release. The first paragraph needs to answer the five *w*'s—who, what, where, when, and why, as well as how. It must also begin with a strong lead sentence that will catch readers' attention and draw them into the rest of the piece. The sentence doesn't have to be clever—it just has to grab the readers' interest.

The remainder of the release should present the details of the story, structured roughly like an inverted pyramid: start with the most interesting or pertinent information, then provide the rest of the details in order of decreasing importance. Whenever possible, provide support with a statistic or quote from the first minister, the minister, or a key stakeholder. Good press releases are typically about one page of five to seven paragraphs in length, with no more than three sentences per paragraph.

Examples of Press Releases

A Good Press Release

The following is a good example of a public sector press release; this was issued by the City of Regina in April 2012 with regards to mobile food vendors.

Feature 5.1

More Mobile Food Vendors to Operate in Downtown Regina: City Introduces Two-Year Pilot Project

April 5, 2012

The City of Regina has implemented new mobile food vending

procedures that will allow mobile food vendors to operate on the streets of downtown Regina starting as early as the end of April. Until now, only sidewalk food vendors were operating in the downtown. The program will be monitored as a pilot project for the next two years.

Vendors must obtain a valid permit to operate on local streets throughout downtown and on a portion of Victoria Avenue between Rose and Smith streets. Vendors may be allowed in the City Square plaza in the future. They can be open between 9 and 2 a.m. daily on a seasonal or year round basis.

The City made the change in response to requests from existing and potential food vendors and the ongoing implementation of the Downtown Neighbourhood Plan. Additional research of trends throughout North America especially in five other major western Canadian cities and contact with a number of stakeholder groups also supported the decision.

For more information, call 777-7000.

Source: City of Regina. 2012. "More Mobile Food Vendors to Operate in Downtown Regina: City Introduces Two-Year Pilot Project." April 5. www.regina.ca/press/news-and-announcements/more-mobile-food-vendors-to-operate-in-downtown-regina-city-introduces-two-year-pilot-project/

While this release does a good job of answering the five *w*'s, two things stand out:

- No area code is provided in the telephone contact information and no email/direct press contact. Readers in other jurisdictions (such as those in the five unnamed western Canadian cities researched for the initiative) might wish to contact the City.
- The release does not specify which City of Regina department will monitor the pilot program—an important detail for individuals and organizations looking to follow up on the initiative.

A Better Press Release

An example of a better press release was issued by the Yukon government in January 2013 on mining exploration:

For Release
January 29, 2013

Yukon Government Gives Mining Exploration Program a Boost

WHITEHORSE—The Yukon government is encouraging mineral exploration by increasing funding to the Yukon Mining Incentive Program. Minister of Energy, Mines and Resources Brad Cathers announced the funding increase last night at the Mineral Exploration Roundup.

"We are increasing funds for the Yukon Mining Incentive Program by $200,000 to a total of $770,000 for 2013/14. This new money will encourage more investment in mineral exploration during a period when raising capital is extremely challenging," Cathers said.

The Yukon Mining Incentive Program (YMIP) provides funding to individuals, partnerships and companies to move forward on their mineral exploration projects. Part of the program's function is to provide a portion of the risk capital required to locate, explore and develop mineral projects to an advanced stage.

"The incentive program has a proven track record at leveraging exploration dollars. In an average year, the grants we issue typically are matched by investors at a ratio of four to one," said Cathers. "The program also provides economic incentive for individuals and companies to operate locally and invest in the Yukon economy."

The program has been instrumental in assisting prospectors who have made some of the most significant recent mineral discoveries in Yukon. For example, several large discoveries and projects in the White Gold District in central Yukon were initially assisted by the program.

YMIP focuses on quality projects; it is a competitive, proposal-driven process that is merit-based. The projects most likely to be funded are ones that have the best chance of succeeding and have the strongest potential to generate additional investment in Yukon's economy.

During the 2011/12 fiscal year, the $570,000 YMIP budget supported 34 exploration projects that ultimately spent a total of $2 million on their operations.

For more information about YMIP or other mining programs supported by the government visit geology.gov.yk.ca. The application deadline for the upcoming year's program is March 31.

–30–

Contact:

Elaine Schiman

Cabinet Communications

867-633-7961

elaine.schiman@gov.yk.ca

Jesse Devost

Communications, Energy, Mines & Resources

867-667-5809

jesse.devost@gov.yk.ca

News release #13-016

Source: Yukon. 2013. "Yukon Government Gives Mining Exploration Program a Boost." January 29. www.gov.yk.ca/news/13-016.html

---

This release is better than the previous example for the following reasons:

- The lead sentence is written in active language and directly answers the "why" question.
- The release effectively uses a quote from the minister in the second paragraph.
- It provides a direct link to mining programs information and the funding application deadline.

The Best Press Release

The best example of a public sector press release is one issued by Saskatchewan's Ministry of Finance in February 2013 on the status of the province's balanced budget:

News Release - February 15, 2013

Saskatchewan Remains on Track for Balanced Budget

Saskatchewan has maintained its enviable position through the first three-quarters of this fiscal year, remaining the only province in Canada on track for a balanced budget.

The government's Third Quarter Financial Report, released today, projects the province will finish 2012–13 with a pre-transfer surplus of $8.8 million in its General Revenue Fund (GRF).

"Given the current world economy, preserving a balanced budget is challenging," Finance Minister Ken Krawetz said. "While Saskatchewan's economy is strong, resource revenue is down because of falling prices. This decline is offset somewhat by record investment and revenue from a growing tax base, which has expanded thanks to higher employment and population growth."

GRF expense is now projected to finish the year at $11.39 billion—up $190.4 million or 1.7 per cent from budget, largely due to higher than expected usage of certain government services and unforeseen weather events, like flooding. The increases include:

- $40 million for the Provincial Disaster Assistance Program (up $110 million in total over Budget);
- $51 million for Teachers' Pensions and Benefits;
- $47 million for AgriStability, AgriInvest and Crop Insurance;
- $10 million for snow removal and ice control on provincial highways;
- $10 million for increased use of the Research and Development Tax Credit in the 2011 tax year;
- $7 million for increased usage of court services, corrections and prosecutions; and
- $4 million for increased usage of the Graduate Retention Program.

"These expenses have been offset by expense management savings identified at mid-year and by an increased dividend from Crown Investments Corporation of Saskatchewan (CIC)," Krawetz said.

"At budget, we expected the Crowns to generate 2012 net income of $346.5 million and that CIC would provide a dividend to the GRF equal to about 90 per cent of this net income, excluding the net income of SaskPower, allowing the corporation to address its long-term infrastructure requirements."

In 2012, CIC Crowns, excluding SaskPower, generated net income of about $135 million more than expected at budget time. About 90 per cent of this increase—$120 million—will be provided to the GRF.

GRF revenue is now projected to finish the year at $11.40 billion—up $104.2 million or 0.9 per cent from budget, largely due to higher than expected tax revenue and the increased CIC dividend.

Government general public debt is forecast to be $3.8 billion at the end of 2012–13, unchanged from budget and from the end of the previous fiscal year.

The province's Growth and Financial Security Fund is now forecast to finish 2012–13 with a balance of $662.7 million.

"Fiscal responsibility continues to be our foundation, a key part of our Plan For Growth to help keep Saskatchewan moving forward," Krawetz said. "Given the volatility of world markets and unforeseen circumstances, we are pleased to be able to maintain a balanced budget."

–30–

For more information, contact:
Jeff Welke
Finance
Regina
Phone: 306-787-6046
Email: jeff.welke@gov.sk.ca
Cell: 306-536-1185

Related Documents
pdf Backgrounder Q3 2012-13.pdf (122.7 KB)
pdf Q3 REPORT 2012-13.pdf (407.1 KB)

Source: Saskatchewan. 2013. "Saskatchewan Remains On Track for Balanced Budget." February 15. www.gov.sk.ca/news?newsId=38eb2bce-7081-4711-a161-607523070228

This release is better than the previous two examples for the following reasons:

- The headline is clear and to the point.
- The body of the release directly answers the five *w*'s.
- The related documents section provides useful files for journalists and the general public: Backgrounder Q3 and Q3 Report.
- The release highlights numbers, saving journalists on tight deadlines from sifting through long reports to find statistics.
- Using bullets makes the numbers stand out and gives news editors ideas for other stories based on the diverse programs listed.
- There is a good distribution of quotes throughout the release.
- It provides links for sharing the document through email and on social media platforms such as Facebook and Twitter.
- The email address of the Ministry of Finance contact is hyperlinked.
- Inclusion of a cellphone number tells journalists that the communications representative will likely be available outside of regular business hours to field questions.

5.2 BACKGROUNDERS

A backgrounder is a relatively short but content-rich document (or subdocument) that provides additional information about a specific issue or initiative.[2] Backgrounders can be stand-alone documents that accompany tactics such as news releases, or independent sections of other tactics such as briefing notes (see chapter 7 for more details). The following are characteristics of good backgrounders:[3]

- a clear purpose, e.g., to lend credibility to a controversial policy decision, to provide historical justification for a decision to cut a program or service
- a concise statement of the issue or subject at hand at or near the beginning of the document
- a short historical overview of how the issue or subject evolved or came to be
- references to as much outside, independent information as possible to justify claims and arguments, establishing the organization's credibility and authority on the issue or subject

- a concluding explanation of why the issue or subject is important today

Examples of Backgrounders

A Good Backgrounder

A good example of a backgrounder was included in a 2011 report by the
Government of the Northwest Territories' (GNWT) Department of Human
Resources on the status of the GNWT's Staff Retention Policy:

<hr>

Feature 5.4

Report on the Staff Retention Policy Year Ending March 31, 2011

Background

In May 2000, the Government of the Northwest Territories (GNWT)
introduced the Staff Retention Policy, which provides a process for
the redeployment of staff whose jobs are eliminated or transferred to
another community. The Policy focuses on the retention of employees
within the public service but does provide layoff as an option where
redeployment is not feasible. The Policy also provides for a retraining
fund, administered by the Department of Human Resources, which
supports the retraining of staff who move from one department
to another. Where an affected employee can be retrained within
their own department, their department covers the retraining costs.
Once a person is identified as affected, their home department and
Client Service Manager work with the employee to identify potential
employment opportunities within GNWT. If a reasonable job offer
cannot be made to the individual during their affected employee period
(up to eight weeks) and layoff notice period (13 weeks), they are given
one of the following layoff options:

- Education assistance for one year to pursue further post-
secondary education
- Separation assistance payment based on years of service
- Severance priority payment based on years of service plus

hiring priority in the GNWT for 18 months after the layoff notice period

- Voluntary Separation Severance, applicable only where an employee's position is transferred to another community or if they choose to terminate their employment to create a vacancy which will be staffed by an employee who has been laid off or will be laid off.

Status

In fiscal year 2010–2011, 51 individuals were identified as "affected employees" under the Staff Retention Policy. Of those:

- 17 were redeployed within the GNWT
- 2 retired or are eligible to retire
- 1 chose Education Assistance
- 9 chose Separation Assistance
- 8 chose Voluntary Separation
- 7 currently are outstanding on the staffing priority list as affected employees
- 1 is on a term/transfer assignment
- 1 is on long-term sick leave
- 5 had their layoff notice rescinded.

Statistics do not include individuals who were potentially affected but where accommodation was made within their departments to place them without the individuals having to seeking government-wide hiring priority.

Source: New Brunswick Department of Agriculture, Aquaculture, and Fisheries. 2011. "Department of Human Resources: Report on the Staff Retention Policy Year Ending March 31, 2011." www.assembly. gov.nt.ca/_live/documents/content/11-05-18td31-166.pdf

While this backgrounder does a good job of providing a succinct history and overview of the 2000 Staff Retention Policy, it is unclear exactly who the audience is for the piece or what purpose it is designed to serve. The statement "The purpose of this issue note is to use data from Staff Retention Policy in fiscal year 2010–2011 to anticipate future trends in affected employees" does not directly identify the intended audience. In addition, while the statistics on affected employees are clear, a chart with year-over-year figures could help a senior decision-maker identify important trends.

A Better Backgrounder
The New Brunswick Department of Agriculture, Aquaculture, and Fisheries' February 2012 submission to the External Review on Northern Shrimp provides an example of a better backgrounder:

Feature 5.5

Submission of the New Brunswick Department of Agriculture, Aquaculture and Fisheries to the External Review on Northern Shrimp
29 February 2012

Background
New Brunswick enterprises were among the first seven traditional offshore license holders in the Northern Shrimp fishery. Not only were they pioneers in this fishery, but in order to obtain those initial licenses, they had to relinquish groundfish allocations, make very significant investments in vessels, and develop a market presence on international markets. In part because of their involvement in Northern Shrimp, New Brunswick license holders were also able to support the development of a midshore shrimp fishery in the Gulf of St. Lawrence and on the Scotia Shelf.

When the resource expanded in the 1990s, a large increase in access was granted. Additional access was provided to inshore fishermen and in the form of special allocations. Large quota increases had negative effects on international shrimp markets, which led to an erosion of the position of both New Brunswick's processors/Northern Shrimp license holders and our midshore license holders. The large increase in access holders was understood, by ourselves and NB license holders, to be contingent on the Last-In/First-Out (LIFO) principle. The decision as presented at the time was that should the resource decline, reductions in access would occur among the new entrants and the viability of the original fleet would be protected. This understanding was based on statements by the Minister of Fisheries and Oceans Canada and has been repeatedly confirmed by subsequent Fisheries and Oceans Ministers; the understanding is also clearly spelled out in the Integrated Fisheries Management Plan (IFMP) for Northern Shrimp in 2003 and again in 2007.

Review

We were initially concerned when, in June 2011, we became aware of a joint announcement by Minister Ashfield, Newfoundland and Labrador Fisheries and Aquaculture Minister Jackman and Minister Penashue that a review of Northern Shrimp allocation rules would be undertaken prior to the 2012 fishing season. As a jurisdiction with direct interests in Northern Shrimp, we were surprised that such an important decision would be made without consultation or even notification to the Province of New Brunswick. We were also surprised that the announced review would appear to involve only the Province of Newfoundland and Labrador.

We were further concerned when DFO modified the provisions of the IFMP in 2011 to allow the special allocation held by St. Anthony Bay Resources Inc. (SABRI), to be fished by the inshore fleet, in a move that is contrary to the IFMP and that effectively constituted a reduction in the overall quota pool available to the offshore fleet.

In December 2011, Minister Ashfield wrote to New Brunswick Minister Olscamp outlining the terms of reference of the external advisory process on rules and management policies in the Northern Shrimp fishery. The terms of reference indicate, inter alia, the review is to consider if appropriate policies, principles, and methodologies were used in the decision making, and to provide additional advice on whether other departmental policies, principles, and tools should have been taken into consideration.

From the New Brunswick perspective, the scope of review proposed by Ernst & Young at the St. John's meeting of January 18, 2012 was an appropriate approach to the issue given the terms of reference provided by Minister Ashfield.

Source: New Brunswick Department of Agriculture, Aquaculture, and Fisheries. 2012. "Submission of the New Brunswick Department of Agriculture, Aquaculture and Fisheries to the External Review on Northern Shrimp." www.dfo-mpo.gc.ca/fm-gp/peches-fisheries/reports-rapports/eap-pce/documents/nb-eng.pdf

The backgrounder could be improved by

- summarizing much of the text using bullets, which would have the additional benefit of better highlighting the main points;
- providing the source for the percentages used; and
- using Next Steps instead of a Conclusion to highlight the ongoing nature of the issue and underscore the strategic direction sought by the New Brunswick government on the issue.

The Best Backgrounder

The best example of a backgrounder is from the Bank of Canada on the topic of e-money, a digital alternative to cash.

Feature 5.6

E-Money

Advances in technology enable a number of innovations that change the way Canadians pay for goods and services. Some products—for example, the debit card—offer a way to access funds in a bank deposit account and can be thought of as electronic payments, or "e-payments." Other innovations offer a way to directly store monetary value in an electronic device or in a communications network. We call those electronic money, or e-money for short.

What Is E-Money?

E-money is a digital alternative to cash.

It is monetary value that is stored and transferred electronically through a variety of means—a mobile phone, tablet, contactless card (or smart card), computer hard drive or servers.

E-money is usually issued by an institution upon receipt of funds and is given a value in a national currency, such as the Canadian dollar.

Examples of e-money include prepaid payment cards that use payment networks such as Visa or MasterCard, or account balances kept at online service providers such as PayPal. Both can be used for a range of purchases in different establishments.

Another type of e-money is decentralized, without an issuer and not denominated in national currencies. The most well-known example is the Bitcoin, a digital currency that is used for transactions directly between users through a computer network.

Why Do People Use E-Money?

People like e-money because it acts like cash: it can be as fast, convenient and confidential.

E-money meets the needs of consumers buying over the Internet who want to keep their personal and financial information private.

In person, people may prefer e-money over having to carry and count bills and coins. Merchants using e-money may save the cost of providing change and processing cash.

Technological progress also helps stimulate innovations. For example, the widespread adoption of the Internet and mobile devices allows for the creation of e-money products that do not require consumers and merchants to purchase card readers, terminals or other payment infrastructure.

E-Money in Canada

There are fewer e-money products in Canada than in other countries. One reason for this is that e-payment systems—for example, contactless debit cards and credit cards—are popular and serve much the same function as e-money products by offering fast and convenient means of payment.

The e-money products we see most frequently in Canada are prepaid payment cards.

E-Money and the Bank of Canada

Understanding and monitoring e-money products is an important part of the Bank of Canada's research agenda.

The Bank of Canada has several reasons to study e-money:

- We design, produce and distribute Canada's bank notes. Although people still use cash, widespread adoption of e-money could change the demand for cash. You can read here about our research on this topic.
- We oversee Canada's payment clearing and settlement systems. The Bank has a specific oversight role for payment systems that are systemically important, and it promotes the safety and

efficiency of other payment systems that may affect the financial or economic welfare of Canadians.

For a more detailed discussion of e-money, please consult "Electronic Money and Payments" and a presentation that the Bank of Canada delivered to the Senate Committee on Banking, Trade and Commerce on 2 April 2014. You can read the statement or presentation slides.

Selected Bank of Canada E-Money
Research:
Charles Freedman. 2003. "Reflections on Three Decades at the Bank of Canada." "Closing Remarks."
In Macroeconomics, Monetary Policy, and Financial Stability, Proceedings of a conference held by the Bank of Canada, June 2003.
Joshua Gans and Hanna Halaburda. 2013. "Some Economics of [Private] Digital Currencies." Bank of Canada Working Paper No. 2013–38.
Gerald Stuber. 1996. "The Electronic Purse: An Overview of Recent Developments and Policy Issues." Bank of Canada Technical Report No. 74.
Warren Weber. "The Efficiency of Private E-Money-like Systems: The U.S. Experience with State Bank Notes".
Jonathan Chiu and Russell Wong. "E-Money: Efficiency, Stability and Optimal Policy"
Ben Fung, Miguel Molico and Gerald Stuber. "Electronic Money and Payments".
Selected e-money reports produced by other central banks:
"Virtual Currency Schemes." A report prepared by the European Central Bank.
A bitcoin primer from the Federal Reserve Bank of Chicago.
Presentation on bitcoin prepared by the Federal Reserve Bank of St. Louis.
April 2014

Source: Bank of Canada. 2014. E-Money. www.bankofcanada.ca/wp-content/uploads/2014/04/E-Money-Backgrounder.pdf

Like the previous backgrounders, this example provides a succinct overview and history of the specific issue at hand. However, what makes this example excellent is the use of key questions as the primary method of organizing the information, background information on why the issue is important to the Bank of Canada, use of bullets to enumerate information, and the inclusion of references that readers can consult for more information.

5.3 FAQs

Frequently asked questions (FAQs, also known as Q&As or questions and answers) are an alternative method of disseminating information about a product, service, initiative, or issue organized around a list of questions and corresponding answers that an organization believes are most likely to be asked by the public.[4] FAQs are fairly ubiquitous and are found either as stand-alone documents or as part of other tactics, such as briefing notes and websites.

Most FAQs follow a standard formula: a set of questions that are designed to segue into answers that address the five *w*'s (who, what, when, where, and why), repetition and further elucidation of key messages throughout the answers, and direction on where to find further information on the subject.

Examples of FAQs

A Good FAQ

A good example of a public sector FAQ was issued by the City of Calgary about its Wall of Windows initiative:

Feature 5.7

City Hall Wall of Windows: FAQs

The City Hall LRT Station's South Platform features a unique display known as the Wall of Windows that celebrates the vibrancy of our city. Below are answers to some of the frequently asked questions about the project. Have a question that's not answered? Please contact us.

Q: What is the Wall of Windows?
A: The City Hall "Wall of Windows" is seven colourful, engaging display boxes located on the exterior of the Administration Building along

the south platform of the newly constructed City Hall LRT station. The total installation spans 140 feet (~42 metres), and each box is 20' wide by 8' high and 4' deep.

Q: Why was the Wall of Windows created?

A: City communicators are constantly looking for new opportunities to communicate with Calgarians about programs and services. Through the refurbishment of the City Hall C-Train station, an opportunity was identified to redesign the face of the Administration Building into an innovative, unique communication space to inform and engage the public.

Q: Who's responsible for the Wall of Windows?

A: The Wall of Windows display boxes are a City-led initiative with the goal of enhancing communication for Calgarians and visitors to the city.

Q: How often will the displays change?

A: The Wall of Windows will reflect an overarching theme that will remain for one year. The content of each display box will reflect this theme in varied and unique ways and will be refreshed every quarter.

Q: Is the City getting into advertising?

A: No, the Wall of Windows is a communication channel to inform Calgarians and visitors of events, activities, culture, or programs found in the city. Offering sections of the space for traditional advertising was considered as a way to offset costs; however, using the space in this way would be in violation of the Development Permit for that site and the existing advertising contract that Calgary Transit has with an external vendor (Pattison).

Q: How can I contribute ideas/art to the Wall of Windows?

A: There is no formal process as of yet. The City will be reaching out to groups for their involvement. However, if you have an idea that you'd like to see in the Wall of Windows please send it to marketing@calgary.ca. If you're interested in becoming one of our featured photographers, please submit your images of Calgary to the YYCPhoto Flickr Group.

Q: What's the cost of the Wall of Windows?

A: The budget to refurbish the City Hall LRT station platforms included renovations to the north entrance to City Hall and allowed for the addition of the Wall of Window display cases. The display cases are a small portion of this total budget. Refurbishing the City Hall platforms is part of a larger current project, which includes adapting all of the 7 Avenue LRT platforms to accommodate future four-car trains and improve the streetscape. This project is financed under Calgary Transit's capital budget.

The cost of design (City creative services staff), printing, and installing (external vendor) the signage material for each box is approximately $3,200. By comparison, each display costs less than a mid-sized, one-day advertisement in a daily newspaper, and far less than a similarly sized billboard.

Q: Are there plans for other Wall of Windows installations around the city?

A: Not at this time. Part of the motivation for developing the Wall of Windows as a communications channel was that it coincided with the refurbishing of the City Hall LRT platforms. However, should another opportunity present itself that offers similar efficiencies and communications effectiveness, it will be considered.

Source: City of Calgary. n.d. "City Hall Wall of Windows—FAQs." www.calgary.ca/CS/CSC/Pages/MyYYC---FAQs.aspx

This is an example of a good FAQ because it answers four of the five *w*'s clearly and concisely:

- *who*: the Wall of Windows is identified as a City-led initiative
- *what*: details about the size of the wall, and the cost of design, printing, and installing signage material for each box
- *where*: the wall is located at the City Hall LRT Station's South Platform on the exterior of the Administration Building
- *why*: addressed by the key messages, "the Wall is a communication channel to inform and engage the public," and "the City of Calgary encourages residents to participate in the Wall of Windows by contributing ideas and art"

The biggest drawback of this FAQ is that it does not answer the when question, that is, when was the project launched? This information is important to include because editors and freelance journalists are more likely to pursue a follow-up story on the project if they can identify an anniversary. A second drawback is that the FAQ does not include any supporting visual images. Website viewers have to click through two hyperlinks to find an image associated with the project. A simple online search produces a media story on the Wall of Windows from September 2012 featuring a captivating photograph of the City of Calgary's acting director of customer service and communications standing in front of the wall. The FAQ would have been improved through the inclusion of a similar image. A third drawback relates to the additional information provided: although the FAQ provides a "contact us" link that directs users to the general City of Calgary contact information and hours of operation page, a better link would have led directly to the initiative's lead contact or the communications department.

A Better FAQ

A better example of a public sector FAQ was issued by the Canadian Food Inspection Agency (CFIA) on the 2009 Organic Products Regulations:

Feature 5.8

2009 Organic Products Regulations: Questions and Answers

Q1: What do the Organic Products Regulations do?

The regulations require mandatory certification to the revised *Canadian Organic Standards (Canadian Organic Production Systems Standards: General Principles and Management Standards* and the *Permitted Substances Lists)* for agricultural products represented as organic in import, export, and inter-provincial trade, or that bear the federal organic agricultural product legend (or logo).

The regulations came into effect on June 30, 2009.

Q2: Are non-food products, such as aquaculture products, cosmetics, fibres, health care products, etc., included in the Canada Organic Regime?

The regulations apply only to food products, animal feed, and products used for the cultivation of plants. Each sector not included in the application of the regulations may continue to make organic claims. However, these products must also meet all other relevant federal legislation.

Q3: How is the Canada Organic Regime structured?

The Canada Organic Regime is based on a third-party service delivery model.

The Canadian Food Inspection Agency (CFIA) was established as the competent authority providing oversight to the system.

Conformity Verification Bodies assess certification bodies to determine if they meet the established criteria prior to recommending that they be accredited by the CFIA. They also monitor accredited Certification bodies for ongoing compliance.

On-farm and facility organic production system verification are conducted by third-party verification officers employed by accredited certification bodies.

Compliance verification and enforcement activities are carried out by the CFIA.

Q4: How do the regulations affect the organic industry?

All persons whose products bear organic claims in inter-provincial and import trade, or who wish to use the legend are required to comply with the regulations. Certification to the Canadian Organic Standards is mandatory for such products.

There is no significant impact anticipated for stakeholders who are presently certified to the voluntary Canadian Organic Standards.

Q5: Are certification bodies identified on product packaging?

Organic operators are required to place the name of their Certification Body on organic product packaging, in accordance with the labelling provisions in the regulations.

Q6: Are there fees for participants in the Canada Organic Regime?

No fees relating to CFIA services or activities are anticipated for the participants in the Canada Organic Regime at this time. The establishment of any future cost-recovery scheme or fees for participants would first be subject to broad consultation with stakeholders.

Q7: What are the requirements for exported products?

Exported products are required to meet the requirements of the importing country. Exported products that do not meet the requirements of the regulations may not be marketed in Canada, and may not bear the organic agricultural product legend. The re-entry of these products into Canada, as organic, is prohibited.

Q8: What are the requirements for imported products

Under the regulations, organic products may be imported under the following conditions:

- Certified to the Canadian Organic Standard;
- Certified as organic in accordance with an agreement, entered

into with another country, regarding the importation and exportation of organic products; and

- Certified as organic in accordance with an agreement, described above, by a certification body recognized by a country referred to above.

All importers of organic products must be able to demonstrate, at all times, that the imported product conforms to the import requirements set out above. The importers must retain all documents attesting to this fact. These documents will be verified by CFIA inspectors.

Q9: How are negotiations for import/export agreements handled under the regulated system?

Negotiation of acceptance of the Canada Organic Regime with Canada's trading partners is the responsibility of the Government of Canada and has been initiated on a priority basis with our key trading partners.

On June 17, 2009, the Government of Canada entered into an agreement on the trade of organic products with the United States.

During the week of June 20, 2011, the Government of Canada entered into an organic equivalency arrangement with the European Union.

Q10: Should there be differences identified in these information exchanges, how will they affect acceptance of the Canadian provisions?

The Government of Canada is seeking comments from the Canadian General Standards Board's (CGSB) Technical Committee for Organic Agriculture on any differences identified. These comments will assist the Government of Canada in negotiating recognition of the Canadian provisions by its trading partners.

Q11: Was the Canada Organic Regime developed to meet the requirements of our trading partners?

Yes. The requirements of our trading partners were considered by the CGSB committee members during the revision process to the organic standard. The structure of the Canada Organic Regime was developed to be in keeping with the organic regulatory systems of our key trading partners.

Date modified: 2012-02-01

Source: Canadian Food Inspection Agency. 2009. *2009 Organic Products Regulations: Questions and Answers.* www.inspection.gc.ca/food/organic-products/labelling-and-general-information/questions-andanswers/eng/1328081120744/1328081195020

Unlike the Wall of Windows FAQ, the Organic Products Regulations FAQ better answers the five *w*'s:

- *who*: the CFIA, which is identified at the top of the website under the Government of Canada logo; the answer to Q3 explains the structure of the third-party service delivery Canada Organic Regime
- *what*: why the regulations require mandatory certification to the revised Canadian Organic Standards
- *when*: June 30, 2009, the date the regulations came into effect
- *where*: anywhere in Canada
- *why*: answered in the reiteration of the key messages, "There is no significant impact anticipated for stakeholders who are presently certified to the voluntary Canadian Organic Standards," "No fees relating to CFIA services or activities are anticipated for the participants in the Canada Organic Regime at this time," and "Any future cost-recovery scheme or fees would first be subject to broad consultation with stakeholders"

The main drawback of the CFIA FAQ is the absence of contact information for CFIA staff and a section that provides direction on how to get more information (e.g., hyperlinks to related policy documents).

The Best FAQ

The best of example of a public sector FAQ comes from Saskatchewan's Department of Government Relations on the Provincial Public Safety Telecommunications Network (PPSTN):

Feature 5.9

Provincial Public Safety Telecommunications Network (PPSTN): Questions and Answers
Radio System

Q. What is a Public Safety radio system?

A. A Public Safety radio system, such as the PPSTN, is specifically designed and operated for the public safety community. Such systems are constructed to address the demanding requirements of public safety communications such as coverage, interoperability, capacity, availability, and reliability.

Q. Who owns the PPSTN?

A. The PPSTN was created pursuant to the PPSTN Agreement between the RCMP, SaskPower, and the Province, represented by the Ministry of Government Relations. The complementary resources, knowledge, experience, skills, and other attributes of each of the parties allow them to successfully operate and manage the PPSTN. The RCMP and SaskPower manage their own users while the Ministry manages all others.

Q. Who are the users of the PPSTN?

A. The over 8,000 radios on the PPSTN are used by the RCMP, SaskPower, municipal fire and police, emergency medical services, volunteer search and rescue chapters, First Nations, Government Relations, Environment, Corrections, Highways, and other provincial and federal government agencies.

Q. Why do we need a Public Safety radio system?

A. SaskTel's FleetNet system was discontinued in December 2010. The PPSTN parties invested in a province-wide, public safety radio system to provide agencies responding to emergencies with a reliable means to communicate with the Sask911 Public Safety Answering Points, dispatch services, and other responding agencies.

Q. What does the PPSTN offer its users?

A. The PPSTN is a public safety grade Project 25 (P25) network that is specifically designed and operated to service the public safety community in the province. Such public safety systems are inherently costly to construct and to operate; however, they provide reliable emergency communications that address requirements such as interoperability, coverage, capacity, and availability to more effectively respond to emergencies in an efficient and coordinated manner.

Q. How much did Saskatchewan's public safety radio system cost?

A. The overall investment in the system was approximately $130 million. More information on costs is available in the annual PPSTN Operating Report at http://www.gr.gov.sk.ca/PPSTN.

Q. Will this new system operate everywhere responders will need it?

A. The system will provide coverage for emergency responses involving most Saskatchewan residents.

Governance of the PPSTN

Q. Why isn't a Crown agency like SaskTel responsible for operating and maintaining the network?

A. The PPSTN is a public safety network; not a commercial network. The PPSTN provides negligible profit-generating potential for commercial Crown corporations because of the expense of operating it.

Crown Investments Corporation supports the proposed governance structure.

Q. What is SaskTel's role in the new network?

A. During the PPSTN planning stages, the Province committed to co-location of facilities with SaskTel, as well using their services and other facilities. A significant portion of PPSTN operating costs are co-location and telecommunications services purchased from SaskTel.

Q. Do the users have any say in the ongoing operation of the network?

A. Yes. The PPSTN has established a User Committee to consult on issues of affordability and system serviceability. The User Committee meets quarterly.

A Single Monthly Provincial Rate

Q. How did the Province arrive at the $40/radio/month to operate on the PPSTN?

A. SaskTel's FleetNet subsidized user fees for "protective services" ranged from $28 to $35 per month. The Ministry did not want the PPSTN to bill appreciably more than what users were paying on FleetNet and therefore, subscriber fees were subsidized down to $40/radio/month.

Q. What are SaskPower and RCMP paying for user fees?

A. Each party is responsible for its own funding sources and for any expenses of their users.

Radio Purchase Plan

Q. What do you mean by "based on basic operational needs"?

A. "Basic operational needs" refers to a sufficient radio communications capacity to meet the basic requirements for primary front-line emergency response units to provide: communication capacity with dispatch services; communication capacity with other primary front-line emergency response units; and, basic on-scene tactical command and control capacity.

Q. What if I need more radios than are provided?

A. Each agency can purchase additional radios, at their cost, using their normal procurement practices. Only PPSTN-approved radios may be used on the PPSTN.

Q. Do Government ministries qualify to receive radios under this plan?

A. No. Government radios will not qualify under this purchase plan. Each Ministry will go through the normal Government budget process to purchase their radios.

Q. When will radios be available and how will we get the best price?

A. The Ministry has a small stock of radios available to meet the basic operational needs of new users and will continue to provide them as long as stock is available.

The PPSTN can identify to you vendors whose radio equipment has been successfully tested on the PPSTN. Standing Offers previously negotiated have expired and there is no current plan to renew them as the bulk of users have now purchased their radios.

Q. My municipality contracts policing services from the RCMP, will I need to pay additional costs for policing services (radios)?

A. No. The RCMP will continue to manage the radios for those municipalities that contract policing services with them.

General Questions

Q. Why is it important for Government to provide financial support to the public safety users in fire and emergency response?

A. It is important because: the success of the PPSTN depends on broad-based user participation; public safety grade radio systems are costly to build and operate as they must meet higher performance and reliability standards; and municipalities and fire departments in rural Saskatchewan have advised Government that the cost of signing onto the network must be affordable in order for them to participate.

Q. Is it mandatory that our municipality participate on the PPSTN?

A. No. Participation is voluntary, however participation is encouraged. Broad participation provides for the highest levels of interoperability resulting in better public safety communications and response.

Q. Will commercial users be allowed on the PPSTN?

A. No. The network is designed solely for public safety and public service agencies.

Q. How do I enquire about applying to get onto the system?

A. Contact the PPSTN office at 1-888-953-3693 or email us at PPSTN@ gov.sk.ca

Q. How do we order the radios?

A. You must apply as a qualifying agency through your jurisdictional authority to order radio equipment supplied as part of this program. Please contact us to learn more about ordering additional radios.

Q. Who pays for shipping of equipment to my agency?

A. The program will cover the costs of shipping the initial order of radios to your agency. All subsequent shipping costs for maintenance and repair will be the responsibility of the agency.

Q. Do I have to buy radio accessories?

A. Program allocated mobile radios come with basic mounting apparatus. Portable radios come with antenna, battery, and one charger per agency. All additional accessories such as vehicle antennas, cabling, microphones, etc. are the responsibility of the agency.

Q. Who pays for mobile installation?

A. The user agency is responsible for all installation, maintenance, and repair costs.

Q. Will there be an installation guide for radios?

A. A video and written installation guide will be provided with the radios.

Q. Does installation have to be done by specific dealers?

A. No, but it is recommended that experienced installers be utilized to ensure proper equipment operation—installation is the responsibility of the agency.

Q. Who do I call for help with the application process and later with the radios?

A. Contact PPSTN at 1-888-953-3693 or e-mail PPSTN@gov.sk.ca

Q. When will I get my radios?

A. After your agency has successfully completed the application process, you will be allocated radios on a first-come, first-served basis.

Q. What kind, type, and quantity of radios will be supplied to my agency?

A. The PPSTN must approve radios to ensure they will operate on the system. Currently Ministry clients use Motorola radios—contact us for details.

Q. Can I purchase additional radios and if so what type and make?

A. You may purchase additional radios at your own cost. Any equipment purchased must be on the approved manufacture list and programmed by the PPSTN.

Q. Will different makes of radios on this system "talk" to each other?

A. Users will be able to communicate with each other utilizing PPSTN-approved radio equipment.

Q. When can we switch over to the new system?

A. Transition or migration is dependent on: network readiness in your area; dispatch centre readiness for your agency; and successful application and readiness process by your agency.

Q. If I wasn't a FleetNet user, can I come onto the new system?

A. Any qualifying agencies may participate.

Q. What do I have to do to get ready?

A. Go to our Forms website at http://www.gr.gov.sk.ca/PPSTN-Forms or contact Government Relations for more information.

Q. Who owns the radio equipment allocated under this program?

A. The Government of Saskatchewan retains ownership, however, the user agency is responsible for all damage, maintenance, and repair costs.

Source: Saskatchewan. Ministry of Government Relations. 2010. "Provincial Public Safety Telecommunications Network (PPSTN). Questions and Answers." www.gr.gov.sk.ca/Default.aspx?DN=bc9a79a6-9136-4cc7-82a5-e9e48f958798

Like the CFIA example, the PPSTN FAQ clearly and directly answers the five *w*'s:

- *who*: the RCMP, SaskPower, and the Ministry of Government Relations are identified as the key partners, and the organizations that use the radios on the PPSTN as users
- *what*: how a public safety radio system aids public safety communications
- *when*: December 2010, the date when the PPSTN was initiated following the discontinuation of SaskTel's FleetNet
- *where*: Saskatchewan

- *why*: answered in the reiteration of the key messages, "it's important for government to provide financial support to the public safety users in fire and emergency response," "success of the PPSTN depends on broad-based user participation," and "public safety grade radio systems are costly to build and operate as they must meet higher performance and reliability standards"

The PPSTN FAQ also stands out for its simplicity of language. Upon first glance, the document appears targeted to public sector organizations that currently use or will potentially use the PPSTN, but the FAQs use very simple language that can be easily comprehended by government officials, stakeholders, and users with little to no technical competency. Finally, the direction for how to get more information is clear and precise: it includes a simple question ("How do I enquire about applying to get onto the system?") and provides a clear and direct answer (a phone number and email address) both in response to the question, and later in the document in answer to another question asking for help with the application process and assistance with the radios. The document also provides a hyperlink to the annual PPSTN Operating Report.

5.4 LETTERS TO THE EDITOR

A letter to the editor (LTE) of a newspaper or magazine is a common method of clarifying an organization's position on a controversial issue of public importance, communicating the rationale for a upcoming or recent policy or program decision, or seeking public support for a new initiative. Usually between 200 and 500 words long, LTEs generally follow the journalistic practice of attempting to answer the five *w*'s of an issue (who, what, when, where, and why, as well as how) and often end with a call to action, which urges the reader to take action.

Examples of Letters to the Editor

A Good Letter
The first example of a letter to the editor is then Minister of International Cooperation Julian Fantino's December 2012 letter to the Huffington Post about the New Democratic Party's stand on economic development in developing countries:

Feature 5.10

Dear NDP: CIDA Does Not Need Your Economic Advice

I read NDP MP Helen Laverdière's piece in the Huffington Post with great interest. I find it ironic that the NDP, a party that wishes to impose a $21-billion carbon tax on Canadians and more than $50-billion in radical spending measures while we face global economic uncertainty, now wants to give advice to developing countries on their economic development.

Let me take this opportunity to enlighten the MP and the NDP about the Canadian International Development Agency (CIDA) and dispel their myths.

Our Conservative government is focused on delivering tangible results for those most in need around the world. As I stated in my speech to the Economic Club of Canada: This means using any and all legitimate tools, and all partners available to us to meet this critical objective, including the private sector. We do not subsidize private sector companies as Laverdière led your readers to believe. We do not subsidize NGOs for that matter. We are an outcomes-driven agency and we will work with all legitimate partners who can help free people from the ill effects of poverty.

CIDA collaborates with developing country governments, civil society, multilateral institutions, and the private sector in all areas of development, such as basic health, education, and food assistance. They are all necessary partners to achieving meaningful development and economic growth that raises people out of poverty. A stronger economy creates more opportunities, more jobs, and allows families to support themselves. We cannot do this without the private sector.

When we speak about the private sector, CIDA is equally speaking about large multinational companies that employ millions of people worldwide, and individual entrepreneurs operating in remote villages in the developing world.

Let me give you an example: Due to CIDA's work, Vu Thi Ha—a terracotta pot factory owner in Vietnam—was able to improve her competitiveness with knowledge gained at a business development course. She is not alone. Between 2007 and 2010, in Vietnam alone, CIDA helped 1,200 small- and medium-sized businesses—90 percent of them owned by women—increase their profits.

I am also proud to say that CIDA works with the extractive sector to ensure it is transparent, accountable, sustainable, and maximizes local benefits. The fact is that constructive NGOs understand this direction. They are working with us towards these objectives and are achieving meaningful results. CIDA's collaboration with Plan Canada and IAMGOLD, for example, will train 10,000 youth in 13 communities of Burkina Faso so they can compete for higher paying jobs in their communities.

Development is not about dependency; it is about helping those in need get a leg up so they can prosper. This is a concept that the tax-and-spend NDP fundamentally do not understand. While the NDP would prefer to fund endless talk shops, I am committed to ensuring our development assistance is accountable, transparent, and results-focused.

The fact is that CIDA is getting real results. Through Canada's generosity, one million girls and boys in Haiti are receiving hot, nutritious meals in school each day. 7.8 million children have been vaccinated against polio in Afghanistan. And 6 million people received critical food assistance in the Sahel region of West Africa where a famine was averted because we acted quickly and decisively. This is a small sample of results we are achieving every day in every corner of the globe.

The NDP should set aside their ideology and rhetoric and support CIDA, our partners, and most importantly, those people living in poverty around the world who aspire to become self-sufficient.

Source: Julian Fantino. 2012. "Dear NDP: CIDA Does Not Need Your Economic Advice." Huffington Post: Politics, December 21. www.huffingtonpost.ca/the-honourable-julian-fantino/cida-fantino_b_2340884.html

The letter answers the five *w*'s as follows:

- *who*: Minister of International Cooperation Julian Fantino in response to an earlier letter to the editor written by NDP MP Helen Laverdière
- *what*: CIDA's mission and core activities in international development, although then Minister Fantino appeared to have a

second goal of critiquing the federal NDP's position on international development

- *when*: December 12, 2012
- *where*: the online Huffington Post, although this particular letter gained some notoriety for also being published on CIDA's website (see Canadian Press 2013) in violation of the federal government's Communication Policy, which states that all information about "policies, programs services and initiatives" must be communicated to the public "in an accountable, nonpartisan fashion consistent with the principles of Canadian parliamentary democracy and ministerial responsibility" (Treasury Board of Canada Secretariat 2012)
- *why*: ostensibly to clarify CIDA's mission and mandate in light of MP Laverdière's earlier letter to the Huffington Post, although then Minister Fantino's political agenda seems as likely a rationale for the letter having been written
- *how*: is the use of specific examples of how CIDA has helped people in developing nations like Haiti and Afghanistan to illustrate CIDA's mission and mandate

A Better Letter

A better example of an LTE is Dawn Klappe's July 2013 letter to the *Kelowna Capital News* on the status of Kelowna's last public post office:

Feature 5.11

July 4, 2013

To the editor:

Canada Post, on June 27, 2013, put up a message on the doors of the last CUPW (Canadian Union of Postal Workers) staffed retail outlet on Banks Road. In a nutshell, they were announcing the "proposed" move of this service to the industrial area of Gaston Road. The notice asked for customer feedback to this change and also placed this notice in the private mailboxes of almost 300 customers that currently rent this service.

Canada Post explains that this newer "smaller retail model" will save money, which they claim they are short of at the moment.

This new model would make our public post office little more than a hole in a wall, with one clerk and longer wait times in line. Not exactly a revenue-generating idea.

The closing and shrinking of offices is all part of Canada Post's strategy to reduce costs and encourage, even force, people to go to private sector outlets. As a rule, these postal counters are not as reliable. They tend to come and go when operators are not happy with Canada Post or not making enough money. Also, it is difficult for these outlets to be as accountable as a public post office.

Instead of downsizing, downgrading, and closing public post offices, Canada Post could expand and leverage its retail network like Australia Post is doing. It could also add new revenue-generating services such as postal banking, which has proved to be money-making in other countries.

Canada Post almost never decides to keep a post office open after giving notice. The corporation does not seem interested in what the public has to say—the public own Canada Post.

Canada Post has failed to tell the public that there are only 30 days in which to respond to this "proposal." Furthermore the corporation doesn't even notify the affected community unless that customer enters the outlet or rents a box, a flagrant disregard of the Canadian Postal Charter.

This is effectively the swan song of Kelowna's only public post office.

Write your MP, call Canada Post and let them know that we, as taxpayers, will not stand by quietly while they destroy the truly last bastion of Canada's history.

Dawn Klappe, President,
Kelowna CUPW

Source: Dawn Klappe. 2013. "Letter: Kelowna's Last Public Post Office Moving Closer to Its Demise." *Kelowna Capital News,* July 4. www.kelownacapnews.com/opinion/letters/214079741.html

This letter does a better job than the previous example of answering the five *w*'s:

- *who*: Dawn Klappe, who identifies herself as president of the Kelowna CUPW, thereby ensuring absolute transparency about her position on the issue at hand

- *what*: Canada Post's proposal to downsize a local outlet in an effort to reduce costs and the potential harm to public good that it might cause
- *when*: June 27, 2013 (provided in the first sentence)
- *where*: Kelowna, specifically the CUPW-staffed Canada Post outlet on Banks Road (if this letter were addressed to the editor of a national newspaper, it might be more appropriate to speak about national trends on downsizing postal operations and to use statistics about how these types of moves have decreased overall revenue, etc.)
- *why*: to encourage members of the public to respond to Canada Post's request for public feedback on the proposed change to the customer service location, many of whom may not have known about the request if they hadn't recently visited the location
- *how*: the letter uses rational arguments and an urgent, passionate tone to motivate people to provide input rather than dismiss the letter as coming from a self-serving union leader

This letter concludes with a call to action, letting readers know that they should contact their MP and Canada Post about the issue.

The Best Letter

The best LTE example was submitted by Mississauga Councillor Nando Iannicca to the *Mississauga News* in March 2013 on the topic of development fees in the downtown core:

Feature 5.12
March 28, 2013
Dear Editor: Re: "Outrageous," letter published in the March 20 edition of The News.
Please allow me to correct the dreadful, yet understandable, error made by Joe Perruccio, who in his letter to the editor incorrectly states that I proposed that "City Centre dwellers should fund its growth," and that downtown "taxpayers should be responsible to fund expansion projects via whatever profit they might make by selling their homes."

I proposed precisely the opposite, to the benefit of residents and homeowners like Mr. Perruccio, who have been paying the freight for the "economic free riders" sitting on land banks in the downtown core.

The articles quite rightly stated that I proposed and "supported the idea of increased levies for downtown partners, perhaps even a mechanism where downtown property owners would pay a percentage of land sale revenues," and that I "suggested charging those who are selling their property, especially those who plan to sell to a developer who wants to put multiple units (such as condominiums) on the land."

I went on to specifically reference the Square One parking lot, the Rogers lands west of Confederation Dr. between Webb Dr. and Burnhamthorpe Rd. W. and the dozen single detached homes on the southwest corner of Hurontario St. and Elm Dr. that just sold for approximately $25 million and are proposing 1,600 condos (yes, you've read that correctly).

I never once referred to homeowners, residents, hard-working taxpayers, those selling their homes, or "City Centre dwellers."

What the letter writer fears, though does not recognize, is that they are really arguing against a land transfer tax for all. How telling and ironic then that, in the same article, our City manager "suggested that a land transfer tax being pushed by Mayor McCallion could help raise the needed funds," and that I have become the poster child for the Mississauga Real Estate Board and all homeowners in the City for arguing against such a tax.

But no hard feelings Mr. Perruccio—with you or the writer of the two very accurate articles. Despite the friendly fire and the fact that you are shooting at your only soldier, reviewing the articles and the facts clearly prove our collective quibble lies with the headline writer who I'm sure upon reflection would certainly agree.

Nando Iannicca
Councillor, Ward 7

Source: Nando Iannicca. 2013. "Councillor Explains." *Mississauga News,* March 28. www.mississauga.com/opinion-story/3133734-councillor-explains/

This letter clearly addresses the five *w*'s:

- *who*: City of Mississauga Councillor Nando Iannicca; the author of the letter he is responding to is Joe Perruccio

- *what*: Iannicca's position on the issue of increased levies for downtown property owners who sell their land to a developer that wants to build multiple units
- *when*: March 2013
- *where*: Mississauga, Ontario, in particular "the Square One parking lot, the Rogers lands west of Confederation Dr. between Webb Dr. and Burnhamthorpe Rd. W. and the dozen single detached homes on the southwest corner of Hurontario St. and Elm Dr."
- *why*: to clarify the author's public position on the proposed use of increased levies on downtown property sales
- *how*: involves the author's careful effort to balance his frustration with the original letter and the reality that appearing enraged over its publishing could damage his public image—"Please allow me to correct the dreadful, yet understandable, error made by Joe Perruccio.... I proposed precisely the opposite" and, later, "reviewing the articles and the facts clearly prove our collective quibble lies with the headline writer who I'm sure upon reflection would certainly agree"

5.5 SPEECHES

Speeches are prepared scripts that spokespersons use to (1) inform or educate members of a targeted audience about a specific undertaking, proposal, or initiative; (2) convince or persuade audience members to change the way they think about a particular proposal, policy, or issue; and/or (3) *actuate* or *motivate* audience members to undertake a specific action that they were not taking previously.[5]

Basic Structure

Most speeches follow a simple structural formula: an introduction, followed by a body in which the bulk of the information is given, and a conclusion or summary. The structure, in other words, basically follows the old dictum, tell them what you're going to tell them, tell them, and then tell them what you told them.

The introduction should make up 10 to 15 percent of the total length of the speech. A standard speech introduction includes three parts: (1) a greeting to acquaint the speaker with the audience (sometimes a joke related to the theme of the speech is useful here); (2) a "hook" or "attention grabber" to make sure the audience is listening attentively and to demonstrate the value of the speech for them; and (3) a summary of the main point(s) of the speech. It is here that the question "why do target audience members need to care about the key message?" needs to be answered.

The body of the speech should comprise between 75 and 80 percent of the total length of the speech, and contain between three and seven main points. A common tactic is to make the most important point first, proceed to the least import point, and then move back to the more important. For example, if the body has five points, with 5 being the most important and 1 the least important, the order of the body would be 5-1-2-3-4.

In the conclusion to a speech, the speaker takes one last opportunity to reiterate the key message of the speech and may leave the audience with a parting, memorable thought or question that reinforces the key message. The conclusion should comprise no more than 10 percent of the total length of the speech.

Drafting

A good way to begin writing a speech is by stating the most important point that needs to be made in the body of the speech. This point must be easily identifiable and easily made to the average member of the target audience. To get this point right, envision a single individual who embodies all of the critical traits of the target audience. With this person in mind, ask yourself: How should I tailor information to meet this person's needs? Do I need to tell personal stories to illustrate the main points? What type or level of language is right for this person and for the substance of the speech?

The point about choice of language underscores the importance of writing a speech as if the writer were speaking aloud. Remember that speech writing is ultimately about writing "oral language." Write as if to explain, tell, or show something to someone—and remember that it doesn't have to be in perfect sentences. Oral language—the way most people talk to each other—doesn't work like that. Most people mix whole sentences with partial ones in order to clarify meaning and emphasize points. When you've finished writing the first point, read it aloud and listen to how it sounds— how the ideas flow, the length of the sentences, the "sound" of the oral language that has been created. Use this process to develop the rest of the main points of the body of the speech.[6]

Another feature of oral language that needs to be conveyed into speech writing is repetition. When speaking, people unconsciously repeat their main points over and over again in different ways to make sure that the people they are talking to remember and understand what they are talking about. Good speeches do the same thing. Key messages are reiterated throughout the speech to increase the likelihood that the audience will retain what it heard and gain the feeling or take the action that the speech was intended to inspire. Remember the old dictum—tell them what you're going to tell them, tell them, and then tell them what you told them.

Links

When the main points of a speech have been drafted and read aloud, a good next step is to link the points together. Remember: the clearer the path between points, the easier it is to make the transition from one idea to the next. A link can be as simple as: "We've explored one scenario for the ending of Block Buster 111, but let's consider another. This time..." or "What follows is the introduction of Main Idea Two." The most important thing is to make sure that the linkages between points are clear and sensible, because "the biggest mistake speakers and writers make is to assume people will *follow leaps of logic....* Spell out to the audience when you are taking a turn in your thoughts with phrases like: 'As an example of this' or 'This brings us to the larger problem of,' and so forth" (WikiHow n.d.).

The Conclusion

Once you have completed the body of the speech, the next task is to draft the conclusion. Good conclusions make the key message of the speech stand out or resonate in audience members' minds. One method of ensuring this is to provide a summary of major points, and then offer a call to action to the audience. For example, the desired outcome of a speech persuading people to vote for you in an upcoming election is that they do so; you can help this outcome occur by calling them to register their support by signing a prepared pledge statement as they leave. A good approach to crafting an appropriate call to action is to revisit the purpose of the speech: Was it to motivate or inspire? Was it to persuade to a particular point of view? Was it to share specialist information? Was it to celebrate a person, place, time, or event?

The Introduction[7]

For most writers, the last step in writing a good speech is composing the introduction. Strong introductions engage audience members—they make them forget about how hungry they are, the temperature in the room, the urge to check their smartphones, etc. The mechanism that engages audience members is called the "hook," which comes in as many forms as there are speeches and audiences. The task of the speech writer is to identify which specific hook will catch the desired audience. One way to do this is revisit the purpose of the speech—Why is it being given in the first place? What exactly are audience members expected to do as a result of the speech? What would appeal to the "average audience member" identified earlier—humour? a story? startling statistics? a thought-provoking or controversial quote? Good speech writers use a particularly engaging hook throughout the speech, even as the basis for setting up the conclusion.

Dlugan (2009) provides a good example of how to craft a strong opening for a speech on raising school safety awareness. A speech on this topic could begin in a number of different ways, for example, "I'm going to talk to you today about security in our schools..." or "School security is an important issue that we must deal with...." Both openings are direct, to the point ... and boring. A better way to begin might be to use a bit of drama and "misdirection" as follows:

Tobacco. [pause]

Alcohol. [pause]

Guns. [pause]

Criminal items seized in a search [slight pause] of a 6th grade locker in a bad school district.

Dlugan (2009) suggests that this opening works better for several reasons:

- it employs a classic technique—the Rule of Three, which states that readers are more likely to absorb information repeated in threes
- "Seized in a search of a 6th..." uses alliteration, an effective tool in oral language
- the pauses after the three opening words add drama; drama is also created because the danger increases with each item (guns are more dangerous than alcohol and tobacco)
- the mid-sentence pause after "search" signals that an important statement is coming up

- the audience thinks these items were seized from a criminal hideout, and is then surprised to learn they were found in a school locker
- this opening provides an excellent segue to the key message of the speech, such as "We must act decisively to prevent this from becoming reality in our schools"

And all this in just 19 words.

Examples of Speeches

A Good Speech

An example of a good public sector speech was delivered by City of North Bay Mayor Al McDonald at a groundbreaking ceremony for the city's airport industrial business park in November 2011:

Feature 5.13

Good morning everyone,

Thank you for attending this historic announcement for the future growth of our great city. This $6-million project was a partnership between all three levels of government. Each partner contributed an equal share. The development of the Aviation Industrial Park was a co-operative effort involving many internal city departments: Planning, Economic Development, Engineering, Legal, Building, and Finance, as well as external partners such as the North Bay Jack Garland Airport, North Bay Hydro, North Bay-Mattawa Conservation Authority, and various utility companies.

On behalf of the City, I wish not only to recognize all those that played a key role in the creation of this Aviation Industrial Park but to also thank them for their commitment to a vision for the future of North Bay.

I would like to thank our funding partners: our federal government, including our MP Jay Aspin and the FedNor Team of Aime Dimatteo, Carmen Demarco, and our local representative Denise Deschamps for their assistance and leadership in assisting our city in this important initiative.

Our provincial government: Minister Rick Bartolucci, Northern Development and Mines, as well as Assistant Deputy Minister Cal

McDonald who is here today on the Minister's behalf, the Northern Ontario Heritage Fund Corporation team, Bruce Strapp and our local representatives Moe Dorie and Siobhan O'Leary, for believing in this important project.

I would like to acknowledge our community partners: North Bay Jack Garland Airport, Manager Jack Santerre, and the North Bay Jack Garland Airport Board of Directors.

The development of this new industrial park at the airport allows us to capitalize on unique assets such as the 10,000-foot runway.

We need to recognize the existing core group of companies that service a wide range of global customers.

We will target companies involved in manufacturing, high-tech, and aviation/aerospace areas that will be the foundation of this Airport Business Park. We have signed our first new tenant, Hy-Power Nano Inc. just two weeks ago.

The Airport Industrial Business Park is a strategic and important investment for the future of North Bay, and, as mayor, I encourage local business to consider this park for future expansions and to promote this for investment by their customers, suppliers, and contacts.

Last but not least, I would like to thank North Bay City Council for their unanimous support of this project. They have never wavered in their support of the Airport Business Park. Our city will benefit long into the future. I thank you for attending today.

Source: City of North Bay. 2011. "Speech Given by Mayor Al McDonald Ground Breaking Ceremony Airport Industrial Business Park." November 18. www.cityofnorthbay.ca/common/pdf/SPEECH%20 FOR%20GROUNDBREAKING%20CEREMONY-AIRPORT%20INDUSTRIAL%20BUSINESS%20 PARK-NOV%2018-2011.pdf

The basic elements of this speech are clear: the purpose of the speech was to thank project partners for their help in establishing the new industrial park; the main audience members were identified (all three levels of government, various City of North Bay departments, and community partners), and key messages were articulated ("This project was a partnership between all three levels of government, as well as many internal City of North Bay departments" and "The development of this new industrial park at the airport allows us to capitalize on unique assets"). With its primary focus on audience/partners, though, the second key message—the "value" that "taxpayers" are likely to expect—is buried.

A Better Speech

An example of a better speech was delivered by the Deputy Head and Librarian and Archivist of Canada at a Conference Board of Canada event in October 2012 on social media in the public sector (see appendix 5.1). This speech provides a textbook illustration of how to plan and organize a speech:

- Ten to 15 percent of the total speech is allocated to an engaging, interesting, and mildly humorous introduction, 10 percent to the conclusion, and 75 to 85 percent to the body.
- The "hook" or "attention grabber" is a set of nine challenging questions—"What is this? What is going on here? What is happening to our traditional ways of operating? Where is my stuff that used to come from publishers? Where is it coming from now? The Web? Who creates it? Is it reliable? Authentic?"
- The main message is clear and is repeated throughout in various forms—"Social media is an opportunity for public administrators to share information with and engage the public, but it must be executed with a mandate of advancing the core missions of our organizations."
- The three main points of content of the body are clearly telegraphed— "tell them what you're going to tell them"—by the speaker at the outset, with "signposts" of progress repeated throughout the speech ("First, what is really changing here?" "Second, I would like to discuss the resulting social transformation," and "Third and finally, I would like to give you a brief overview of how Library and Archives Canada is adapting to social media").
- The conclusion is clearly identified ("In closing, I would like to suggest that..."), and the main point is clearly reiterated ("the rise of social media for government and non-governmental organizations represents both a rupture and continuity with our past").
- The speech concludes with a memorable parting thought for the audience—"we cannot simply implement new methods for the sake of change. The element of continuity must be within our guiding visions, the raison d'être of our organizations, to ensure that whatever adaptations we choose to undertake, they will be done to advance the core missions of our organizations."

The Best Speech

The best speech example was delivered by City of Whitehorse Mayor Dan Curtis to city council on the topic of the 2013 operating budget (see appendix 5.2). The purpose of the speech is clear: to persuade councillors—and, more broadly, Whitehorse residents—of the need for a modest increase in property taxes to pay for increased service and infrastructure requirements. The key message is consistent with this purpose: "To achieve a balanced budget and meet the increased service and infrastructure requirements, the City of Whitehorse must modestly increase property taxes and user fees while implementing spending reduction measures."

In terms of who the message is intended for, members of Whitehorse council are clearly the primary target audience. But this speech is in the "best" category because it is also very clearly intended to be heard by residents of Whitehorse ("the budget is responding to stakeholder requests to extend transit service for people who work or take classes past 7:00 p.m.").

In terms of structure, giving the speech the subheading of "Managing Our City's Growth Responsibly" immediately establishes growth as a central message, and it is repeated in some form in almost every paragraph of the speech. The context section is an example of a very useful way of providing an introduction to a speech, and the bullets in the conclusion are an effective way to "tell them what you told them."

Feature 5.14

John F. Kennedy's 1963 speech, delivered in Cold War–era Berlin is considered to be one of the best public speeches ever given. In a 2013 article for the *Globe and Mail*, Andrew Cohen provides some insight into why the speech was so effective.

JFK, Berlin, 1963: The Right Time. The Right Place. The Right Message.

On June 26, 1963, John F. Kennedy went to West Berlin and gave a speech for the ages. It was the loudest and longest in a life of great ovations. It was also the last.

Fifty years later, Mr. Kennedy in Berlin remains one of the spectacles of the Cold War. Here was an exquisite meeting of man, moment and momentum, creating a dazzling piece of theatre. Presidents have come to Berlin since to declaim and decry, but none like this.

Today, in a time when political speeches are wreathed in banality, euphemism and cliché, Mr. Kennedy in Berlin evokes the lost art of oratory. It reminds us that great speeches matter when delivered in the right place at the right time—and also, how they can go dangerously awry.

In June of 1963, Mr. Kennedy was surging. On two consecutive days earlier that month, he had given the most important speeches of his presidency, addressing the two most important issues of his time. In Berlin, he would give a third.

On June 10, Mr. Kennedy addressed nuclear arms at American University in Washington. He praised and humanized the Russians and saluted a mutual commitment to peace. He declared a moratorium on the testing of nuclear weapons and embraced negotiations on a nuclear test ban treaty. His message was less about winning the Cold War than ending it.

On June 11, Mr. Kennedy addressed civil rights from the Oval Office. He did what no president had ever done: He cast civil rights as a matter of morality.

He urged Americans to think of civil rights "as old as the scriptures and as clear as the American Constitution," and asked them to examine their consciences on race. Then he announced unprecedented civil rights legislation.

Some advisers urged him to cancel his upcoming visit to Europe, which included three days in West Germany. He refused. He wanted to be seen in West Berlin, which had been isolated inside East Germany since the Russians had erected the Berlin Wall in August 1961.

On the morning of June 26, Mr. Kennedy drove to the Brandenburg Gate. He peered into the East, grey and sullen. He had already begun jotting down phrases and practising them in German, not terribly successfully.

At 12:50 p.m. he spoke from the steps of Rathaus Schoeneberg, before hundreds of thousands of Berliners filling Rudolph Wilde Platz— leaning out windows, standing on roofs, clinging to streetlamps. He had come to the front line of the Cold War, observed its fundamental injustice, and it angered him.

"There are some who say that communism is the wave of the future," he said. "Let them come to Berlin. And there are some who say in Europe and elsewhere we can work with the Communists. Let them come to Berlin. And there are even a few who say that it is true that communism is an evil system, but it permits us to make economic progress. Lass' sie nach Berlin kommen. Let them come to Berlin."

Twice, memorably, he punctuated his narrative with the refrain: "Ich bin ein Berliner!"

The Berliners roared, deep and guttural. Kennedy had never seen a crowd as big or rapturous. He thought the people would have rushed the wall had he ordered them. While not given to emotionalism, the mood emboldened him to discard most of his prepared remarks and to speak extemporaneously.

That was dangerous. McGeorge Bundy, his national security adviser, was aghast listening to a hawkish JFK. "Mr. President, I think that went too far," he told him as he left the platform. In the moment, Mr. Kennedy had moved from conciliatory to confrontational, and Mr. Bundy worried it might kill the talks over nuclear arms.

That afternoon, at the Free University in Berlin, a chastened president returned to the theme of peace. Soviet Premier Nikita Khrushchev, Mr. Kennedy's interlocutor, understood the nature of spectacle, ignored the first speech and accepted the second.

As a student of history, Mr. Kennedy knew the confluence of events—the crowd, the Wall, the time—were unique. Some compared his feverish appearance to the triumphal passage of a Roman emperor. "We'll never have another day like this as long as we live," he mused.

Mr. Kennedy would live to see the Limited Nuclear Test Ban Treaty, his proudest achievement. But in his last five months there would be no more speeches like this or the others that tumultuous June, when Pope John died, the Profumo scandal broke and the Buddhist monks in Vietnam began burning themselves alive in protest.

Mr. Kennedy was exhilarated by Berlin. As he departed that afternoon, he said that one day he would leave a note to his successor, "to be opened at a time of some discouragement."

It would have three words: "Go to Germany."

Source: Andrew Cohen. 2013. "JFK, Berlin, 1963: The Right Time. The Right Place. The Right Message." *Globe and Mail,* June 25. www.theglobeandmail.com/news/world/jfk-berlin-1963-the-right-time-the-right-place-the-right-message/article12815970/#dashboard/follows/

LEARNING ACTIVITIES

Activity 5.1: Critical Assessment

This assignment is intended to help you develop your ability to assess and distinguish the relative quality of various core communications tactics. To begin, work with a partner to find three examples each of press releases, backgrounders, FAQs, letters to the editor, and speeches that interest you. Next, work with your partner to assess the relative strengths and weaknesses of your samples, summarizing your work in a 2,500 word analysis (500 words per tactic). Remember that the goal of this assignment is not to summarize the information presented in the product, but to respond critically to it.

Activity 5.2: Tactic Development

In chapter 4, you were asked to identify a new initiative that a public sector organization is using to achieve a strategic goal—an initiative new enough that few communications materials have been generated to date. Building on activity 4.4 and earlier exercises, develop the following:

- one press release designed for print media (500 words/one page maximum)
- one backgrounder designed for a website (1,000 words/two pages maximum)
- one FAQ designed for a website (10 questions and answers/one page maximum)
- one letter to the editor of a local newspaper (250 words maximum)
- one speech to be delivered to a public audience by a senior organizational spokesperson (e.g., minister, deputy minister) (500 words maximum)

Ensure that these tactics are consistent with the key messages you developed as part of activity 4.4.

FURTHER READING

Bennett and Jessani *The Knowledge Translation Toolkit: Bridging the "Know-Do" Gap; A Resource for Researchers* (2011), especially section 5, is a great source of examples, templates, and guides for crafting basic communications tactics.

ONLINE RESOURCES

The Washington-based Communications Consortium Media Center provides a treasure trove of tips, tools, and resources for creating standard press kits (www. ccmc.org/node/16138), as does Communicate & Howe!'s excellent site (www. communicateandhowe.com/2013/11/29/nonprofit-communicators-toolbox-traditional-tools-tactics/). Susan Doyle provides a comprehensive overview of press release writing in government on her Writing for Government website (web.uvic.ca/~sdoyle/E302/Notes/index.html). Doyle also provides a very good overview of government correspondence, as does Rob Parkinson's "Format Guidelines for Letters" on his Writing for Results website (writingforresults. net/Acro_3/4_msg/2_format/letters.pdf).

QUESTIONS FOR CRITICAL REFLECTION

1. What are the relative strengths and weaknesses of the tactics covered in this chapter?
2. Is there a common method or standard way of distinguishing between good, better, and best communications tactics?

KEY TERMS

backgrounder: A relatively short but in-depth stand-alone document that provides additional information about a specific issue.

FAQs (frequently asked questions): A list of questions and answers that is typically used to prepare spokespersons to engage with the media or general public about a product, service, or initiative.

letter to the editor: A method of clarifying an organization's position on a controversial issue of public importance, communicating the rationale for an upcoming or recent policy or program decision, or seeking public support for a new initiative that involves submitting an open letter to the editor to a newspaper or magazine for publication in a special letters section.

press release: A document used to communicate key messages to the public through a media intermediary.

speech: A prepared script that a spokesperson uses to address a targeted audience about specific topics.

NOTES

1 This section is adapted from Susan Doyle's "Notes on Writing a Press Release," a section of her excellent Writing for Government website (http://web.uvic.ca/~sdoyle/E302/index.html).

2 This section is based on Bill Stoler's article, "Press Kit Elements That Work" (www.publicityinsider.com/presskit.pdf).

3 These points are based on National Association of Social Workers' "How to Write and Use an Effective Backgrounder in Public Relations" (www.socialworkers.org/pressroom/mediatoolkit/toolkit/backgrounder.pdf).

4 This section is adapted from Rob Parkinson's Q&As, a section from his excellent Writing for Results website (writingforresults.net/tplt_3/Acro/lmb/Min/enclosre/Qs_&_As.pdf).

5 This section is adapted from Susan Dugdale's "How to Write a Speech," a section from her excellent Write it Out Loud website (www.write-out-loud.com/howtowritespeech.html).

6 Dlugan (2009) provides some useful examples of various speech outlines.

7 This section is adopted from Julie Linkins's article, "How to Write a Good Introduction to a Speech" (www.ehow.com/how_5844162_write-good-introduction-speech.html#ixzz1ffUloj7y).

WORKS CITED

Bennett, Gavin, and Nasreen Jessani, eds. 2011. *The Knowledge Translation Toolkit: Bridging the "Know-Do" Gap; A Resource for Researchers.* Ottawa: IDRC.

Canada. Department of Fisheries and Oceans. 2012. "Submission of the New Brunswick Department of Agriculture, Aquaculture and Fisheries to the External Review on Northern Shrimp." www.dfo-mpo.gc.ca/fm-gp/peches-fisheries/reports-rapports/eap-pce/documents/nb-eng.pdf

Canadian Food Inspection Agency. 2009. *2009 Organic Products Regulations: Questions and Answers.* www.inspection.gc.ca/food/organic-products/labelling-and-general-information/questions-andanswers/eng/1328081120744/1328081195020

Canadian Press. 2013. "Fantino's Office Linked to 'Editorials' on Government Website." *CBC News: Politics,* May 30. www.cbc.ca/news/politics/story/2013/05/30/pol-cp-cida-fantino-partisan-letters.html

City of Calgary. n.d. "City Hall Wall of Windows—FAQs." www.calgary.ca/CS/CSC/Pages/MyYYC---FAQs.aspx

City of North Bay. 2011. "Speech Given by Mayor Al McDonald Ground Breaking Ceremony Airport Industrial Business Park." November 18. www.cityofnorthbay.ca/common/pdf/SPEECH%20FOR%20GROUND-BREAKING%20CEREMONY-AIRPORT%20INDUSTRIAL%20BUSI-NESS%20PARK-NOV%2018-2011.pdf

City of Regina. 2012. "More Mobile Food Vendors to Operate in Downtown Regina: City Introduces Two-Year Pilot Project." April 5. www.regina.ca/press/news-and-announcements/more-mobile-food-vendors-to-operate-in-downtown-regina-city-introduces-two-year-pilot-project/

City of Whitehorse. 2013. "Mayor's Speech—Operations Budget 2013: Managing Our City's Growth Responsibly." www.city.whitehorse.yk.ca/modules/showdocument.aspx?documentid=3044

Cohen, Andrew. 2013. "JFK, Berlin, 1963: The Right Time. The Right Place. The Right Message." *Globe and Mail,* June 25. www.theglobeandmail.com/news/world/jfk-berlin-1963-the-right-time-the-right-place-the-right-message/article12815970/#dashboard/follows/

Dlugan, Andrew. 2009. "Speech Preparation #3: Don't Skip the Speech Outline." Six Minutes: Speaking and Presentation Skills. http://sixminutes.dlugan.com/speech-preparation-3-outline-examples/

Doyle, Susan. 2013. Writing for Government. http://web.uvic.ca/~sdoyle/E302/index.html

Dugdale, Susan. n.d. "How to Write a Speech." Write-Out-Loud.com. www.write-out-loud.com/howtowritespeech.html

Fantino, Julian. 2012. "Dear NDP: CIDA Does Not Need Your Economic Advice." Huffington Post: Politics, December 21. www.huffingtonpost.ca/the-honourable-julian-fantino/cida-fantino_b_2340884.html

Iannicca, Nando. 2013. "Councillor Explains." *Mississauga News,* March 28. www.mississauga.com/opinion-story/3133734-councillor-explains/

Klappe, Dawn. 2013. "Letter: Kelowna's Last Public Post Office Moving Closer to Its Demise." *Kelowna Capital News,* July 4. www.kelownacapnews.com/opinion/letters/214079741.html

Library and Archives Canada. "Social Media in the Public Sector, 2012. Remarks by the Deputy Head and Librarian and Archivist of Canada." www.bac-lac.gc.ca/eng/news/speeches/Pages/social-media-in-the-public-sector-2012.aspx

Linkins, Julie. n.d. "How to Write a Good Introduction to a Speech." www.ehow.com/how_5844162_write-good-introduction-speech.html#ixzz1ffUloj7y

National Association of Social Workers. 2008. "How to Write and Use an Effective Backgrounder in Public Relations." www.socialworkers.org/pressroom/mediatoolkit/toolkit/backgrounder.pdf

Northwest Territories. Department of Human Resources. 2011. "Department of Human Resources: Report on the Staff Retention Policy Year Ending March 31, 2011." www.assembly.gov.nt.ca/_live/documents/content/11-05-18td31-166.pdf

Parkinson, Rob. n.d. "Briefing Notes for the Honourable John Smith, Minister for International Trade." Writing for Results. writingforresults.net/tplt_3/Acro/lmb/Min/enclosre/Qs_&_As.pdf

Saskatchewan. 2013. "Saskatchewan Remains On Track for Balanced Budget." February 15. www.gov.sk.ca/news?newsId=38eb2bce-7081-4711-a161-607523070228

Saskatchewan. Ministry of Government Relations. 2010. "Provincial Public Safety Telecommunications Network (PPSTN). Questions and Answers." www.gr.gov.sk.ca/Default.aspx?DN=bc9a79a6-9136-4cc7-82a5-e9e48f958798

South West Community Care Access Centre. 2013. "Briefing Note: Access to Care for High Risk Seniors and Adults with Complex Health Needs." www.ingersoll.ca/Portals/Ingersoll/Documents/Our%20Town%20Hall/Minutes%20and%20Agendas/2013/Agenda/06_10_2013/Access.pdf

Stoler, Bill. n.d. "Press Kit Elements That Work." *Bill Stoller's Free Publicity: The Newsletter for PR-Hungry Businesses.* http://www.publicityinsider.com/presskit.pdf

Treasury Board of Canada Secretariat. 2012. *Communications Policy of the Government of Canada.* www.tbs-sct.gc.ca/pol/doc-eng.aspx?id=12316&section=text

WikiHow. n.d. "How to Write a Speech." www.wikihow.com/Write-a-Speech

Yukon. 2013. "Yukon Government Gives Mining Exploration Program a Boost." January 29. www.gov.yk.ca/news/13-016.html

PUBLIC EVENT PLANNING

CHAPTER OVERVIEW

This chapter introduces a four-step process for managing public events. Step 1 involves formulating clear objectives for an event. Step 2 focuses on developing the specific activities needed to implement the event strategy in a way that integrates objectives and messages. Step 3 involves delivering the event and assessing its impact on target audiences. Step 4 concludes the process with an evaluation of the effectiveness of the event to demonstrate its contribution to the organization's objectives and to document lessons learned. The chapter concludes with an activity that provides an opportunity to put the event management process outlined throughout the chapter into practice.

LEARNING OBJECTIVES
By the end of this chapter, you will be able to

- explain what events are and how they factor into public sector organizations' communications activities;
- conduct the research necessary to identify the target audience and key messages for a public event;
- plan a public event by interpreting event research results to senior management and formulating public event strategy;
- develop a public event in a way that integrates policy, objectives, messages, and communications techniques;
- pre-test a public event strategy to ensure maximum impact;
- design and deliver a public event; and
- evaluate the effectiveness of an event to measure its contribution to an organization's objectives and to document lessons learned.

INTRODUCTION

Public events are an important tactic in Canadian public sector communications because they are one of the few in which information is directly transmitted and disseminated to targeted audience members in their own communities. The most common types of public events are announcements, speeches, news conferences and exhibitions. This chapter introduces a four-step process for managing public events, which was originally developed by the Canada School of Public Service.[1] Step 1 involves formulating clear objectives for an event. Step 2 focuses on developing the specific activities needed to implement the event strategy in a way that integrates objectives and messages. Step 3 involves delivering the event and assessing its impact on target audiences. Step 4 concludes the process with an evaluation of the effectiveness of the event to demonstrate the contribution to the organization's objectives and to document lessons learned.

6.1 STEP 1: EVENT PLANNING

Event management begins with planning and involves eight activities: (1) defining event objectives; (2) identifying the target audience; (3) refining key messages; (4) determining the event type; (5) identifying the event location; (6) developing a budget; (7) creating a promotional strategy; and (8) developing an event critical path.

Event Objectives

As noted in chapter 4, clear objectives are critical for any communications activity, as they describe exactly what an organization wants to accomplish, and provide the benchmarks for evaluating the success of an activity. Event objectives are no different: they need to flow directly from the overall strategic communications plan that the event is designed to support. Objectives for public events are developed on three levels: output, outtake, and outcome. Output objectives define the tangible services or goods that a communications activity will produce. Examples of communications outputs include websites, half-page ads in all local newspapers in a specific region, or reaching 60 percent of a target population with a specific message by a specific date. Outtake objectives are used to define the awareness/comprehension and retention/recall of core themes and messages that an organization wants target audience members to have or take away as a result of a particular communications activity. Examples of outtake objec-

CHAPTER 6

---

tives include achieving a 5 percent increase in public awareness of policy X, having 85 percent of the population of region Y understand the behavioural implications of a new hunting regulation, and getting 95 percent of a province's population to understand new municipal voting procedures one year after their introduction. Outcome objectives define the extent to which an organization would like members of a target audience to alter their preferences and behaviour as a result of changes in their awareness, retention, and comprehension of the core themes or messages included in a communications activity. Typical outcome objectives could include increasing voter turnout rates in a given municipality by 10 percent as a result of their increased awareness of the importance of voting, or decreasing the number of driving regulation violations by 5 percent in a 12-month period as a result of increased understanding of new changes to the regulations.

Target Audience and Key Messages

The next two activities in the event planning stage involve (1) defining exactly who the target audience for the public event will be in terms of size, location, core demographic characteristics, information requirements, and priority; and (2) refining key messages for the event, including a brief rationale for each. Target audiences and key messages need to directly correspond to and support the results of the stakeholder analysis and key message development conducted during the strategic planning process discussed in more detail in chapters 3 and 4.

Event Type

In public sector communications, the four most common event types are (1) **announcements**, scripted statements designed to inform the public about a new initiative or the organization's position on a policy, program, service, activity, or initiative; (2) **speeches**, prepared bodies of text delivered by an organizational spokesperson to an audience and/or the media at an event or a news conference; (3) **news conferences**, events held with invited media for the purpose of delivering an announcement or discussing an occurrence of important news value; and (4) **exhibitions**, temporary or permanent venues where one or more exhibitors convey particular educational or promotional messages to target audiences by means of exhibits or displays (e.g., trade and consumer shows, open houses, public fairs and festivals, conferences and conventions).

Selection of the specific event type is dependent on a number of considerations:

- approach of the initiative (proactive or reactive, low or high profile)
- nature and scope of the target audience (national versus local, narrow versus broad, level of education, size, etc.)
- complexity of the issue or information disseminated
- need for key stakeholder support
- enhancement opportunities, i.e., opportunity to modify an existing event to achieve dual objectives
- communications impediments, such as media hostility to the initiative or department, public indifference, or competing regional, sectoral, or international interests
- timing of event, i.e., time needed to properly produce the event, anticipated elapsed time for the intended objectives to be achieved, optimal timing for disseminating further information to reinforce the event
- need for ministerial involvement, including the minister's role to date and preferred level of involvement, public perception of the minister, his/her language capability, etc.

For example, an announcement or participation in an exhibition might be an appropriate choice for an initiative that has a relatively low profile, a localized target audience, little need for key stakeholder support, few communications impediments, and no need for ministerial involvement. Conversely, a news conference or major speech by a minister might be an appropriate choice for an initiative that has a national audience, needs to generate key stakeholder support, has a short deadline to get the message out, and if the minister has been personally linked to the initiative.

Event Location

Once the event type has been determined, the location for the event can be chosen based on a few critical questions:

- Is the location central to the target audience?
- Does the facility represent the image you want to project for the event?

- Are dates available for the public event?
- Does the facility have the capacity to expand (or flexibility to reduce) its space if required?
- Are conditions attached to using the facility? (i.e., does the facility have exclusive arrangements with catering, A/V, security and other contractors?)
- Is there a cut-off date for cancelling the booking and not losing your down payment?
- Does the facility have a mandate that could cause your event to get "bumped" from the schedule?

Once location possibilities have been narrowed down, try to conduct on-site inspections to ensure that the locations meet your objectives and requirements. Factors to consider when conducting on-site location inspections include the following:

- Pay attention to how the facility representative(s) interacts with you. Unexpected challenges are bound to arise over the course of your event and it is easier to cope if you are working with flexible people.
- If you are considering using a municipally owned facility, be sure the representatives are aware of your event's economic impact. A number of municipal facilities have a mandate to promote tourism/convention spending and are thus more flexible when negotiating to meet this mandate.
- Most of the time, facility operators are not flexible about space rates, especially municipal facilities that are under pressure to generate revenue; however, operators are usually somewhat flexible about providing added value items such as half-price move-in/move-out days.
- Food and beverage costs are often negotiable, especially if you plan on holding several large food functions at the facility.
- Meeting room costs are very often negotiable. If you are booking a large number of hotel "room nights" or spending a lot on other space and services, you may be able to negotiate free or discounted meeting rooms, as well as a break on set-up charges

for your meeting rooms. Most facilities will throw in ice water, table drape, pens, and notepads at no charge.

Budget

Most public sector communications strategies include at least some notional budgetary allocation for specific communications tactics. Using this allocation, a basic budget for a public event can be constructed with the following categories: exhibit space (industry average allocation is 29 percent of total budget); design and construction/rental (16 percent); show services, such as drayage, A/V, electrical, Internet (17 percent); travel (13 percent); shipping (12 percent); promotion (12 percent); and other (1 percent). As with any communications budget, be sure to contact staff in finance to ensure consistency with departmental/governmental expenditure rules and regulations. See appendix 6.1 for a more detailed event budgeting template.

Promotional Strategy

With event objectives defined and budget set, a promotional strategy can be developed to ensure that key messages reach target audience members. Specific promotional tactics for public events include media advisories, press releases, web pages and social media, direct mail/email campaigns, print ad purchases, telemarketing, and partnerships with stakeholders/other governments/trade associations.

Critical Path

The last step in the planning stage of the event management process involves creating a **critical path** for the event, a document that defines event objectives, outlines critical milestones, provides contact information for suppliers, and lists the key tasks, responsibilities, and completion dates for all personnel involved in the planning, development, delivery, and evaluation of the event. Critical paths can be useful tools for event mangers as they can be used for ongoing team meetings and eventually for event evaluation. Appendix 6.2 contains a template for creating a critical path for any public sector event. Table 6.1 provides a checklist that can be used when planning a public event.

TABLE 6.1: PLANNING CHECKLIST

Show name:				
Show dates:				
Show location:				
	Estimate	Cost	Variance	Comments
Space rental				
Space				
Deposit				
Other				
Subtotal				
Exhibit				
Design				
Fabrication/purchase				
Exhibit refurbishing				
Graphics design				
Graphics production				
Refurbishing				
Rental				
Shipping preparations				
Storage (pro-rated)				
Insurance (pro-rated)				
Other				
Subtotal				
Shipping				
To show				
From show				
Show to show				
Customs broker				
Other				
Subtotal				
Personnel expenses				
Salaries				
Staff training				
Staff incentives				
Pre-show dinner				
Staff attire				
Transportation				
Hotel				
Food/entertainment				

6.2 STEP 2: EVENT DEVELOPMENT

The development stage of the event management process begins with putting together a team of individuals responsible for developing and delivering the event. Depending on the event, team members could include minister's and deputy minister's staff, program staff and subject matter experts, communications advisors, speech writers, media relations staff, creative services, administrative support staff, and external contractors and suppliers. In addition to event team creation, the development stage includes the following activities: creating event kits, shipping, selecting and liaising with contractors, registering, and pre-testing.

Event Kits
Depending on the event type, organizers may wish to consider creating an event kit for participants that includes key materials such as copies of speeches and news releases, brochures, promotional materials (e.g., pens and USB sticks), water bottles, and exhibit venue documentation (e.g., maps and local attractions).

Shipping
For large events like media conferences, major public speeches, and exhibits, event materials may have to be shipped well ahead of the event itself. The following are points to remember about shipping:

- The exact shipping address and earliest date for arrival of materials should be confirmed with the event organizer.
- Whenever possible, use the event's official transportation contractor, as they have priority over other carriers at the loading dock. They also have representatives on-site before, during, and after the event if you have problems with your shipment.
- Some events charge extra for drayage, or moving your booth from the loading dock to the booth and back again at the close of the show.
- Labels should be prepared in advance for post-show shipping.
- Always remember to keep records of all shipping documents.

Pre-event Promotion
For exhibits and conferences, host organizations sometimes provide promotional services at no charge or for a nominal fee, such as inclusion in direct mail campaigns, website listings and links, and invitations that can

be overprinted with your organization name. To take advantage of these, carefully review the exhibitor services manual issued by event organizers (typically three months prior to the event) for key deadlines, formats, and other critical details.

Contractor Selection and Liaison

Large events often involve working with a range of contractors, such as event planners, display decorators, audio/visual production people, security staff, telephone and Internet service providers, temporary staffing, caterers, and material handling staff. Some events have exclusive facility contractors that have pre-established event pricing; others will have to be negotiated via open contracting processes. Regardless of how they are sourced, the key to working successfully with event contractors is providing clear and concise direction regarding the service to be performed, agreeing in writing to deliverables, and following up regularly to ensure that your event needs remain top of the contractor's mind. To set this tone, the items listed below are key:

- Meet in person with contractors whenever possible. Written and electronic communication cannot take the place of face-to-face meetings for establishing and engendering trust, resolving conflicts, or maintaining long-term contact.
- Develop a clear description of the work to be performed and the expected level of service prior to key meetings with contractors.
- Meet with suppliers to review due dates and go over specifications they need to do their job effectively.
- Implement a supplier reporting system that provides regular reports on the status of the event.
- Meet with all contractors and key suppliers one month prior to the event to review planning details.
- Set clear timelines for move-in/move-out as well as other logistical deadlines that affect the operation of the event.
- Provide regular feedback to the supplier on the quality of their work.

Registration

Large events, such as conferences, workshops, exhibitions, and press conferences usually require some type of registration system to capture critical information about participants for such things as identification, material distribution, security, event follow-up, and evaluation. Most often, public sector event organizers tend to outsource the registration process to an outside contractor. Below are some registration considerations if the event is small enough to manage in-house:

- Ensure that the database used to track participants includes fields for all critical information: first name/last name, employer/organization, position with employer/organization, email address, primary phone contact, and method of payment (if applicable).
- Choose a system that allows you to "pre-populate" as many fields as possible in the database. When inputting a postal code, for instance, a city and province should fill in automatically.
- Attendees of conferences and open houses often arrive within a short period of time. Ensure that you have sufficient staff and procedures in place to process the anticipated numbers of people with minimal wait time.
- Send badges and related event information to VIPs in advance.

Pre-testing

For most events, a pre-production test of major activities is recommended to ensure consistency with original objectives and champion (e.g., minister, deputy minister, key stakeholder) expectations. Activities that might be pre-tested include the creative components of the activity (e.g., images, colours, text), key messages, and display design. Table 6.2 provides a checklist that can be used for event development in general.

TABLE 6.2: DEVELOPMENT CHECKLIST

Criteria	Yes	No
Has an event team been established?		
Has a team leader been appointed?		
Has a detailed production schedule been prepared?		
Has a detailed production budget been prepared?		
Have the intended audiences been identified?		
Has the best message to reach each audience been defined?		
Has the best type of event to communicate the intended messages been identified?		
Can this event be effectively tied in with another event?		
Should this message be tied in with another message?		
Has the timing been identified?		
Is the audience large enough or significant enough to warrant the event?		
Will the event meet the requirements of the audience?		
Does the event support the overall objectives of the organization?		
Given the audience, is the proposed content and format appropriate?		
Will this event reach the audience?		
Will there be sufficient event materials available?		
Has an event promotion plan been prepared?		
Will there be a participant registration system in place?		
Have the event components been pre-tested?		

6.3 STEP 3: DELIVERY

The third step in the event management process is implementing the event. The main activities involved in this stage include selection of an on-site manager, event staff training, risk management, and organizing security.

On-Site Manager

An on-site manager should be appointed for any event, regardless of size and scope, to ensure that all critical activities proceed as planned and that contingency plans can be executed if required. Depending on the size and scope of the event, on-site managers might also be responsible for

- acting as the primary liaison for the event organizer to address all issues pertaining to the event;
- ensuring a smooth set-up and operation of the event;
- conducting the pre-event briefing, orientation, and training;
- distributing entry passes;
- coordinating the distribution of event materials to the event site;
- maintaining an inventory of supplies at the event;

- ensuring that on-site promotional activities are executed in the prescribed manner and identifying additional promotional opportunities at each event;
- conducting on-site troubleshooting to resolve event issues;
- conducting daily risk assessment audits, and creating emergency preparedness strategies;
- conducting on-site evaluations to determine the effectiveness of the event; and
- preparing reports to recommend improvements for events.

Regardless of the size of the event, it is good practice to set out the responsibilities of the on-site manager as clearly as possible as if it were a formal job description or employment contract.

Event Staff Training

The success of any event requires a well-trained and -informed staff, which can be achieved through three activities: a pre-event briefing, an on-site orientation session, and the production of an orientation manual.

Pre-event Briefing

All event staff should attend a pre-event briefing, the purpose of which is to review the objectives and goals of the event, all of the event activities, and the role that each team member will play in achieving the event objectives. If event staff are not familiar with your organization or its programs and services, it is a good idea to have a senior manager (or even the minister) participate in the briefing session to reinforce the importance of the event in meeting organizational objectives and to help keep team members focused on results.

On-Site Orientation Session

An on-site orientation session should be conducted the day before the event. To be effective, the session needs to be both informative and fun, as exhibit personnel often have a "been there, done that" attitude. One way to address this potential challenge is to draw on their expertise in some way to ensure that they feel included and that they attend the session. Orientation session agenda items should include emergency procedures, policies, media relations, show promotional programs, and exhibiting tips. The session should not be longer than one hour, including time to distribute show passes, name badges, and any other critical items.

Orientation Manual

Depending on the size and complexity of the event and the potential for future repetition, the creation of an orientation manual should be considered. Orientation manuals can itemize the activities that will take place at each event location and serve as a central reference for event team participation. In addition, good manuals also set out operating parameters and guidelines, ensuring that all personnel have access to the same information. A basic orientation manual may include an event summary, schedule, and map(s); the exhibit theme and objectives; exhibit partners; a floor plan; programs and promotions; the names of the site manager and exhibit hosts personnel; installation and dismantling procedures; exhibiting tips; media/VIP relations; exhibit security; emergency procedures and accident report forms; and location details (e.g., accommodations, attractions, dining, weather, travel information).

Risk Management

Risk management is the goal of managing the risk attendant to the success of any event involves safeguarding people, property, reputations, and assets by identifying as many risk factors as possible in the entire scope of an event's operations, presenting alternate solutions, and making cost-effective recommendations. Managing event risk typically involves the following:

- *Analyze the severity, scope, and timing of the crisis.* Has the incident or crisis already occurred and you are just now considering how to mitigate the consequences? If the crisis is still occurring, is it getting worse with each passing minute? Can you reduce it by acting immediately? If it is a looming crisis, when will it occur? What exactly is at stake? Lives? Reputations? Money? Attendance? Client satisfaction? How rapidly must you respond? Are there identifiable actions and events that could trigger a crisis?

- *Generate solutions.* Produce a list of all possible solutions, no matter how implausible or costly they may initially seem. Your goal in this step is to ensure you have considered every possible angle. Consider the following: Who can help? What can they offer—skills, equipment, money, influence, or moral support? When can they offer it?
- *Prioritize the solutions* by considering how effectively and completely a particular option would solve the crisis or mitigate its consequences, how difficult it would be to implement the solution, how much it would cost to implement the solution, and how quickly the option could be implemented.
- *Choose the best solution or solutions.* Often you can simultaneously implement more than one solution. Sometimes one solution can be identified as a backup in case the other proposed solution fails.
- *Inform those who need to know.* Make a list of those who need to know how you are solving or have solved the crisis. Disseminate the information as quickly as possible; consider those who should be briefed in person versus those who can be briefed by other means.

At the end of the day, the art of managing event risk involves developing the humility of admitting when you don't know something and asking for help when you need it.

Security

No matter how secure an event is designed to be, some breaches of security—theft, for example—are bound to occur. The following steps can be taken to maximize event security:

- Ensure that boxes are not marked in any way to indicate their contents. Use a numbering system with a manifest to keep track of contents.
- Make sure that someone who is knowledgeable about the shipment is on-site to receive the goods.
- Purchase sufficient insurance coverage for important materials during shipment, show, and return shipment.

- Ensure that all bills are as specific and detailed as possible, and that anyone authorized to remove items is listed and a copy is left with the security office/guard.
- Never leave small, easy-to-pocket items (personal or corporate) in high-traffic areas or in the event space overnight. Notebook computers, purses, and handheld devices are common targets of theft.
- Hire additional booth-specific security coverage for off-show hours from a reputable, insured, and bonded firm if the contents of the booth are valuable.
- Be especially careful during move-out, when many people are coming and going and when people's guards are down.

By using the proper risk management techniques, you can significantly reduce the odds of a breach in security. Table 6.3 provides a checklist for public event delivery.

TABLE 6.3: DELIVERY CHECKLIST

Criteria	Yes	No
Is the event on budget and schedule?		
Did the event receive all of the appropriate approvals?		
Did the event produce the intended communications activities?		
Is the message reaching all of the intended target audiences?		
Did the event communicate the objectives it was intended to address?		
Is the event achieving the desired audience impact?		
Does the target audience believe the message?		
Are there components of the event that are more or less effective?		
Are there new tactics that should be added to the event?		
Should more or fewer resources be directed at a particular target audience or geographic area?		
Has the public environment evolved/changed in such a fashion that would require an adjustment to the event?		
Was on-site training provided?		

6.4 STEP 4: EVALUATION

The fourth and final step of the event management process involves evaluating the success of the event. More specifically, event evaluation involves answering the following key questions:

- Did the event reach the target audience?
- Did the event meet its objectives?

- Did the target audience find the event to be informative and interesting?
- Did the event address the requirements of the originator and the department?
- What is the return on investment (ROI) (cost per participant reached)?
- Was the event produced within budget?

As with any evaluation of a communication activity, event evaluation needs to start by revisiting the original objectives and baselines of the event. Once these have been re-established, indicators of event performance can then be selected.

As will be discussed in detail in chapter 8, for output objectives, measures are likely to focus on assessing whether the event was aimed at and communicated to the target audience. Techniques employed involve analyzing media coverage, including the number of articles and interviews related to the event (perhaps compared with the number of releases issued), prominence of the coverage, and the messages conveyed. Other outputs might be to measure how quickly media start using the key messages of a campaign against what was planned, or to assess the size and characteristics of the audience being reached, the number visiting an event, or the number of hits on a website.

For outtake objectives, measures are likely to focus on the degree to which the audience is aware of the message, and has retained and understood it. Techniques might include interviewing members of the target audience (for instance, prior to and following the event), qualitative research, and gauging media uptake of key messages.

For outcome objectives, measures are likely to focus on the degree to which the event actually changed people's opinions, attitudes, and behaviour; for example, did they stop smoking, join an organization, or start wearing a seat belt? Techniques might include detailed interviewing and focus groups among target audiences, research among representative samples of media and other opinion leaders, or simply observation of people's behaviour. Other outcomes would offer straightforward qualitative proof; for example, by how much enquiries increased or support rose, or how many products/publications sold. It is necessary to monitor, but not research these obvious results. Benchmark research is a prerequisite for determining whether and to what extent attitudes or behaviour have altered (outcome) in line with objectives.

TABLE 6.4: EVALUATION CHECKLIST

Criteria	Yes	No
Was the event completed on budget and on schedule?		
Did the event produce the communications activities that were intended?		
Did the message reach the intended audience?		
Did the public believe the message?		
Did the event communicate the objectives it was intended to address?		
Did the event achieve the desired audience impact?		
Did the event address the requirements of the organization?		
Has the impact/effectiveness of the event been documented?		
Were the results of the evaluation made available in time for them to be useful?		
Did the results of the event justify the cost of the event?		
Was it determined how the event could have been improved?		
Were actionable findings and recommendations produced as a result of carrying out the evaluation?		
Have the results of the evaluations been added to the organization's public environmental analysis database?		

LEARNING ACTIVITIES

The Government on Web 2.0 Initiative

This activity provides an opportunity to put the event management process outlined in this chapter into practice. It begins by providing essential background on the fictional Government on Web 2.0 initiative and then presents a series of exercises that allow you to apply the skills and knowledge gained in the course of this chapter to real-world event management problems. The exercise concludes with a capstone exercise that requires learners to apply skills and knowledge from the chapter in a less directed fashion.

Background

Imagine that you are a communications planner working in the fictitious federal Department of Small Business, which has recently introduced a Government on Web 2.0 initiative in the latest speech from the throne. The initiative involves the design and delivery of a one-window service website that provides information to small businesses about the department's programs and services, which include assistance in hiring, training, and retention of employees; helping export small business products and services;

providing market information; ensuring small business compliance with taxation and customs regulations; and registering small business owners in courses to learn how to sell products and services to government. Small businesses are defined as organizations with fewer than 500 employees.

The Department of Small Business's primary program objectives are to assist small businesses with start-up and help them achieve continued success. The department's communications objective is to raise awareness of its programs and services to 75 percent amongst small businesses. Another objective is to have 25 percent of small businesses registered with the department over the next three years.

The departmental headquarters are located in the National Capital Region and it has regional offices located throughout the country. Your deputy minister formed a task force to develop a strategy to oversee the development and implementation of the department's Web 2.0 program over the next year. The director general of communications, who sits on the task force, assigned you responsibility for managing all public events (announcements, news conferences, speeches, and exhibits) in support of the program.

Your first assignment on this file was to conduct an analysis of the strategic environment for the initiative. Key findings from your analysis were as follows:

- Awareness of the Department of Small Business averages 50 percent across the country. Awareness is highest in Ontario (65 percent) and lowest in British Columbia (30 percent).
- Only 10 percent of small businesses are registered with the department. Registration is highest among businesses in the manufacturing sector (25 percent) and lowest among businesses in the hospitality industry (2 percent).
- On average, 125,000 new small businesses are started each year. Of these, 40 percent cease operation within one year and a further 25 percent after the second year.
- On average, the department receives 10 inquiries a day about the program.
- Ninety percent of small businesses have access to the Internet.

Activity 6.1: Potential Event Opportunities
As the communications planner for the department's Government on Web 2.0 initiative, you have convened a brainstorming session with the five other

individuals also appointed to this file: the minister's press secretary, the departmental speech writer, the Government on Web 2.0 program manager, the regional communications coordinator, and the creative services manager. After assigning a role to each member, your first task as a group is to identify potential opportunities to use public events in support of the Government on Web 2.0 initiative over the next year. For each opportunity, identify

- the specific type of event (e.g., announcement, news conference, speech, or exhibition) that would be appropriate; and
- a short rationale to explain why each event is appropriate.

Activity 6.2: Potential Audiences

Building on the results of exercise 6.1, your next task as a group is to identify potential target audiences for the initiative in general and the potential event in particular. To understand more about the target audiences, your group must identify the specific types of information that should be collected about audience members and how that information could be collected (i.e., which specific research tools would be most useful).

Activity 6.3: Define Objectives

This exercise requires groups to establish SMART objectives for the initial announcement of the Department of Small Business Government on Web 2.0 initiative. (SMART stands for "specific," "measurable," "achievable," "relevant," and "timely." This concept is used to guide the development of objectives.) The following table can be used to structure your group's work:

TABLE 6.5: DEFINING OBJECTIVES WORKSHEET

Condition	Characteristics	Justification
Specific	audiences, messages, desired response, timetable	
Measurable	awareness, understanding, support	
Achievable	possible given the public environment, timing, and available resources	
Relevant	to the organization's mandate	
Timely	can be achieved to the overall objectives	

Activity 6.4: Pre-testing Speeches

Using the Development Checklist (table 6.2) introduced earlier in this chapter, work with your group to identify how you would pre-test an exhibit and a major speech by the minister to the upcoming Government Technology Exhibition and Conference (GTEC) that outline the Department of Small Business' Government on Web 2.0 initiative. Be sure to identify the research tools you would use to pre-test the exhibit and speech. For each tool, identify the types of feedback you would be looking for.

Activity 6.5: Crisis Management

Each group has been impacted by one of the "disaster" scenarios described below. For this exercise, use the Delivery Checklist (table 6.3) to discuss how your group would deal with the situation when it occurred and what steps you would take to minimize the risk of a similar occurrence in the future.

Group 1 scenario: You have scheduled an announcement of the Department of Small Business Government on Web 2.0 initiative to be held in front of several small businesses in the market area. On the day of the event, a major rainstorm with raging winds blows over your backdrop, damaging your signage and computer display.

Group 2 scenario: The Department of Small Business is hosting a one-day symposium attended by approximately 300 small business owners. Your keynote speaker, the clerk of the Privy Council, cancels one hour before the scheduled speech.

Group 3 scenario: You have scheduled a news conference to announce the one-millionth registration for the Web 2.0 project. As you arrive at the office of the particular small business, located across the street from an embassy, you observe that a civil rights demonstration attended by approximately 1,000 protesters and police is taking place.

Group 4 scenario: You are an exhibitor at a Government of Canada Info-Fair in Ottawa that will be attended by more than 10,000 participants over a two-day period. It is three hours before the show. Your exhibit structure (pop-up exhibit) has still not arrived. You are unable to contact the person delivering the exhibit structure.

Activity 6.6: Evaluation

Working in groups, develop a strategy to explain how you would evaluate the event developed for the Department of Small Business Government on Web 2.0 initiative.

Activity 6.7: Capstone

The prime minister is very excited about the success of the Department of Small Business Web 2.0 initiative and wants to profile this success story at an upcoming government-organized summit being held in a lesser-known local resort area in six months' time. Adopting the four-step methodology outlined in this chapter, work in your group to research, plan, develop, deliver, and evaluate one of the following three tasks:

- Task 1: the initial press conference and announcement of the summit and the Department of Small Business's involvement
- Task 2: the 5,000 square foot Department of Small Business exhibit at the summit
- Task 3: the keynote speech by the prime minister about the Web 2.0 program at the summit

Use the following guidelines to help structure your work:

TABLE 6.6: EVENT PLANNING WORKSHEET

Step 1: Research	• This was the research that was done...
	• This is what we found...
Step 2: Planning	• SMART objectives for the specific event
	• identification of target audiences
	• themes and messages
	• activities
	• budget
Step 3: Development	• production schedule
	• event materials
	• promotion
	• pre-test
Step 4: Delivery	• training
	• event report
Step 5: Evaluation	• tools
	• evaluation report (mock-up)

FURTHER READING

Two very good, comprehensive treatments of event management are Johnny Allen, William O'Toole, Robert Harris, and Ian McDonnell's *Festival and Special Event Management*, 5th edition (2011) and C. A. Preston's *Event Marketing: How to Successfully Promote Events, Festivals, Conventions, and Expositions*, 2nd edition (2012). Joe Goldblatt's *Special Events: A New Generation and the Next Frontier* (2011) provides an excellent overview of event planning in the 21st century, with chapters on green events and corporate social responsibility, and links to a wealth of online event planning resources.

ONLINE RESOURCES

BizBash.com offers comprehensive event planning news, ideas, and resources, including search engines for venues and suppliers. Communicate & Howe! provides a number of tips and tools for public event planning on its excellent website (www.communicateandhowe.com/2013/11/29/nonprofit-communicators-toolbox-traditional-tools-tactics/).

QUESTIONS FOR CRITICAL REFLECTION

1. Are public events still relevant in this age of widespread electronic communications?
2. What factors would make you decide to attend a public event rather than accessing the information by other means (e.g., online)?

KEY TERMS

announcement: A scripted statement designed to inform the public about a new initiative or an organization's position on a policy, program, service, activity, or initiative.

critical path: A document that defines event objectives, outlines critical milestones, provides contact information for suppliers, and lists the key tasks, responsibilities, and completion dates for all personnel involved in the planning, development, delivery, and evaluation of an event.

exhibition: A temporary or permanent venue where one or more exhibitors convey particular educational or promotional messages to target audiences by means of exhibits or displays examples include trade and consumer shows, open houses, public fairs and festivals, conferences, and conventions.

news conference: An event held with invited media for the purpose of delivering an announcement or discussing an occurrence of important news value.

public event: A communications tactic at which information is directly transmitted and disseminated to target audience members in their own communities. The most common types of public events are announcements, speeches, news conferences, and exhibitions.

risk management: The goal of managing the risk attendant to the success of any event, which involves safeguarding people, property, reputations, and assets by identifying as many risk factors as possible in the entire scope of an event's operations, presenting alternate solutions, and making cost-effective recommendations.

NOTE

1 With permission, this chapter is based on event management training materials developed by the Canada School of Public Service.

WORKS CITED

Allen, Johnny, William O'Toole, Robert Harris, and Ian McDonnell. 2011. *Festival and Special Event Management.* 5th ed. Milton: Wiley Australia.

Goldblatt, Joe. 2011. *Special Events: A New Generation and the Next Frontier.* Hoboken, NJ: Wiley.

Preston, C. A. 2012. *Event Marketing: How to Successfully Promote Events, Festivals, Conventions, and Expositions.* 2nd ed. Hoboken, NJ: Wiley.

CHAPTER 7

BRIEFING NOTES

CHAPTER OVERVIEW

This chapter examines the briefing note, one of the most ubiquitous communications tools in Canada's public sector today. It begins by describing the three main types of briefing notes used today: the information note, the meeting note, and the decision note, and goes on to provide some general guidance on how to write and present notes. The chapter also includes a discussion of a fourth type of briefing note: the issue note, which is a highly specialized note used to address gaps in understanding or expectations between public sector organizations and key stakeholders. It concludes with an activity that gives learners an opportunity to develop briefing note writing and editing skills.

LEARNING OBJECTIVES
After completing this chapter, you will be able to

- describe the three most common types of briefing notes used today: the information note, the meeting note, and the decision note, as well as the highly specialized issue note;
- identify the main components of the information, meeting, decision, and issue notes;
- understand some of the basic principles of writing good briefing notes; and
- write and edit an information note, a meeting note, and a decision note.

INTRODUCTION

Briefing notes are perhaps the most ubiquitous communications tool in Canada's public sector today. They are used at all levels of public sector organizations to quickly and succinctly inform decision-makers about emerging and/or critical issues and to provide focused and considered advice on how to deal with those issues. This chapter begins by describing the three main types of briefing notes used today: the information note, the meeting note, and the decision note, and goes on to provide some guidance on how to write and present notes. It concludes with a discussion of a fourth type of briefing note: the issue note, which is a highly specialized note used to address gaps in understanding or expectations between public sector organizations and key stakeholders.

7.1 TYPES OF NOTES

Information notes are designed to bring senior decision-makers up to date on new or emerging issues of concern to them or the organization for which they are responsible. Information notes may be initiated as a result of media coverage of an issue, release of a report on a related topic, or policy or regulatory changes. Information notes typically include the following kinds of information: the current and emerging status of an issue; key supporters and detractors of an issue; and next steps—not necessarily recommendations, but upcoming key actions or events others may need to be aware of with regards to the issue. **Technical notes** are a special type of information note that provide synopses of scientific or technical issues for decision-makers. Technical notes can cover topics such as public infrastructure project updates, new scientific findings or research progress status, financial or econometric analysis, environmental research, and legal analysis.

    Meeting notes are designed to prepare decision-makers for an important upcoming meeting or event, such as a legislative or cabinet committee meeting, an invitation to address a special interest group, or a meeting with a counterpart in another department or broader public sector organization regarding a matter of shared interest. In general, meeting notes include additional information about the audience or key players who have initiated or are participating in the meeting or event. Depending on the nature of the event, good meeting/event notes generally include key information about the players attending or driving the meeting or event; analysis on key issues likely to be discussed at the meeting; an overview of questions the decision-maker may be asked at the meeting; next steps or recommendations for action at the meeting, if required; and (potentially) key messages or speaking points.

House notes are special kinds of meeting notes that prepare cabinet members to respond to issues raised in the legislature, either during question period or committee hearings. House notes typically include a brief summary of the key facts that is focused on the context and timing of the issue being raised; key messages stating the government's position and action on the issue; a list of the questions most likely to be asked about the issue, as well as recommended answers; and sufficient background to prepare the cabinet member for any additional questions.

Decision notes are designed to help prepare decision-makers to make choices about critical or emerging issues. They typically include three options with corresponding rationales and pros and cons; a proposed course of action; financial and other key implications of the action (even if the action is to maintain the status quo); analysis of the possible adverse consequences or criticism that could stem from the recommended action, as well as the best means of addressing them; and any additional political or operational considerations, such as other agencies and departments affected by the recommended action. See appendix 7.1 for sample formats of each type of briefing note.

7.2 WRITING BRIEFING NOTES

Writers of briefing notes should know four things before beginning:

- Why was the note requested in the first place?
- What are the needs of the recipient?
- Who is the "ultimate audience"?
- What are the sources of the note's content?

The most important thing that briefing note writers need to know is why a note was requested in the first place: What event in the internal or external environment prompted the request? What development may be looming on the horizon? A clear understanding of the context for writing the note will go a long way toward determining its parameters, including how much background is required, which other parties need to be consulted, and how urgent the timelines are—all of which will help focus the content at the writing stage and keep the note to a reasonable length. Some key questions can help to determine why a note was requested: What is the purpose of the note—to bring a decision-maker up to speed on a critical or emerging issue, prepare a decision-maker to attend an important meeting, or advise a decision-maker on how an important decision should be made? Does your organization have a publicly stated position on the issue? How closely related is the issue at hand to your organization's strategic mandate and agenda?

Note writers must also understand how well a note recipient understands the subject matter at hand. This helps determine how much background is needed and the degree to which that information needs to be analyzed and distilled for the reader to digest. For example, a decision-maker who knows the issue very well will likely need only new key information, whereas a new staff member or elected official will need additional context and background for the new information to make sense.

It is important to remember that the decision-maker for whom a briefing note is prepared may not be the only audience for that note; in some cases, briefing notes need to be written with an "ultimate audience" in mind, such as a stakeholder group or community affected by an organization's programs or policies, another government, or the media. Knowing whom the ultimate audience for a briefing note is helps determine how a note is written, because it forces writers to become more familiar with the needs of that audience.

The best way to gain some of these insights is to ask—the individual who generated the request for the note, a colleague, a supervisor, an acquaintance who many have worked with the requester, etc. Avoid making assumptions about what a recipient may or may not know or whom an ultimate audience is. Omitting key background information could have very real and damaging consequences—especially if the briefing note is for a hot-button issue or for question period.

In terms of content, the information included in most briefing notes is not new. Most feature content covered in other places, including communications strategies, cabinet submissions, previous briefing notes, correspondence, etc. In addition to these, other sources that are useful to consult when writing a briefing note include the following:

- throne speeches
- the "House book" prepared for ministers at the beginning of each legislative session, which includes notes on all key departmental issues, programs, and services
- Hansard debates

- reports from legislative committees
- public correspondence
- media clippings on the issue gathered by the communications branch—in particular, analysis from credible regular commentators on the issue
- ministry website and the minister's official and personal websites
- official websites of the opposition and the opposition critic
- position papers created by the opposition and stakeholders directly involved in or affected by the issue
- public statements made by the opposition and stakeholders directly involved in or affected by the issue

7.3 NOTE FORMAT

Most briefing notes are organized into four main parts: purpose, summary, analysis, and conclusion. The *purpose* of a briefing note is typically defined by the title of the note, a concise statement of the issue or topic, or a short section containing a description of the purpose. The *summary* often includes a succinct synopsis of facts related to the issue or topic, a description of the current situation, an overview of the organization's previous actions and current position on the issue, the identification and explanation of key players/stakeholders involved in the issues, and any relevant background information. The *analysis* might include a description of options that could be used to deal with an issue, and key considerations related to proceeding with those options. The *conclusion* might include a recommended option or next steps, key messages, and speaking points. The format of any given briefing note will ultimately be determined by four things: the purpose of the note, the writer, the recipient's needs and preferences, and the organization's formatting requirements.

Purpose

The title of a briefing note needs to provide a succinct summary of the topic addressed in the note. It does not need to reflect the analysis of data or to be a precursor to a recommendation; however, it should prepare the reader for that discussion. The following title is drawn from a fictitious federal government briefing note on adult literacy:

Feature 7.1: Briefing Note Title

Briefing Note for the Minister: Standing Committee Report on Raising Adult Literacy

Source: Theresa McKeown. n.d. "Example of a Briefing Note." Public Sector Writing. www.publicsectorwriting.com/wp-content/uploads/2010/03/EXAMPLE-Briefing-Note-for-Information.pdf

---

Most briefing notes include a short section of two to three sentences that describes the purpose of the note. This section is used to answer the basic question, why was this briefing note requested in the first place? The purpose section needs to include both a description of the nature of the note and the subject matter up front so that the note's purpose is immediately clear to the reader. Note how the following example clearly signals the content of the note to come and lays the foundation for recommended next steps:

Feature 7.2: Briefing Note Purpose

Purpose

The purpose of this note is to inform the Minister of the June 12, 2003, tabling and issues related to a Standing Committee report on Raising Adult Literacy. As the report is critical of the government's literacy initiatives, the Minister may receive questions from the media and/or in Question Period.

Source: Theresa McKeown. n.d. "Example of a Briefing Note." Public Sector Writing. www.publicsectorwriting.com/wp-content/uploads/2010/03/EXAMPLE-Briefing-Note-for-Information.pdf

---

The following example is from a federal government briefing note on gun show regulations that illustrates the use of a title and issue statement:

Feature 7.3: Briefing Note Title and Statement

Memorandum for the Minister

Gun Shows Regulations: Options
(Decision Sought)

Issue

Options for proceeding with the current *Gun Shows Regulations* (the regulations).

Source: David McKie. 2012. "Memo Warned Toews of Risks in Dropping Gun Show Rules." *CBC News: Politics.* November 13. www.cbc.ca/news/politics/story/2012/11/13/pol-gun-show-briefing-notes-power-politics.html

Summary

The summary section of a briefing note concisely and succinctly describes the circumstances that prompted the briefing note to be generated in the first place. The section should not include all of the background information describing the events that led to the current situation (which is described in a different part of the note, discussed below), but needs to capture the crux of the issue. The current situation section from the federal adult literacy briefing note (see below) demonstrates how a good summary section concisely addresses four main points: the problem being addressed, where the problem originated, why it is important, and, in the case of a decision note, the range of alternatives available.

Feature 7.4: Briefing Note Summary Section

Current Situation

On June 12, the Standing Committee on Human Resources Development and the Status of Persons with Disabilities is tabling its report on *Raising Adult Literacy Skills: The Need for a Pan-Canadian Response.* It is anticipated the Opposition and media will focus on three findings of the report:

1. The government is not doing enough or demonstrating leadership to address the national problem of illiteracy in Canada.
2. The social and economic costs of illiteracy are an estimated $10 billion annually, according to the 1988 Canadian Business Task Force on Literacy report.
3. The federal and provincial governments should develop a pan-Canadian accord on literacy and numeracy skills development.

Source: Theresa McKeown. n.d. "Example of a Briefing Note." Public Sector Writing. www.publicsectorwriting.com/wp-content/uploads/2010/03/EXAMPLE-Briefing-Note-for-Information.pdf

A useful tool for judging how much and what kind of information should be included in the current situation section is to answer this question: What has happened that requires action or a decision now, or requires the briefing note audience to be updated?

In addition to a description of the current situation, most briefing notes have a background section that presents an overview of the relevant facts that led to the need for the briefing. Because background sections are typically longer than other sections, information is usually presented in bullet point format that focuses on the presentation of key facts rather than presenting a narrative. The background section of the federal note on adult literacy reads as follows:

Feature 7.5: Briefing Note Background, Example 1

Background

While recognizing provincial/territorial and private sector responsibilities, the Committee concludes that the federal government has not demonstrated leadership in this "national" problem. The first of 20 recommendations is that the Minister of Human Resources Development Canada meet with provincial/territorial labour market and education ministers to develop a pan-Canadian accord on literacy and numeracy skills development.

According to the report, this accord should:

- identify provinces and territories as having primary responsibility for education and labour market training;
- establish joint funding levels and funding duration;
- determine the means of delivery, set goals, and establish methods for evaluating outcomes.

If a pan-Canadian accord is not possible, the committee states the Government of Canada should negotiate bilateral agreements with willing provinces/territories. In its dissenting opinion on the report, the Bloc Québécois supports a bilateral approach as long as it has an "opting-out with compensation" provision.

The report also outlines the following:

- In 1988, a Canadian Business Task Force on Literacy estimated the annual cost to business of illiteracy in the workforce at $4 billion and the cost to society at $10 billion.
- In 1987, the National Literacy Secretariat was founded to fund literacy initiatives and provide an infrastructure to support literacy activities across Canada (resource centres, electronic networks and communication systems, provincial and territorial coalitions); all funded partially or entirely by the National Literacy Secretariat (NLS).
- In 1997, the federal government increased to $30 million the annual allocation of the NLS, and targeted the additional money to family literacy, workplace literacy, and new technology.
- In 1999–2000, most provincial and territorial governments expanded policy statements on adult literacy or developed positions, if they did not already have one. However, provision (i.e., funding) to learners did not increase in most parts of the country.
- The January 2001 Speech from the Throne pledged an increased commitment to skills and learning with a specific mention of literacy but no federal policy was announced.
- In the September 2002 Speech from the Throne, the federal government indicated that it would build on its investments in human capital, including literacy.
- Participants at the November 2002 National Summit on Innovation and Learning, adopted 18 priority recommendations one of which included the establishment of "a pan-Canadian literacy and essential skills development system, supported by federal, provincial and territorial governments. Establish programs to improve literacy and basic skills based on individual and community needs and interests."

Source: Theresa McKeown. n.d. "Example of a Briefing Note." Public Sector Writing. www. publicsectorwriting.com/wp-content/uploads/2010/03/EXAMPLE-Briefing-Note-for-Information.pdf

The background section of the Gun Show Regulations note reads as follows:

Feature 7.6: Briefing Note Background, Example 2

Background

In Canada, there are approximately 300 gun shows held annually. While general provisions exist under the *Firearms Act* (the Act) which relate to storage and display requirements, there are no regulations currently in force specific to the temporary display of firearms at gun shows.

Originally developed and laid before each House of Parliament in 1998, but not brought into force, the *Gun Shows Regulations* outline requirements for individuals and businesses wishing to sponsor and participate in gun shows. Essentially, the regulations: i) require the sponsor to secure the approval of the Chief Firearms Officer (CFO) and notify local law enforcement prior to an event; ii) require the sponsor to ensure the security of the location and firearms therein, and that the gun show will not endanger the safety of any person; and, require exhibitors to ensure the security of his or her table or booth and the firearms therein.

Law enforcement is generally in favour of implementing the regulations, as they would help ensure that firearms are properly secured and displayed at gun shows.

Firearms advocates have expressed concern that the regulation of gun shows is unnecessary as the majority of gun show sponsors and exhibitors generally meet safety requirements set out in the *Gun Show Regulations*. Firearms advocates are also concerned that the CFO's discretionary powers under the regulations are too broad.

Between 1998 and 2008, the *Gun Show Regulations* were deferred on nine occasions for such reasons as reducing the administrative burden for individuals and sponsors participating in gun shows and allowing government officials to review the appropriateness of the proposed standards for those wishing to sponsor a gun show.

In 2010, the regulations were deferred for a 10th time, until November 2012, to allow officials time to consult with stakeholders and determine the need for and the content of the regulations. Possible amendments to be considered include requiring sponsors to inform as supposed to secure the approval of the CFO.

Source: David McKie. 2012. "Memo Warned Toews of Risks in Dropping Gun Show Rules." *CBC News: Politics.* November 13. www.cbc.ca/news/politics/story/2012/11/13/pol-gun-show-briefing-notes-power-politics.html

When writing background sections for briefing notes, it is useful to keep the following in mind:

- *Understand the objective.* Understanding completely what the reader needs from the briefing note will keep the section focused on the elements required for a decision or for complete information. Asking some key questions, such as why the note was requested, why it was requested now, and who has an interest at stake in the issue, will help filter out background information that does not serve the objective of the note.
- *Know the audience.* All briefing notes should be prepared with an understanding of how well the recipient understands the subject matter and the nuances of the issue. The best way to find out how much they know is to ask those who work mostly closely with them. Making assumptions about or guessing what they may or may not know could have critical consequences if the audience is unprepared for difficult questions from colleagues or the media.
- *Apply political acumen.* Applying a certain degree of political acumen will help filter out information that truly isn't relevant to the decision or issue at hand.

Analysis

Most briefing notes that are designed to prepare decision-makers for action (e.g., to attend a meeting or make a decision) include a section on key considerations that outlines the strategic elements of the issue at stake. Depending on the issue, these could include a description of the

- key legal, financial, regulatory, or policy issues connected with the issue and/or any recommended course of action;
- principal political issues connected with the issue and/or any recommended course of action;
- key stakeholders affected by or likely to be affected by the issue and/or any recommended course of action;
- positions on either side of the issue within government and/or any recommended course of action;
- new problems that may be created by the recommended action (or inaction);

- potential criticism that the recommended action does not go far enough;
- potential consequences or backlash if a recommended course of action fails; and
- the best means of handling adverse consequences.

To illustrate, the key considerations section of the federal Gun Show Regulations note reads as follows:

Feature 7.7: Briefing Note Key Considerations

Considerations

In the absence of the *Gun Show Regulations,* the regulations prescribing storage and display requirements under the Act apply. These regulations, among other things, require that businesses either ensure that their premises have both an electronic security alarm and locks on all windows and doors or, alternatively, have security measures in place that are approved, in writing, by the CFO. In the context of a gun show, each participating business would be required to ensure premise security, including, at times, obtaining written CFO approval.

The *Gun Show Regulations* relieve the administrative burden that would be placed on businesses participating in a gun show by allowing a sponsor to obtain universal CFO approval of the proposed security measures for a gun show location.

In the absence of the *Gun Show Regulations,* the business regulations would also require all firearms on display to be secured to either a permanent structure or a wall. The *Gun Show Regulations* reduce the security requirements for exhibitors by allowing firearms to be attached to the structure or table on which they are displayed.

In the absence of the *Gun Show Regulations,* there is limited monitoring or tracking of public safety incidents associated with gun shows. However, the RCMP has received anecdotal reports of unsafe storage and has recorded one incident where the activities at a gun show could have endangered public safety (guns were not securely fastened to the display tables).

The CFO community has noted unsafe display of firearms across the country. CFOs have also noted incidents where exhibitors were criminally charged in relation to the trafficking and unauthorized possession of firearms at gun shows.

From a risk management perspective, gun shows are not a significant public safety concern. However, this could change in the future and, should a significant incident occur, there could be criticism that the regulations were not implemented.

Section 118 of the *Firearms Act* requires the Minister of Public Safety to lay proposed amendments to regulations before each House of Parliament for consideration if the amendments are material or substantial. Should the government decide to either repeal or amend the *Gun Show Regulations,* the coming into force date of the legislation may need to be deferred again in order to allow both the House and Senate to adequately examine the repeal or amendment legislation.

Source: David McKie. 2012. "Memo Warned Toews of Risks in Dropping Gun Show Rules." *CBC News: Politics.* November 13. www.cbc.ca/news/politics/story/2012/11/13/pol-gun-show-briefing-notes-power-politics.html

Conclusion

Recommended Course of Action

Decision notes are typically distinguished by a special section that sets out a recommended course of action. Such sections typically begin with an overview of options currently available, providing a short rationale and the major implications (financial, legal, and political) of each. They then proceed to a recommended course of action. Recommended course of action sections should avoid introducing new thoughts or ideas, as all concepts should have been presented and analyzed in the key considerations, discussion, or analysis sections. The recommendation needs to be tied to evidence that has already been presented and analyzed. The federal note on adult literacy recommends the following approach to dealing with the release of the adult literacy report:

Feature 7.8: Briefing Note Recommended Course of Action

Next Steps

A Question Period card is being prepared for the Minister. Questions and Answers are also being prepared in anticipation of possible media scrums. The official government response will be developed in the form of a Memorandum to Cabinet, which your officials have the lead on.

Until such time as the official government response is developed and approved by Cabinet, the following tactical approach could be considered in response to questions:

- Thank the Standing Committee for its work (the government will study the Report closely and respond officially to its findings and recommendations).
- Point out that the Committee acknowledged the more than $30 million the federal government gives annually to the National Literacy Secretariat as well as the government's targeted funding on family literacy, workplace literacy and new technology.
- Remind inquirers of the government's Throne Speech commitment to build on our investments in human capital, including literacy.
- And reiterate that the government will continue to work with all partners to address the problem although provinces and territories have constitutional responsibility for education and private and volunteer sector organizations and employers also have a role to play.

Source: Theresa McKeown. n.d. "Example of a Briefing Note." Public Sector Writing. www. publicsectorwriting.com/wp-content/uploads/2010/03/EXAMPLE-Briefing-Note-for-Information.pdf

Key Messages

Briefing notes that are designed to prepare decision-makers for action usually include a section on key messages, that is, the most important things your organization has to say on the issue at hand. As discussed in chapter 4, **key messages** are clear, concise "chunks" of information written as they would ideally appear in a media quote or sound bite. As a result, key messages need to be easy for the speaker to say, which will make them easy for the audience to understand and remember. While most of a briefing note is written for the reader's eye, key messages should be written for the listener's ear.

Some briefing notes—especially House notes—consist almost completely of key messages. Just as it is important to know the level of background detail desired by the audience, it is also important to learn how detailed and comprehensive the recipient wishes the key messages to be, and who might be hearing those key messages.

In many cases, key messages will have already been developed for other communications products (e.g., earlier notes on similar, related issues; communications strategies). Tracking existing key messages is necessary in order to ensure a consistent approach to the issue, or, if the situation has changed, to be aware of past approaches. It also helps avoid the duplication of work. In those few cases where no key messages already exist,

- identify all of the points the briefing note recipient needs to communicate on the issue, then focus on the most important points;
- determine what the briefing note recipient's audience needs to hear from your organization;
- simplify the messages by removing scientific language and jargon, and ensure that you use active language;
- include evidence or statistics to substantiate the message; and
- edit the messages down to short declarative statements.

The federal note on adult literacy suggests the following key messages be used in response to the release of the committee's adult literacy report:

Feature 7.9: Briefing Note Key Messages

Suggested Response

- We thank the Standing Committee for its work; we'll study the Report closely and respond officially to its findings and recommendations.
- The Committee acknowledged the more than $30 million we give annually to the National Literacy Secretariat and our targeted funding on family literacy, workplace literacy and new technology.
- In the Speech from the Throne, we committed to build on our investments in human capital, including literacy.

Source: Theresa McKeown. n.d. "Example of a Briefing Note." Public Sector Writing. www.publicsectorwriting.com/wp-content/uploads/2010/03/EXAMPLE-Briefing-Note-for-Information.pdf

7.4 ISSUE NOTES AND THE ISSUES MANAGEMENT PROCESS[1]

Issues are "gaps" that exist between an organization's expectations and those of its stakeholders (Issue Management Council n.d.). **Issues management** is an "anticipatory, strategic management process that organizations [use to] detect and respond" to gaps in expectations (Dougall 2008). An organization engages in issues management if its "decision-makers are actively looking for, anticipating, and responding to shifting stakeholder expectations and perceptions likely to have important consequences for the organization" (ibid.). An **issue note** is special kind of briefing note that public organizations use in the issues management process to provide senior decision-makers with the strategic and tactical communications advice needed to resolve critical and emerging issues that have particularly high public profiles. This section provides some background on the public sector issues management process in general and concludes by describing the role and preparation of issues notes in particular.

Stage 1: Identification

For most public sector organizations, the issues management process begins with regular and ongoing scanning of the operating environment in order to identify emerging and/or critical issues within that environment, or the "gaps" between an organization's own performance expectations and those held by key audiences. The purpose of conducting regular and ongoing scanning is to identify issues early in their life cycle so they can be more readily managed. As Dougall explains,

> if the organization's issues management process detects an issue in the earliest stage, more response choices—such as service modification, the introduction of new conduct codes or anticipatory collaboration with key interest groups—are available to decision-makers. As the issue matures, the number of engaged stakeholders, publics and other influencers expands, positions on the issue become more entrenched and the strategic choices available to the organization shrink. If and when the issue becomes a crisis for the organization, the only available responses are reactive and are sometimes imposed by external parties. (2008)

A thorough scanning process needs to be built upon "the systematic, multi-method collection and review of potentially relevant data from industry, government and academic sources" (ibid.) and all forms of media—print, TV, radio, and online publications. Chapter 9 provides some suggestions for how to set up a regular and ongoing scanning mechanism for use in social media.

Stage 2: Monitoring

Once an issue has been identified, the next step in the issues management process involves **monitoring**, the systematic tracking of an issue using a variety of methods and sources. The purpose of monitoring is to give an organization better insight into, and knowledge of, the nature, scope, and likely impact of an issue to better inform strategic decision making and response. Monitoring can vary from watching how an issue is covered by the media on a day-to-day basis, to content analysis to determine issues significant to stakeholders, to focus group or public opinion polling to determine issue scope and legitimacy. If the issue involves new or unknown stakeholders, monitoring should also involve stakeholder analysis to understand what key audiences know, how they feel about an issue, and how they are likely to respond to what the organization is, or is not, saying or doing.

Stage 3: Analysis and Response

During the analysis stage of the issues management process, senior decision-makers decide whether an issue requires some type of response from their organization. The two most critical components of this decision are probability of occurrence (how likely is the issue to affect the organization) and organizational impact (how could if affect the organization's mandate, reputation, service/program offerings, funding, etc.) (Dougall 2008).

If an issue is likely to occur and is likely to have an impact on an organization, decision-makers must then decide how to respond. A good place to start is by defining exactly what the organization wants to achieve—in other words, by crafting realistic and measurable objectives. Ideally, issue response objectives should be developed at the output, outtake, and outcome levels, and should be based on clear and specific baseline data. As Dougall (2008) observes, defining clear and measurable objectives in the issues management process is critical, because one of the "greatest barriers to effective issues management [is] the lack of clear objectives.... The scanning, monitoring, prioritization and strategic decision-making steps have no value unless action is taken toward achieving specific and measurable objectives."

The Issue Note
Once the objectives have been crafted, the task of determining the actual content of the response can begin. The Government of Ontario's issue note template provides a useful guide for thinking through and documenting the content of an issue response:

Issue Description
This section usually begins with a sentence that concisely and accurately describes the issue, references where the issue arose (e.g., media, courts, by-election), and anticipates the question most likely to be raised about the issue.

Context
Depending on the complexity and sensitivity of the issue, an issue note might also include a context section that provides some basic background; bullet-style information on the issue, such as how the issue is related to the government's mandate; significant legal and/or financial implications of the issue; what other governments are doing with regards to similar issues; and so on. Unlike background information sections in other briefing notes, the purpose of the context section in an issue note is to provide sufficient information to give a spokesperson the minimal amount of knowledge needed to speak with relative authority on the issue.

Strategic Considerations
This section should identify all key stakeholders involved with the issue and present a basic overview of the stakeholder's basic position on the issue, a brief description of the rationale for that position, and the anticipated reaction of the stakeholder.

The strategic considerations section should also describe how the media—print, radio, TV, social—has covered the issue to date. Depending on the issue and the time available, information contained in this section could include media quotes that illustrate the positions of key stakeholders, public officials, and those who support or oppose the initiative; the results of any content analysis performed to document the depth and nature of treatment (see chapter 3 for more details); and/or the scope and extent of coverage.

Key Messages

As with other briefing notes, key messages in issue notes are short, simple statements that are written to be read by a decision-maker or spokesperson directly from the note in the legislature, during a media scrum, when responding to a question, and so on. Depending on the issue, these messages may also include key facts that can be used to support the messaging. Depending on their size and number, these can either be included directly in the key messages section or attached as a fact sheet or backgrounder.

When drafting key messages for issue notes, it is most important to identify whom the speaker and audience will be. The key messages need to be written in plain, simple language; should avoid bureaucratic and technical jargon and acronyms; and should not get into program details. The following are examples of the forms that typical messages take: "We're doing a good job," "We have consistently shown our commitment to...," "We're aware of the problem and have to fix/are fixing/are looking into it," and "We are reviewing ... and we're calling on the federal government to join us in this task."

Issue Strategy

The strategy section is designed to provide a high-level overview of how an organization plans to respond to the issue (reactively or proactively) and what tactics it intends to use to communicate its position to the public/media. Issue strategies typically identify who the main spokesperson/people will be, what role the minister will play (if appropriate/relevant), what supporting products (news releases, fact sheets, Q&As) will be generated, and what media relations will be employed (what media will be specifically targeted; will there be a press conference and if so, what kind; timing, etc.). If the issue strategy is designed to address an issue arising from legislative proceedings (e.g., a question posed during question period or a committee hearing), the issue strategy should also include some points about how the issue will be dealt with in the legislature as a whole.

Action Plan

The action plan details the specific, tangible steps the organization intends to take to address the issue. Depending on the nature of the issue, these steps could include meetings with key stakeholders on specific days, details of a news release, timing of a news conference, creation of a task force, and the launch of public consultations.

An Issue Note Example

Appendix 7.2 contains an example of a fictitious issue note written to prepare senior decision-makers at Ontario's transportation agency Metrolinx to respond to an auditor general's report that was critical of the costs of a new fare-card system.

Stage 4: Evaluation

Ideally, evaluation of issues management activities should be identical to the task of communications evaluation discussed in chapter 8. To be effective, both need to "begin with the end in mind," meaning that they should have very clear and specific objectives, ideally at the output, outtake, and outcome levels, clear and specific baselines, and reliable indicators of performance that are appropriate to the objectives. For example, a simple indicator of output performance might be the total number of communications products (e.g., issue notes, press conferences, social media broadcasts) produced in response to an issue. A simple indicator of outtake performance might be the total number of visits to a website to measure audience exposure, or a public opinion poll to measure audience comprehension of an issue strategy's key messages. A simple indicator of outcome performance could be a focus group or a series of key informant interviews to assess whether and to what extent the target audience has changed its behaviour as a result of increased issue awareness and retention.

LEARNING ACTIVITY

Activity 7.1: Writing a Briefing Note

In chapter 4, you were asked to identify a new initiative that a public sector organization is going to use to achieve a strategic goal—an initiative new enough that few communications materials have been generated to date. In chapter 5, you developed five specific tactics (a press release, a backgrounder, an FAQ, an LTE, and a speech) for this initiative. The point of this activity is to develop briefing note writing and editing skills.

For this activity, develop

- one information note to bring a senior decision-maker in your chosen organization up to date on the status of your chosen initiative (1,000 words/two pages maximum);

- one meeting note to prepare a senior decision-maker to attend a face-to-face meeting with a disgruntled but important stakeholder about the initiative (1,000 words/two pages maximum); and
- one decision note, providing a senior decision-maker with three options regarding the future of the initiative—Option 1: maintain status quo, Option 2: expand initiative, Option 3: cancel initiative (1,500 words/three pages maximum).

ONLINE RESOURCES

Susan Doyle provides a good tutorial on writing briefing notes for public sector organizations on her Writing for Government website (web.uvic. ca/~sdoyle/E302/Notes/WritingBriefingNotes.html), as does Theresa McKeown's "Memoranda and Briefing Notes" on her Public Sector Writing site (www.publicsectorwriting.com/wp-content/uploads/2011/09/ Briefing-Notes-versus-Memorandum.pdf).

For practice on writing briefing notes, try Doyle's briefing note assignments at (web.uvic.ca/~sdoyle/E302/Work/index.html) and Rob Parkinson's "How to Fix a Four-Page Memo" on his Writing for Results site (writingforresults.net/Acro_3/4_msg/2_format/4-p_memo.pdf).

QUESTIONS FOR CRITICAL REFLECTION

1. What qualities are busy public sector decision-makers most likely to value in a briefing note?
2. What qualities are most likely to be valued in a briefing note writer?

KEY TERMS

decision note: A document designed to help prepare decision-makers to make choices about critical or emerging issues.

House note: A special kind of meeting note designed to prepare cabinet members to respond to issues raised in the legislature, either during question period or committee hearings.

information note: A document designed to bring senior decision-makers up to date on new or emerging issues of concern to them or the organization for which they are responsible.

issue note: A special kind of briefing note that public organizations use in the issues management process to provide senior decision-makers with the strategic and tactical communications advice needed to resolve critical and emerging issues that have particularly high public profiles.

issues: "Gaps" that exist between an organization's expectations and those of its stakeholders.

issues management: An "anticipatory, strategic management process that organizations [use to] detect and respond" (Dougall 2008) to gaps in expectations.

meeting note: A document designed to prepare decision-makers for an important upcoming meeting or event, such as a legislative or cabinet committee meeting, an invitation to address a special interest group, or a meeting with a counterpart in another department or broader public sector organization regarding a matter of shared interest.

monitoring: The systematic tracking of an issue using a variety of methods and sources.

technical note: A special type of information note that provides synopses of scientific or technical issues for decision-makers.

NOTE

1 This section is based on Elizabeth Dougall's excellent paper, "Issues Management," found on the Institute for Public Relations website (www.instituteforpr.org/topics/issues-management/).

WORKS CITED

Dougall, Elizabeth. 2008. "Issues Management." Institute for Public Relations. www.instituteforpr.org/topics/issues-management/

Doyle, Susan. 2013. "How to Write a Briefing Note." Writing for Government. web.uvic.ca/~sdoyle/E302/Notes/WritingBriefingNotes.html

Issue Management Council. n.d. "Clarification of Terms." http://issuemanagement.org/learnmore/clarification-of-terms/

McKeown, Theresa. n.d. "Example of a Briefing Note." Public Sector Writing. www.publicsectorwriting.com/wp-content/uploads/2010/03/EXAMPLE-Briefing-Note-for-Information.pdf

McKie, David. 2012. "Memo Warned Toews of Risks in Dropping Gun Show Rules." *CBC News: Politics.* November 13. www.cbc.ca/news/politics/story/2012/11/13/pol-gun-show-briefing-notes-power-politics.html

Parkinson, Rob. n.d. "How to Fix a Four-Page Memo." Writing for Results. writingforresults.net/Acro_3/4_msg/2_format/4-p_memo.pdf

CHAPTER 8

EVALUATION

CHAPTER OVERVIEW

This chapter provides an overview of the key research tools that public sector organizations use in professional communications evaluation to establish baselines and populate indicators at the outtake and outcome levels, namely, unstructured interviews, questionnaires, structured interviews, focus groups, and content analysis.

LEARNING OBJECTIVES

After completing this chapter, you will be able to

- explain what a baseline is, what activities are needed to establish one, and what role they play in communications evaluation;
- identify and describe the three types of objectives used to direct communications activities;
- identify and describe the most common types of indicators used to measure communications activities;
- explain the relationship between objective level and indicator selection; and
- develop a strategy to evaluate a public sector communications initiative.

INTRODUCTION

In communications, **evaluation** is the process by which organizations measure to see if a particular activity has achieved the standards or expectations set out in a specified objective. As discussed in chapter 3, the evaluation process in public sector communications ideally begins well before any communications activity actually takes place with the development of objectives that clearly and precisely define what an organization wants to achieve, the establishment of baselines that provide accurate measures of current conditions against which future change can be measured, and the selection of indicators that can deliver useful and reliable data about tactic performance. As the Institute for Public Relations says, "These [objectives] have to come first. No one can really measure the effectiveness of anything unless they first figure out exactly what it is they are measuring that something against" (Institute for Public Relations [IPR] 2002, 13).[1]

At the output level, the evaluation process in public sector communications is typically quite straightforward: an organization identifies and then uses some method to determine the quantity of tangible goods and/or services produced by a specific communications activity, and then assesses how that number compares with the standards or expectations set out in the communications objective. Part of what makes output evaluation in communications relatively straightforward is the fact that, in most cases, baselines are set at zero value. The following table illustrates a basic output-level evaluation process, building on the material discussed in chapter 3:

TABLE 8.1: OUTPUT-LEVEL EVALUATION EXAMPLE

Output-level objective	Baseline	Performance indicator used	Performance achieved	Evaluation result
21 of 21 national print media outlets to cover minister's speech within 48 hours	No coverage	Communications staff to review national dailies	15 of 21 national print media outlets cover speech within 24 hours; remaining 6 within 48 hours	Objective achieved; activity successful
All 26 major stakeholders contacted through social media activities (Facebook, Twitter) during eight-day period	No contacts	Communications staff to follow up directly with stakeholders	18 of 26 stakeholders contacted	Objective not achieved; activity unsuccessful Recommendation: review objective and methodology
80 percent of department staff to attend training sessions over three-week period	No staff trained	Attendance taken by staff at sessions	84 percent of department staff attended training session	Objective achieved; activity successful

Source: Adapted from United Kingdom. Government Communication Network. 2012. *Evaluating Government Communication Activity: Standards and Guidance,* pp. 19–20. London: Cabinet Office.

The evaluation process at the outtake and outcome levels in public sector communications is usually more complex and challenging because accurate baselines are more difficult to establish (for example, trying to establish existing levels of key message awareness/retention or comprehension) and indicators must be more sophisticated in terms of the quality and quantity of data they need to gather (for example, trying to measure changes in the behaviour of target audience members as a result of exposure to a key message). This chapter showcases some of the key research tools that public sector organizations use in communications evaluation to establish baselines and populate indicators at the outtake and outcome levels, namely, unstructured interviews, questionnaires, structured interviews, focus groups, and content analysis. Chapter 9 builds on this discussion with a review of tools used to evaluate social media–based communications activities.

8.1 UNSTRUCTURED INTERVIEWS

Unstructured interviews are one of the most informal methods of data collection in communications research and evaluation. An **unstructured interview** can be defined as an exchange between a researcher and a subject that does not have a pre-established format, with the exception of some key questions or topics that the researcher has formulated in advance. According to Minichiello and colleagues, "unstructured interviews allow questions based on an interviewee's responses and proceeds like a friendly, non-threatening conversation. They rely on social interaction between the researcher and informant to extract information. However, because each interviewee is asked a different series of questions, this style can lack the reliability and precision of a structured interview" (1990, 19).

Unstructured interviews are appropriate for collecting data on baselines and indicators related to communications outtakes and outcomes, typically as part of preliminary efforts to establish permanent baselines and/or indicators. For example, recall from chapter 3 the following outtake metrics at the awareness, recall, and retention/comprehension levels:

TABLE 8.2: OUTTAKE METRICS

Outtake type	Metric
Awareness	The number of users who recognize specific communications products/activities
Recall	The number of users who recall viewing specific communications products/activities and accurately describe them
Retention/ comprehension	The number of users who understand the key message, like the key message, and think the message was clear and engaging

Source: Adapted from United Kingdom. Government Communication Network. 2012. *Evaluating Government Communication Activity: Standards and Guidance*, p. 20. London: Cabinet Office.

Here, unstructured interviews with selected members of a target audience could be used to develop a question on communications product/ activity recognition for inclusion in a future survey; a sense of whether or not users are able to recall a specific message from an activity; or a series of questions on message comprehension that could be used for a future focus group.

8.2 QUESTIONNAIRES, STRUCTURED INTERVIEWS, AND SURVEYS

A **questionnaire** is a tool used in research to gather targeted information from subjects or respondents that consists of a series of written questions and/or other prompts. Questionnaires can be used as the basis for both structured interviews and surveys. In a **structured interview**, a researcher uses a questionnaire to pose questions or prompts to a respondent and records the respondent's answers. In **survey research,** the questionnaire is presented or sent to respondents (in person, or by phone, email, or Internet) to be filled out and returned for analysis.

Questionnaire Development

There are five steps to follow when creating a questionnaire for use in communications evaluation. The first step is to develop a list of general questions that could be used to generate the desired data. For example, at the outcome level, the following questions could be used to generate data about the outcome metrics discussed in chapter 3:

TABLE 8.3: OUTCOME METRICS

Outcome type	Metric	Possible question
Opinion	The number of users who • like the activity/messages • think the message was relevant to them • think the activity/message was clear and engaging • understand the key/supporting message that the activity was promoting	Did you like the message used in the activity? Is the message relevant to you? Why? Is the message clear and engaging? Did you understand the message in the activity?
Attitude/preference	The number of users who feel that the activity/message had an impact on their • views/attitudes/feelings in general; and/or • views/attitudes/feelings about the organization	Did the message have an impact on your views, attitudes, or feelings about the issue? In what way? Did the message have an impact on your views, attitudes, or feelings about the organization? In what way?

Source: Adapted from United Kingdom. Government Communication Network. 2012. *Evaluating Government Communication Activity: Standards and Guidance,* pp. 20–21. London: Cabinet Office.

The second step is to determine which questions will be included in the questionnaire. Three criteria can be used to do so: (1) Is the question directly related to the baseline or indicator in question? (2) Does the question have a good chance of generating the desired data? and (3) Is it easy for respondents to answer the question? Unstructured interviews would be an appropriate tool to use to answer these questions.

Once the range of questions has been determined, the third step in questionnaire development is to determine the precise format of each question. Open questions provide no restrictions on the content respondents can provide or the manner in which they can reply. As such, they are useful for giving respondents full latitude when providing answers. This same latitude, however, makes analyzing answers time-consuming and difficult. In most situations—particularly those in which the questionnaire will be given to a large number of people—a better, more manageable alternative is the closed or fixed-alternative question, which forces respondents to choose from a prescribed list of responses. The following are examples of types of closed questions:

• **Fill-in-the-blank:** This type of question has a simple answer, usually a name, frequency, or quantity, which is the kind of information these questions allow researchers to obtain.

- **Binary response:** This type of question is ideal for obtaining factual information that falls into the yes-no or true-false category of answer.
- **Scaled-response:** These consist of a list of alternative responses that increase or decrease in intensity in an ordered fashion. These kinds of questions can be further defined as balanced, unbalanced, and rating and ranking.
- **Unscaled-response:** When answering this type of question, the respondent is asked to choose one or more options from a list. One of these options should be "Other," so that the respondent is not forced to select an answer with which he or she is not completely satisfied.

Appendix 8.1 contains additional examples of question types that can be adapted for use in questionnaires.

The fourth step in questionnaire development focuses on question phrasing. If questions are poorly worded, then respondents may either refuse to answer them or give incorrect answers. The following are general rules to ensure that questions are well worded:

- Avoid loaded words that trigger an emotional response or a strong association.
- Avoid ambiguous words that can be interpreted in more than one way.
- Don't use double-negative questions that ask people to disagree with a negative statement.
- Don't use leading questions that encourage the respondent to answer in a certain way, typically by indicating which is the "right" or "correct" answer.
- Avoid "threatening" questions, that is, questions that make respondents afraid or embarrassed to the give an honest answer.
- Don't use double-barrelled or compound questions that ask two or more questions in one.
- Do ask questions in the language of your respondents, using the idioms and vernacular appropriate to the sample's level of education, the vocabulary of the region, and so on (Adler and Clark 1999).

Adler and Clark (1999) provide the following examples of wording to avoid when formulating questions for questionnaires and some suggestions for revision:

TABLE 8.4: QUESTIONNAIRE WORDING OPTIONS

Type of question	Original	Revised
Ambiguous	How many times in the past year have you seen or talked with a doctor about your health?	We are going to ask about visits to doctors and getting medical advice from them. How many office visits have you had this year with all professional personnel who have MD degrees or who work directly for a doctor in the office, such as a nurse or medical assistant?
Double-negative	Do you disagree with the view that the prime minister has done a poor job dealing with foreign policy issues this past year?	What do you think of the job that the prime minister has done dealing with foreign policy issues this past year?
Double-barrelled	What is your opinion of the province's current economic situation and the measures the premier has taken recently?	What is your opinion of the economic situation in the province at present? What do you think of the measures that the premier has taken in the past month?
Leading	Like most former leaders, the current prime minister faces opposition as well as support for his economic policies. How good a job do you think the prime minister is doing in leading the country out of the economic crisis created by the national debt?	Are you aware of the prime minister's policies to reduce the national debt? If so, what is your opinion of them?
Threatening	Have you ever smoked marijuana?	Different people use different terms for marijuana. What do you think we should call it so you understand us? *(If no response or awkward phrase, use "marijuana" in the following questions. Otherwise use respondent word(s).)* _____ is commonly used. People smoke _____ in private to relax, with friends at parties, with friends to relax, and in other situations. Have you, yourself, at any time in your life smoked _____?

Source: Emily Stier Adler and Roger Clark. 1999. *How It's Done: An Invitation to Social Research,* p. 246. Belmont, CA: Wadsworth.

Once the wording of the questions has been determined, the next step in questionnaire design is to ensure that questions are ordered in the most effective sequence. Coopman (2006) summarized four of the most common methods of sequencing as follows:

- **Funnel:** This is the most common method of sequencing, where the questionnaire begins with broad, open questions and moves to narrower, more closed questions. The funnel method is appropriate when the researcher knows the topic well and feels free to talk about it.
- **Inverted funnel:** A method of sequencing in which the questionnaire begins with narrow, closed questions and moves to broader, more open questions. The inverted funnel method works well when subjects are likely to need help recalling information or must be motivated to talk.
- **Diamond:** This method of sequencing combines the funnel and inverted funnel approaches, beginning with specific, closed questions, transitioning to general, more open questions, and then closing with specific, closed questions. The diamond method is particularly useful when subjects are likely to be reluctant to or have difficulty discussing topics at any length.
- **Tunnel:** This method of sequencing describes a questionnaire in which all the questions have the same degree of openness. The tunnel method allows for little probing and variation in question structure. It can be useful for simple, surface information interviews, but not for in-depth interviews.

Most questionnaires finish with an open question that allows respondents to provide input on anything else that they feel may be relevant.

The final step before using the questionnaire involves pre-testing—trying out the questionnaire on a small number of respondents (ideally a selection of the respondents who will ultimately be questioned) in order to identify problems and eliminate them. Once the questionnaire has been fully developed and tested, it can then be used as either the basis for a structured one-on-one interview or a survey.

Structured Interviews[2]

A *structured interview* is a method of data collection in which the researcher poses prepared questions to a respondent and records the respondent's answers. Like speeches, structured interviews have three parts: an opening or introduction, a body, and a conclusion or closing.

The opening of a structured interview typically includes a relatively informal introductory component and a more formal orientation component. During the introduction, the researcher attempts to "break the ice" with the respondent, establish a rapport, and set an appropriate tone for the balance of interview. The more formal orientation describes the purpose of the interview, the topics the researcher intends to cover, the expected length of the interview, and information about how the interview results will be used and confidentiality.

The body of the structured interview is composed of the questions that have been developed for the questionnaire.

The structured interview's closing brings the interview to an end. The closing can be signalled at the end of the body with a preface to the last question, such as "My final question…" During the closing itself, researchers sometimes briefly summarize key findings or conclusions to ensure that they are correct, review the purpose of the interview, and reiterate how the interviewee's confidentiality will be maintained.

Surveys

In most large public sector organizations, the task of conducting surveys to gather data on public opinion is contracted out to professional polling companies, such as Nanos Research, Strategic Counsel, Ipsos Canada, and EKOS Research. In smaller organizations, though—especially those in the broader public and non-profit sectors—communications professionals sometimes use versions of simple convenience polls to get a "'quick read' of people's views, feelings or sentiments regarding a particular issue" (Lindenmann 2006, 9). There are three steps involved in basic convenience polling.

Step 1: Population Selection and Sampling Plan

The first step in conducting a basic convenience poll is to determine the target population for the survey, i.e., which members of that population are going to be in the sample group that is surveyed, and how members of that sample group are going to be chosen. There are two basic kinds of samples—probability samples and non-probability samples. **Probability samples** are collected in a way that gives every variable selected an equal chance of being included. As such, probability samples can be used to make statistical inferences about the population from the sample. The four main types of probability samples are outlined below:

- A **simple random sample** involves the selection of required respondents at random from the sampling frame.
- A **systematic sample** involves choosing a starting point in the sampling frame, and then choosing every nth variable from that point onward. For example, with a 20,000-entry telephone directory as the sampling frame, and a required sample size of 500, you might choose every 40th person in the directory so that the sample includes individuals whose names end with all letters of the alphabet.
- A **stratified sample** involves dividing the population into groups that share a particular characteristic and then using random selection within each group to establish the sample. Stratified samples are used extensively in public opinion polling where response by region is important.
- A **proportionate sample** is similar to a stratified sample in that the population is divided into groups and the sample from each group is derived by random selection. The difference from proportionate sampling, though, is that the sample size selected from each group is roughly proportionate to that group's size in the overall population.

Non-probability samples are collected in such a way that every variable does not have an equal chance of being included. In other words, non-probability samples are used when there is no intention or need to make statistical generalizations about the population beyond the sample surveyed. The three main types of non-probability samples are outlined below:

- A **convenience sample** involves choosing the nearest and most convenient persons to act as respondents until the desired sample size is reached.
- A **quota sample** involves dividing the desired sample size into representative groups and then using convenience sampling to achieve the quota for each group.
- In a **purposive sample**, the principle of sample selection is based on the researcher's judgment, interest, and experience.

Most simple surveys conducted to get a "'quick read' of people's views, feelings, or sentiments regarding a particular issue" (Lindenmann 2006, 9) rely on convenience samples.

Step 2: Delivery

Surveys can be administered in a number of ways—by phone, email, Internet, and in person. Most large-scale surveys conducted by professional firms are administered by phone. Most small-scale convenience polls are administered either in person or online. There are some distinct advantages of using web-based surveys: "Large samples are possible in a short amount of time; usually studies can be carried out much more quickly and far more cheaply than using other methods; data can be analyzed continuously; that is, one can 'port' directly into statistical tools and databases as the completed questionnaires are returned" (Lindenmann 2006, 6). Disadvantages of web-based surveys include the fact that respondents are not chosen at random, thereby subjecting the survey to potential problems with bias and validity of results. As Lindenmann points out, convenience polls do offer some value and are worth considering "if all you need at a given point in time is a 'quick read' of people's views, feelings or sentiments regarding a particular issue and if you recognize that the data you collect in this manner is little more than a rough, informal 'sounding board' pertaining to a handful of people's opinions" (ibid.).

Application 8.1: Google Docs

Google Docs offers a free and relatively simple survey service that allows you to create a custom survey with an unlimited number of questions per survey, as well as unlimited responses. To create a survey using Google Docs, follow these steps:

- Become a member and log-in to the site at docs.google.com.
- Once logged in, click on the Create button on the left side of the screen and choose "Form" from the drop-down menu.

Google Docs then presents a template in which to create questions and designate response types (e.g., multiple choice, checkbox, text, drop-down). Note that Google Docs also lets users designate if a particular question is required; if a question is marked as required, respondents cannot proceed with the survey until they have submitted an answer. When you have finished entering the survey questions, you can then designate how you would like responses to the survey captured (either in a new Google Docs spreadsheet, or on a new sheet in an existing Google Docs spreadsheet). This capability allows you to track and conduct basic analysis of survey responses. For larger, more complicated surveys, Google Docs also allows you to conduct more advanced analyses, including numerous statistical calculations that range from basic descriptive functions, such as count, mean, median, and mode, to more advanced functions, such as standard deviation, probability, correlation coefficients, and covariance. When complete, the survey you've created can be distributed indirectly via Google+, Twitter, or Facebook, or directly to designated email addresses.

Step 3: Final Review and Test-Run

When you're satisfied with the survey, test it by asking colleagues or friends to act as respondents. Remember that a fresh look at your questionnaire from a new perspective will help get any "bugs" out before it is sent to an entire sample group.

8.3 FOCUS GROUPS[3]

A **focus group** is a special kind of structured interview in which a researcher interviews a small number of key informants (usually between eight and twelve) at one time (usually during a 60- to 90-minute period). In public sector communications, focus groups are often used to identify and discuss at length the attitudes and motivations of individuals about specific issues or to test key components of communications strategies (i.e., messaging) prior to rollout. They are particularly useful for gaining insight into baselines and indicators at the outtake and outcome levels. Focus groups are popular because they are a relatively cost-effective alternative to conducting a full-scale public opinion survey, results can be generated almost immediately, and issues can be explored in more depth as required.

The first step in setting up a basic focus group is to determine the number of groups to use and the size of each group. In general, a minimum of two focus group sessions should be conducted to ensure that results are not idiosyncratic or biased. In terms of group size, eight to ten participants is most common, although five to seven members can work well for creative sessions designed to maximize the free flow of information, and ten to twelve members can work well for a simple "brainstorming" session.

Once the number and size of groups is set, group composition can be determined based on the desired profiles, for example, youth, seniors, women, supportive/opposed stakeholders, and knowledge of issue/message. Budget permitting, participants should be offered some type of remuneration or acknowledgement—a cash payment, small honorarium, transit tokens, etc.—for their time.

In terms of how focus groups actually operate, Krueger (2009) describes a typical sequence of focus group activities as follows:

- The group is introduced and begins sharing information in response to an opening question.
- Introductory questions ask the group members to share their experiences in terms of the general topic of the focus group.
- Transition questions help the group see the topic in a broader scope and how opinions on various aspects of the topic may be diverse.
- Key questions (usually five or six), which are carefully crafted to get at the essence of the desired information, are then asked.
- Ending questions prompt participants to summarize their positions, provide feedback concerning the moderator's interpretation of the group results, and seek any information that may have been missed.

Most focus group sessions work best with an independent, third-party moderator or facilitator who can orient the group at the start of the session, put the group "at ease" by making it comfortable and "safe" for participants to express themselves freely, ensure that all topics are covered, ensure that the discussion does not stray from the issue at hand, and manage the "edges" of the conversation by drawing out quiet participants and shutting down overbearing participants who monopolize discussion. Budget permitting, one or two additional people to act as recorders can ensure that as much of the discussion as possible is noted.

8.4 CONTENT ANALYSIS

As discussed in chapter 2, **content analysis** is a highly adaptable technique for gathering and analyzing the content of non-scholarly media products in both print (newspapers, magazines, correspondence, social media) and non-print formats (films, television programs, photographs). In communications evaluation, content analysis can be an important tool for establishing baselines for specific communications activities or gathering indicator data at the outtake and outcome levels. For example, recall from chapter 3 that a common metric for measuring the outcome of a communications activity is media attitude toward the activity, or the key message embedded within the activity. Content analysis can be used to determine the level of positive versus negative coverage of that activity or message. Content analysis can also be used to measure end-user outcomes. For example, it could be used to assess incoming correspondence for the level of positive versus negative reaction to a new activity or message

This section examines the five steps involved in conducting basic content analysis: (1) develop a research question, (2) determine content population and sampling strategy, (3) define the recording unit, (4) develop a coding system and recording sheet, and (5) conduct analysis and report results.

Step 1: Develop a Research Question

A good research question is critical to the success of content analysis. A good **research question** defines exactly what a research activity is designed to achieve in clear, unambiguous terms and anticipates what would constitute a good answer. The following is a hypothetical scenario that illustrates how a good research question can be developed for content analysis.

In 2011, a communications team in Saskatchewan's Department of Parks, Culture, and Sport was asked to work with policy and program staff on the development of a new amateur sport funding policy for the province. One of the first things the team wanted to better understand was what kinds of issues were being reported in the media since the Saskatchewan Party government was elected to office in 2007, especially issues raised by key stakeholders such as amateur sport organizations. After a brainstorming session, the team came up with the following research question: What kinds of issues affecting amateur sport organizations in Saskatchewan have been reported in the local, provincial, and national print media since January 2008?

Step 2: Determine Content Population and Sampling Strategy

Once a good research question has been developed, the next step in content analysis involves identifying and selecting content to analyze. Common sources for print media content include online databases such as ProQuest's Canadian Newsstand, which contains the full text of 21 Canadian daily newspapers from the past 20 years, and Google News, which aggregates content from more than 4,500 English-language sources.

To continue with the fictitious example above, the team determined that the content for the amateur sport funding issues project would be print articles from local, provincial, and national media published since January 2008 that made mention of any issue related to amateur sport in Saskatchewan, especially those connected to amateur sport organizations. To identify these articles within a database, the team used the specific search term "Saskatchewan amateur sport," which yielded a population of 2,216 articles within Canadian Newsstand. To create a more manageable sample size, the team restricted search results to the past 12 months, which produced 139 articles, and then added the additional search term "issue" to "Saskatchewan amateur sport." This sampling strategy produced a manageable 36 articles. The team then scanned the 36 articles and was satisfied that a sufficient number of key issues affecting amateur sport funding and specific amateur sport organizations were covered.

Step 3: Define the Recording Unit

Once the general population for content analysis has been determined and a sample strategy has produced a workable number of articles to analyze, the next step in content analysis is to extract content to analyze using a specific **recording unit**, which is the word, phrase, or person that is the focus of content analysis. After doing a quick review of the 36 articles, the fictitious communications team decided that it could use "public funding" as the recording unit. Adding this term to the original search parameter "Saskatchewan amateur sport" produced a subsample of 15 articles.

Step 4: Develop a Coding System and Recording Sheet

The heart of content analysis involves reviewing the content for specific instances of the chosen recording unit according to a semi-formalized set of rules or **coding system**. For the fictitious example, the team read each of the 15 articles produced by the search parameters "public funding" and "Saskatchewan amateur sport" and recorded how many times "public funding" was mentioned. It then went back and tried to determine whether coverage of the public funding issue was positive or negative. The team did this by counting the number of positive or negative adjectives that were used in the same sentence as and in connection with the term "public funding." The result was that for every positive adjective used in connection with public funding, there were three negative references.

Step 5: Conduct Analysis and Report Results

The last step in content analysis involves analyzing and reporting results in a way that clearly and directly answers the research question—Which issues affecting amateur sport organizations in Saskatchewan have been reported in the local, provincial, and national print media since January 2008? To continue with the fictitious case, the team was able to report that the most common issues related to amateur sport organizations covered in local, provincial, and national print media since January 2008 were the state of public funding, with 17 specific mentions; child safety, with 12 specific mentions; and the state of public infrastructure for amateur sport, with 11 specific mentions. Based on further analysis, it was also able to report that when public funding was mentioned in connection with a specific amateur sport organization, three out of four references were negative. The team concluded that media coverage of amateur sport funding in Saskatchewan has been overwhelmingly negative in nature, particularly when specific amateur sport organizations are involved in the conversation. Appendix 8.2 provides a useful summary of communications evaluation measurement tools.

LEARNING ACTIVITIES

For the following activities, work with a partner to identify a well-known communications campaign for a public good or service that you have an interest in. Then develop three to five objectives (outtake or outcome, or a combination of the two) that the campaign could plausibly have been designed to achieve.

Activity 8.1: Communications Campaign Questionnaire

For this activity, develop a questionnaire that could be used to help evaluate your chosen communications campaign. Make sure that your questionnaire includes

- 10 to 15 questions;
- a mix of question types—at least four of the five open and closed types identified in this chapter (include a 250 to 500 word rationale for your choice of question types); and
- a sequencing pattern that corresponds to the potential target audience (include a 250 to 500 word rationale for your choice of sequencing pattern).

Activity 8.2: Content Analysis

For this activity, analyze the content of selected stories in print media to evaluate whether or not your chosen campaign was successful in achieving its objectives. In writing up your content analysis, be sure to clearly identify and justify

- a clear, unambiguous research question;
- a defined content population and sampling strategy that will yield at least 50 print stories;
- a recording unit; and
- a clear coding system and recording sheet; and to include
- a detailed analysis of whether and how the campaign was able to achieve its objectives (1,500 to 2,000 words).

FURTHER READING

One of the best sources of information for understanding the public sector communications evaluation process is the United Kingdom's Government Communication Network's *Evaluating Government Communication Activity: Standards and Guidance* (2012). Another good source in this regard is the Institute for Public Relations' 2002 *Guidelines for Measuring the Effectiveness of PR Programs and Activities*.

In chapter 11 of their very comprehensive *Research Decisions: Quantitative, Qualitative, and Mixed Methods Approaches*, Palys and Atchison provide a thorough and well-sourced guide to conducting analyses of text, images, and audio and video content (2014).

ONLINE RESOURCES

The Washington-based Communications Consortium Media Center hosts one of the most comprehensive sites on media evaluation (www.ccmc.org/work/media-evaluation). Research to Action's "Guidelines for Evaluating

Nonprofit Communications Efforts" (www.researchtoaction.org/2013/03/ guidelines-for-evaluating-nonprofit-communications-efforts/) is a very good, interactive site that includes access to a variety of tools, resources, and tips on evaluating communications activities.

QUESTIONS FOR CRITICAL REFLECTION

1. How important is the evaluation process to the overall quality of communications in public sector organizations?
2. Based on your knowledge and experience to date, how large a role do you think evaluation plays in public sector communications initiatives?

KEY TERMS

binary response: A type of closed question that has a simple yes-no or true-false answer.

coding system: Used in content analysis, a semi-formalized set of rules that guides the process of reviewing media content for specific instances of the chosen recording unit.

content analysis: A highly adaptable technique for gathering and analyzing the content of non-scholarly media products in both print (newspapers, magazines, correspondence, social media) and non-print formats (films, television programs, photographs).

convenience sample: A method of non-probability sampling that involves choosing the nearest and most convenient persons to act as respondents until the desired sample size is reached.

diamond: A method of questionnaire sequencing that combines the funnel and inverted funnel approaches, beginning with specific, closed questions, transitioning to general, more open questions, and then closing with specific, closed questions.

evaluation: The process by which organizations measure to see if a particular activity has achieved the standards or expectations set out in a specified objective.

fill-in-the-blank: A type of closed question that has a simple answer, usually a name, frequency, or quantity, which is the kind of information these questions allow researchers to obtain.

focus group: A special kind of structured interview in which a researcher interviews a small number of key informants (usually between eight and twelve) at one time (usually during a 60- to 90-minute period).

funnel: A method of questionnaire sequencing that begins with broad, open questions and moves to narrower, more closed questions.

inverted funnel: A method of questionnaire sequencing that begins with narrow, closed questions and moves to broader, more open questions.

non-probability sample: A method of collecting data in such a way that every variable does not have an equal chance of being included.

probability sample: A method of collecting data in such a way that every variable selected has an equal chance of being included.

proportionate sample: A method of probability sampling in which the population is divided into groups and the sample from each group is derived by random selection, with the sample size selected from each group being roughly proportionate to that group's size in the overall population.

purposive sample: A method of non-probability sampling in which the principle of sample selection is based on the researcher's judgment, interest, and experience.

questionnaire: A tool used in research to gather targeted information from subjects or respondents that consists of a series of written questions and/ or other prompts.

quota sample: A method of non-probability sampling that involves dividing the desired sample size into representative groups, and then using convenience sampling to achieve the quota for each group.

recording unit: The word, phrase, or person that is the focus of content analysis.

research question: An expression of inquiry that defines exactly what a research activity is designed to achieve in clear, unambiguous terms and anticipates what would constitute a good answer.

scaled-response: A type of closed question in which the answer consists of a list of alternative responses that increase or decrease in intensity in an ordered fashion. These kinds of questions can be further defined as balanced, unbalanced, and rating and ranking.

simple random sample: A method of probability sampling that involves the selection of required respondents at random from the sampling frame.

stratified sample: A method of probability sampling that involves dividing the population into groups that share a particular characteristic and then using random selection within each group to establish the sample.

structured interview: A method of data collection in which the researcher poses prepared questions or prompts to a respondent and records the respondent's answers.

survey research: A research technique in which a questionnaire is presented or sent to respondents (in person, or by phone, email, or Internet) to be filled out and returned for analysis.

systematic sample: A method of probability sampling that involves choosing a starting point in the sampling frame, and then choosing every nth variable from that point onward. For example, with a 20,000-entry telephone directory as the sampling frame, and a required sample size of 500, you might choose every 40th person in the directory so that the sample includes individuals whose names end with all letters of the alphabet.

tunnel: A method of questionnaire sequencing in which all of the questions have the same degree of openness.

unscaled-response: A type of closed question in which the respondent is asked to choose one or more options from a list.

unstructured interview: An exchange between a researcher and a subject that does not have a pre-established format, with the exception of some key questions or topics that the researcher has formulated in advance.

NOTES

1 This section is based on the introduction to the Institute for Public Relations' *Guidelines for Measuring the Effectiveness of PR Programs and Activities* (2002).

2 This section is adapted from Stephanie J. Coopman's "Conducting the Information Interview" (www.roguecom.com/interview/index.html).

3 This section is based on the New York State Teacher Centers' excellent online tutorial, "Focus Groups" (www.sjsu.edu/people/fred.prochaska/courses/ScWk242Spring2013/s2/New York State Teachers Focus Groups.pdf).

WORKS CITED

Adler, Emily Stier, and Roger Clark. 1999. *How It's Done: An Invitation to Social Research.* Belmont, CA: Wadsworth.

Coopman, Stephanie J. 2006. "Conducting the Information Interview." Rogue Communication. www.roguecom.com/interview/index.html

Institute for Public Relations. 2002. *Guidelines for Measuring the Effectiveness of PR Programs and Activities.* Gainesville, FL: Institute of Public Relations.

Krueger, Richard. 2009. *Focus Groups: A Practical Guide for Applied Research.* Thousand Oaks, CA: Sage.

Lindenmann, Walter K. 2006. *Public Relations Research for Planning and Evaluation.* Gainesville, FL: Institute for Public Relations.

Minichiello, Victor, Rosalie Aroni, Eric Timewell, and Loris Alexander. 1990. *In-Depth Interviewing: Researching People.* Hong Kong: Longman Cheshire.

Palys, Ted, and Chris Atchison. 2014. *Research Decisions: Quantitative, Qualitative, and Mixed Methods Approaches.* Toronto: Nelson Education.

United Kingdom. Government Communication Network. 2012. *Evaluating Government Communication Activity: Standards and Guidance.* London: Cabinet Office.

CHAPTER 9

WEB 2.0 AND PUBLIC SECTOR COMMUNICATIONS

CHAPTER OVERVIEW

This chapter focuses on what communications professionals need to know in four areas of practice—research, analysis, communication, and evaluation—that have been particularly affected by Web 2.0 technologies. With respect to research, this chapter focuses on the skills and tools needed to scan the Web 2.0 environment for intelligence on emerging issues and policy networks. In terms of analysis, it focuses on assessing the strategic significance of information generated by research, and determining how best to respond from an organizational point of view. For communication, it explains some of the key expectations that public sector organizations have when communicating in the Web 2.0 environment, as well as how to craft effective messages for that environment. Finally, in terms of evaluation, this chapter focuses on how to evaluate the success or failure of Web 2.0 communications.

LEARNING OBJECTIVES
After completing this chapter, you will be able to

- scan social media for intelligence on emerging policy and communications issues;
- assess the strategic significance of information generated by social media research and determine how best to respond from a strategic point of view;
- craft policy and communications initiatives for the Web 2.0 environment; and
- evaluate the success or failure of social media activities.

INTRODUCTION

Web 2.0 is the "Internet-based tools and services [like Facebook, YouTube and Twitter] that allow for participatory multi-way information sharing, dialogue, and user-generated content" (Treasury Board of Canada Secretariat [TBS] 2011). In contrast, **Web 1.0** was an early stage in the evolution of the Web distinguished by a static, top-down approach to usage and user interfaces. The **Internet** is defined as the global system of interconnected private, public, academic, business, and government computer networks linked by a broad array of electronic, wireless, and optical networking technologies. The **World Wide Web** is the system of interlinked hypertext documents (text, images, videos, and other multimedia) accessed via the Internet using a Web browser. In Canada, Web 2.0 technologies have affected governance in all areas and at all levels, from national public consultations, to municipal program design, to provincial service delivery (see Roy 2006; Borins et al. 2007; McNutt and Carey 2008; Borins 2011; Lacharite 2011). Web 2.0 technologies have also profoundly affected how public sector communications is conducted. As the case of Ontario's new drivers' rules outlined below illustrates, Web 2.0 technologies have forced public sector organizations to change how they conduct communications research, how they analyze the strategic significance of research intelligence, which tactics they use to communicate with the public, and how they evaluate the success or failure of a specific communications initiative.

On November 18, 2008, Ontario's Minister of Transportation Jim Bradley introduced "tough new legislation that would, if passed, make the province's roads safer for all drivers" (Ontario 2008). Among other things, the bill promised a total ban on alcohol consumption for new drivers, a limit of one teenage passenger in the car of a new driver at any time, and zero tolerance for speeding. Once announced, the bill received high-profile support from organizations such as Mothers Against Drunk Driving (MADD) and the Canadian Automobile Association (CAA), as well as equally high-profile opposition, particularly from Ontarians living in small and rural communities. As NDP Opposition Critic Peter Kormos stated, "In rural Ontario, in Northern Ontario, a vehicle is a fact of life in terms of getting from point A to point B" (Ferguson 2008).

The bill also touched a nerve with young Ontarians, particularly those drivers whose behaviour the bill sought to regulate. Within three days of its introduction, a group of Ontario youth led by Hamilton high school student Jordan Sterling created a Facebook page called "Young Drivers Against New Ontario Laws" as a means of organizing opposition to the bill. Sterling and his colleagues were opposed to being treated differently than other Ontario drivers simply because they were young.

Sterling's Facebook page went "viral" (Campbell 2008). Three hours after it was created, over 200 people had joined. Media coverage from Global News, CTV, and CBC, and other online attention pushed an additional 14,500 people to join by the end of the second day. On the third day, "all the personal blogs, political commentators and discussion forums began to link directly to Jordan's Facebook group," and by day's end 65,000 people had joined. Although traditional media had stopped covering the issue by the third day, membership grew to 95,000 people by the fourth. The power of Facebook status updates "propelled steady growth [in membership] for the next week and a half" (ibid.).

By early December 2008, over 150,000 people had joined the "Young Drivers Against New Ontario Laws" Facebook page. At this point, Ontario government officials seemed to acknowledge the political significance of the movement. On December 8, 2008, Premier Dalton McGuinty announced that his government would withdraw the parts of the proposed legislation that would limit young drivers in Ontario to having only one other teenage passenger in the car. The rest of the restrictions on new drivers—including a total ban on alcohol consumption and zero tolerance for speeding—would proceed. The Standing Committee on General Government conducted four days of public hearings on the revised bill between March 9 and April 11. It passed third reading on April 22, received royal assent on April 28, and came into force in 2010.

Some observers believe that the Ontario government "blinked" because it listened to the feedback it received about the impact the restrictions included in the original bill would have had on rural and urban young drivers (e.g., driving with friends was essential to get to school, extracurricular activities, and employment). Others, however, have argued that "the Ontario Cabinet, including Premier McGuinty, saw the Net Generation response to the proposed driver's license restrictions as a wake-up call" (Borins 2011, 12) to the political significance of Web 2.0 technologies such as Facebook. Until the mid-2000s, the communications landscape was still dominated by the print and broadcast media. Facebook was primarily a youth-only site. Twitter was still in its infancy—and a much-maligned infancy at that.

Older social media users—parents, politicians, established business own-ers, and even professional communicators—had not yet become the active users that they are today. That seemed to change around the time of the Ontario new drivers' rules situation outlined above. The flood of Web 2.0 technologies—Facebook, Twitter, YouTube, LinkedIn, etc.—combined with the explosive rate of uptake by Canadians of all ages combined in the latter part of the 2000s to make Web 2.0 technologies a credible, inextricable, and politically powerful part of governance processes in this country. As McNutt describes:

> The Internet and the Web have changed the means by which actors participate in policy-making activities. All government's estab-lished partners are using the Internet and the Web to enhance their usual activities, including their involvement in the policy process (Margetts, 2009). Think tanks and policy research institutes are using the Web to promote specific policy alternatives to a wider audience of information consumers than ever before (McNutt & Marchildon, 2009). Academics are publishing online and in open-access journals where their research has greater impact (Antelman, 2004; Hajjem, Harnad, & Gingras, 2005). The private sector is us-ing the Internet to improve productivity, target new retail markets, and improve service delivery (Baily & Lawrence, 2001). Nonprofit organizations are developing online presences to communicate and fundraise (Waters, 2007). Internet-based advocacy groups are using the Internet and the Web to organize, protest, and build coa-litions (Eagleton-Pierce, 2001). In sum all traditional policy actors engaged in policy-making activity have moved online, producing various sectoral and issue-based policy networks. (2012, 321)

Public sector communications have not been spared from this "move online." As one Government of Ontario communications official put it at a 2012 Conference Board of Canada gathering, it is no longer possible "to just ignore legitimate people on social media. It's tantamount to ignoring some-one who's just asked you a question to your face. Organizations need people who understand that and who understand what is proper and what is not on social media. Because let me tell you, your reputation can be wiped out in a moment if you're not on top of your game" (Skeaff 2012).

What exactly do public sector communications professionals need to know about Web 2.0 technologies? What do they need to know to be able to communicate effectively in the Web 2.0 environment? This chapter focuses on what communications professionals need to know in four areas of practice—research, analysis, communication, and evaluation—that have been particularly affected by Web 2.0 technologies. With respect to research, it focuses on the skills and tools needed for scanning the Web 2.0 environment for intelligence on emerging issues and policy networks. In terms of analysis, it focuses on assessing the strategic significance of information generated by research, and determining how best to respond from an organizational point of view. For communication, this chapter explains some of the key expectations public sector organizations have when communicating in the Web 2.0 environment, as well as how to craft effective messages for that environment. Finally, in terms of evaluation, it addresses how to evaluate the success or failure of Web 2.0 communications. For those new to the Web 2.0 environment, the Key Terms section at the end of the chapter describes the Web 2.0 technologies that are most relevant to the conduct of public sector communications today: social networking sites (Facebook, Google+), professional networking sites (LinkedIn), multimedia sharing sites (YouTube, Flickr, Instagram, podcasts), blogs (Twitter, Tumblr), and **wikis.**

9.1 RESEARCH 2.0

As the case of Ontario's new drivers' rules makes clear, public sector organizations must develop the capacity to identify and track issues in the Web 2.0 environment that are likely to affect them and their relationship(s) with key audiences, and to gather intelligence in that environment about key policy actors' needs and goals. This section describes some of the key research tools that communications professionals can use to achieve these goals in the Web 2.0 environment—platform-specific search engines, Web 2.0 search engines, RSS feeds, pre-programmed aggregators, and customizable aggregators.

Platform-Specific Search Engines

Each of the major Web 2.0 platforms provides both basic and advanced search functionality. These engines are useful for finding basic information about individuals, organizations, and groups that have a presence on the platform, as well as items they have posted on those platforms. Facebook, for example, allows users to search for people, places, and things from a basic search window located at the top of the user's profile page. In addition to this basic search engine, Facebook also allows users to conduct more advanced searches within different areas of the platform, such as people, pages, groups, events, posts by friends and posts by everyone.

Application 9.1: Facebook Search

Once you have registered as a member, log-in to Facebook (www.facebook. com) and type a term into the search window at the top of the screen. For this application, use the name of either a prominent public service representative (the prime minister, or a premier or mayor, for example) or a public sector organization. Scan the resulting Facebook page, paying particular attention to the number and types of followers, pictures, links, and likes on the page. Based on these results, how would you describe your chosen individual or organization's Facebook "presence"? What appear to be the main objectives of the page (e.g., to drive traffic to other web pages, promote certain key messages, share information)?

LinkedIn also offers both basic and advanced search functionality. For advanced searches, users can search for people using a keyword, first and last name, location, job title, company, or school.

Application 9.2: LinkedIn Search

Once you have registered as a member, log-in to LinkedIn (www.linkedin. com) and type a term into the search window at the top of the screen. For this application, search for a prominent public service representative (the prime minister, or a premier or mayor, for example). Scan the resulting LinkedIn page, paying particular attention to how the individual describes his or her professional responsibilities, as well as the network suggested by LinkedIn through the "People Similar" and "People Also Viewed" results on the right side of the page. How would you describe your chosen individual's LinkedIn presence? His or her network?

Additional filters allow users to refine search results by industry, LinkedIn group affiliation, relationships, language, professional function, company size, seniority level, interests, years of experience, and Fortune 500 status.

Twitter's advanced search engine allows users to conduct Boolean searches of Twitter content (all words, exact phrases, any words, etc.), people searches (from specific accounts, mentions specific accounts, etc.), places, and retweets. As discussed in more detail in the evaluation section below, Twitter's search engine also allows users to search content for basic sentiment (positive, negative, questions).

Application 9.3: Twitter Search

Once you have registered as a member, log-in to Twitter (https://twitter.com) and type a term into the search window at the top of the screen. For this application, try using the name of a prominent public service representative (the prime minister, or a premier or mayor, for example). Scan the individual's site. How would you describe your chosen individual's Twitter presence? What does he or she tweet about? Who is following him or her? Who is he or she following? What about his or her visual presence—how do the posted pictures and videos (if any) contribute to or enhance his or her Twitter "presence"?

Web 2.0 Search Engines

A number of websites, such as Social Mention and BoardReader, offer more advanced search engines that allow users to search content across multiple social media platforms concurrently. Social Mention, for example, allows users to search the content of over 100 social media platforms at one time, including mainstream platforms such as Facebook, Twitter, and YouTube.

Social Mention produces basic intelligence on social media content, including the number of times a search phrase is mentioned, a breakdown of search phrase mentions by social media platform, the top "users" of the search term (i.e., the accounts that mention a search phrase the most), and the number of times top related search terms are used. Social Mention also provides insight into how users feel about and act on the search phrase, as discussed in more detail in the evaluation section below.

Application 9.4: Social Mention Search

Go to Social Mention (www.socialmention.com) and type the name of a prominent public service representative (the prime minister, or a premier or mayor, for example) or organization in the search window.

Scan the results. Who is "mentioning" your individual or organization and what kinds of "mentions" are being made (e.g., blogs, comments, events)? How long is the average mention? How many unique authors of mentions are there? Based on your assessment, how would you describe your chosen individual or organization's social media "presence"—what key messages are being disseminated, who is receiving them, and what actions are resulting? Conduct an advanced search of your chosen individual/organization and limit your results to one particular result source (e.g., blog, microblog, bookmark, comment)? Do the results differ if you change the result source? How?

BoardReader is similar to Social Mention but focuses on gathering content posted only on Web forums and message boards. According to BoardReader, this service is unique because Web forums and message boards are "part of the Internet known as the 'Invisible Web' which poses many problems to traditional search engine spiders. The dynamic content is usually very deep and hard to search. In addition, many of these sites change their locations, servers, or url's [sic] almost daily presenting special searching challenges" (BoardReader n.d.).

Application 9.5: BoardReader Search

Go to BoardReader (boardreader.com) and type the name of the individual or organization you used for your Social Mention search (application 9.4) into the search window. Scan the results. Are the search results on BoardReader different than those on Social Mention? If so, how do they differ? What kinds of results are returned on BoardReader? Who are the authors?

RSS Feeds

Creating a Rich Site Summary (RSS) subscription feed is a slightly more advanced way of finding content in the Web 2.0 environment. **RSS** is a web service that uses standard Web feed formats to publish frequently updated information found in blog entries, news headlines, audio, and video. RSS feeds work like this: users sign up for an RSS "reader" or aggregator service, such as Reedah (www.reedah.com), Feedly (feedly.com), Google Reader (www.google.com/reader), or My Yahoo! (ca.my.yahoo.com). The purpose of the aggregator is to collect the desired Web content for viewing in one location.

The next step in setting up an RSS feed is designing and entering a search query into a Web search engine that specializes in Web 2.0 content, such as the news section of the Google search engine, which will retrieve desired content from Web 2.0 sites. Google News searches the headlines of more than 4,500 English-language news sources worldwide, including online news sources, blogs, podcasts, and video blogs, making it one of the most powerful and popular Web 2.0 search engines available. **Blogs** are websites published on the Internet to disseminate information or provoke conversation. **Podcasts** are digital media broadcasts that users subscribe to and download or stream online. Users may have to try a few different search strings to produce the desired results, adjusting the search engine to better account for such variables as popularity, source of content and geographical focus of content.

Once the search results are generated, the next step in the feed creation process is to create a new "subscription" in the aggregator. In Reedah, the easiest way to do this is to paste the URL of the Google News search results into the Feed URL box on the Add New Subscriptions page. Every new item that fits within the query parameters is delivered automatically to Reedah for viewing. Users can also set the reader to send an alert by email every time a new item is deposited in the reader. RSS feeds are especially useful in public sector communications research for conducting regular and ongoing environmental scans for specific emerging and ongoing issues.

Pre-programmed Aggregators

RSS technology is the foundation of a number of websites that provide automated aggregations of Web 2.0 content that is especially relevant to Canadian public sector communications. PoliTwitter, for example, is a non-partisan service that allows users to track content posted by members of Parliament on Twitter, Facebook, YouTube, Flickr, and various blogs. It also allows users to search Hansard for content.

Application 9.6: PoliTwitter Search

Go to PoliTwitter (politwitter.ca) and see which politicians are "trending" on the main page. What are they talking about on social media? Why do you think the top three individuals trending on the PoliTwitter main page are so popular?

Type the name of your member of Parliament in the search window at the top of the page. Based on the search results, what kind of social media presence does he or she have? If you limit your search results to Twitter or Google News, what kinds of results return? What happens if you limit your search results to Hansard? Are they consistent with the image being advanced in other media?

Gov.politwitter is a companion site to PoliTwitter that allows users to track the Web 2.0 activity of major Canadian public sector institutions and organizations.

Application 9.7: Gov.politwitter Search

Go to the Stats section of the gov.politwitter.ca page and see which Canadian government organizations are "trending." Which have the largest following at the moment and why do you think the organization is so popular? What messages are they disseminating? Scroll down through the Stats page and compare and contrast which organizations are popular on the different media platforms being tracked on gov.politwitter (i.e., YouTube, Facebook, Twitter). What do you think accounts for the differences?

Canadian Blogosphere offers a slightly different kind of aggregator service: it is set up to search popular Canadian blogs—including political blogs—and produces results that can be ranked according to popularity, topic, and author.

Application 9.8: Canadian Blogosphere Search

Go to the Stats section of the gov.politwitter.ca page and see which Canadian government organizations are "trending." Which have the largest following at the moment and why do you think the organization is so popular? What messages are they disseminating? Scroll down through the Stats page and compare and contrast which organizations are popular on the different media platforms being tracked on gov.politwitter (i.e., YouTube, Facebook, Twitter). What do you think accounts for the differences?

Customizable Aggregators

There are a number of web-based companies, such as HootSuite, Radian6, and Syncapse, that provide users with the tools to program their own aggregators in order to create Web 2.0 "dashboards." HootSuite (www. hootsuite.com), for example, allows users to search for content across a variety of platforms (Facebook, Twitter, Google+, LinkedIn, etc.) and report results in real time in one location for easy reading—the so-called "dashboard."

Application 9.9: Create a HootSuite Dashboard

Once you have registered, go to the HootSuite main page (www.hoot-suite.com) and add a new "Stream" from a network on which you are a registered user (e.g., Facebook, Twitter, or LinkedIn). Once in the new stream, enter the name of a prominent public sector representative or organization and scan the results. Repeat this process until you have three or four streams on your dashboard and can follow updates in real time.

HootSuite offers a basic dashboard service free of charge, as well as a premium version that allows users to refine and customize tracking strategies and searches. Radian6 and Syncapse provide similar services.

9.2 ANALYSIS

Once information from the online environment has been generated using tools such as those described above, public sector organizations have to assess this information for its strategic value—both to the organization and to its key audiences. Since its release in 2009, the United States Air Force's Web Posting Response Assessment Tool has become the gold standard for how public sector organizations assess the strategic value of postings in the Web 2.0 environment and determine how best to respond to those postings (Scott 2008). The tool was originally designed to help the Air Force monitor social media postings made by its 330,000 personnel around the world to ensure their safety and security, and allow them an inexpensive, efficient, and meaningful way to communicate with family and friends at home (Shachtman 2009). It has since been adopted by organizations across the public and non-profit sectors, including Ontario's Ministry of Labour (Skeaff 2012). The Air Force's original assessment tree is shown below, as is the one derived from it by the Ontario Ministry of Labour.

FIGURE 9.1: UNITED STATES AIR FORCE WEB POSTING RESPONSE ASSESSMENT TOOL

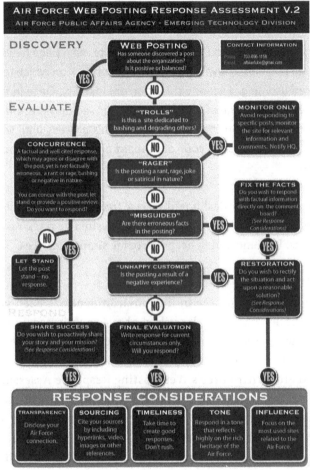

Source: Air Force Public Affairs Agency. n.d. "Air Force Web Posting Response Assessment." http://www.afpc.af.mil/shared/media/document/AFD-091210-037.pdf

FIGURE 9.2: ONTARIO MINISTRY OF LABOUR POSTING RESPONSE CHART

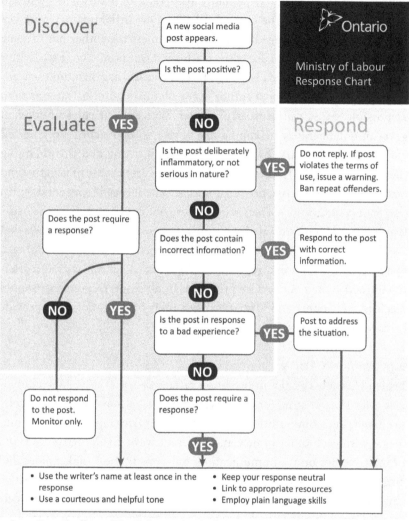

Source: Bruce Skeaff. 2012. "The Challenges of Leadership: Overcoming Obstacles on the Path to Social Media Success." Paper presented at the Public Sector Social Media 2012 Conference.

The first step in the process that underlies both decision trees is to assess whether an online posting is positive or negative. If positive, organizations are encouraged to monitor or rebroadcast if the post speaks directly, clearly, and honestly about its mission and values. If a post is positive, but contains erroneous or misleading information, organizations are encouraged to respond directly with the correct information.

Negative and incorrect posts can be categorized in one of three ways: deliberately inflammatory, factually incorrect, or motivated by a bad service experience. In the case of a deliberately inflammatory post, organizations are encouraged not to respond unless the author has in some way violated the terms of use of the platform it was posted on (e.g., Twitter or a government agency's website). In these cases, organizations are encouraged to report the post author to the platform administrator as soon as possible. Most platforms like Twitter have explicit rules of conduct governing deliberately inflammatory posts and take action on reported violations quickly, first by issuing a formal warning and then banning the person from any future activity on the site. In the case of negative and factually incorrect posts, organizations are encouraged to respond with a post that contains the correct information, but does not address the negative emotions communicated in the original post. In the case of posts that are motivated by a bad service experience, organizations are encouraged to address the situation directly by apologizing (if appropriate) and offering to rectify the poor service provided. In all cases, respondents should disclose their name and affiliation with their organization, and provide links to relevant sites.

9.3 COMMUNICATION

British Columbia's chief information officer says that Web 2.0 technologies offer the potential for public sector organizations "to speak directly to citizens and communities, and for public service employees to communicate with each other in new and different ways. By doing so, we stand to improve not only communication, but consultation, stakeholder and citizen engagement, policy development and service delivery" (British Columbia 2009, 1). To unlock this potential, chief information officers across Canada's public sector recommend that public sector employees follow some basic ground rules when communicating in the Web 2.0 environment, including:

- Clearly state in your personal Web 2.0 account profile that "the views expressed are your own and not those of your employer." As the Government of Canada makes clear, however, this kind of disclaimer "does not absolve you of your obligations as a public servant, including your duty of loyalty" to your employer (TBS 2011).

- Only share information from your workplace that is publicly available, such as illustrations, photographs, videos, or logos found on public websites, unless specifically authorized to do so.
- Do not share personal information about others from your workplace (such as the deputy minister or minister) unless you have the explicit consent of the individual(s) to whom the information relates.
- "Divert work-related conversations to official channels," such as emails or phone calls to work addresses and numbers, "so that there is a record of any guidance provided or decisions taken" (TBS 2011).
- Only link official email addresses to Web 2.0 accounts if such accounts are going to be used exclusively for professional networking.
- Refrain from any activity that might bring into question the "non-partisanship and impartiality of the public service" (TBS 2011).

The Government of British Columbia's use of social media policy is one of the best guides to communicating in the Web 2.0 environment for public sector employees in Canada.

Feature 9.1: Use of Social Media in the BC Public Service: Policy Summary No. 33

Subject Area Description

Social media has changed the way people communicate. Social media is about participation, conversation and knowledge sharing, and is becoming a powerful tool for both professional and personal purposes. Social media forums are used for communication, collaboration, multimedia, reviews and opinions, entertainment and other information aggregation platforms. Some examples include: LiveJournal, Twitter, LinkedIn, Flickr, Facebook, Digg, YouTube, Yelp.com, WikiAnswers and Second Life.

Social media and collaboration tools create the potential for the Province to speak directly to citizens and communities, and for public service employees to communicate with each other in new and different ways. By doing so, we stand to improve not only communication, but consultation, stakeholder and citizen engagement, policy development and service delivery.

Areas of Concern

The primary area of concern for using social media is the failure to protect information which may be personal, sensitive or confidential and if disclosed may cause damage or harm to individuals or the reputation of government.

Many factors amplify this concern:

- Unauthorized use or disclosure of government information is a security and/or privacy breach. (PS#16 Protection of Sensitive Information)
- Personnel may not be provided with adequate awareness and training regarding sensitive and personal information.
- Personnel may inadvertently post personal information and be in violation of the Freedom of Information and Protection of Privacy Act (FOIPPA).
- Unauthorized use of copyrighted material is an infringement of intellectual property rights.
- When sharing information or providing advice online necessary records may not be captured, retained and filed in accordance with government records management.
- Where personnel use social media sites as a government employee, and wish to provide personal comments on sites, they may contravene the Standards of Conduct and bring the public service into disrepute or be misinterpreted as being an official representative of the B.C. government.

Personnel may incorrectly assume an expectation of privacy for personal, non-work related activity on government systems. All information stored or transmitted on government systems is the property of government.

This Policy Summary offers guidance on using social media and is intended to guide personnel in understanding their responsibilities and obligations according to the Information Security Policy and government standards.

Intended Outcomes

The policies or guidelines associated with the use of social media are intended to:

- Improve awareness of privacy and security considerations when using social media.
- Ensure sensitive and personal information is identified and managed appropriately.
- Ensure personnel are aware of their roles and responsibilities as a government employee when using social media.
- Support appropriate information and records management.

Responsibilities of All Personnel
Things to do:

- Be aware of and understand security policy, standards and guidelines for protecting sensitive and personal information.
- Understand and familiarize with the BC Public Service Philosophy and CISO guidelines on the use of social media.
- Attend information security and social media awareness, education and training opportunities.
- Examine information in view of privacy, intellectual property, records management and confidentiality requirements before making it available on social media.
- Instill confidence and trust and not bring the public service into disrepute.
- Follow your ministry's approval procedure prior to use of social media.
- Involve Public Affairs Bureau when using trademarks or official marks, such as government logos, product brands or other marks.
- Have approval by Intellectual Property Program, Treasury Board or ministry legislative authority where copyright material requires a license.

Things to avoid:

- Engaging in any activity that could be perceived as an official act or representation of government unless authorized to do so.
- Engaging in political activities at work. Employees must be able to retain the perception of impartiality in relation to their duties and responsibilities.

Things to pay attention to:

- Ensure records management practices are understood and followed.

Things to report:

- Actual and suspected security incidents and events as required by the Information Incident Management Process.
- File a General Incident or Loss Report (GILR) within 24 hours of a security incident.

Responsibilities of Management
Things to do:

- Ensure that sensitive and personal information is defined.
- Consult on any suspected or actual information security concerns with the Ministry Information Security Officer (MISO).
- Ensure personnel receive suitable training and regular reminders of privacy and security requirements when using social media.
- When a security or privacy breach has occurred, review and revise related social media policies and processes as needed.

Things to establish procedure for:

- Approval processes where required for any materials being used on social media sites.

Things to be aware of:

- When and how personnel use social media.
- Appropriate use of information and information technology resources by personnel.

Things to reinforce with personnel:

- Adherence to policies, standards and guidelines in using social media.

- Protection of personal and sensitive information.
- Ensure the use of the Information Incident Management Process when required.
- Ensure the staff awareness of the BC Public Service Philosophy and CISO guidelines on the use of social media.

Source: British Columbia. Office of the Chief Information Officer, Ministry of Citizens' Services. 2009. "Policy Summary No. 33: Use of Social Media in the B.C. Public Service." www.cio.gov.bc.ca/local/cio/informationsecurity/policy/summaries/33_social_media.pdf

Twitter

Twitter is one of the most popular and valuable Web 2.0 technologies used in Canada's public sector today. According to Alain Lemay, there is "enormous value for government organizations to use Twitter. There are areas where Twitter can get critical information out to the people who need it faster than any other means available. Just to name a few examples, Twitter has been effectively used for crisis communication, public health coordination and public safety improvement" (n.d., 4). To make the most of Twitter, Lemay recommends that public sector organizations abide by the following 15 "commandments":[1]

1. *Thou shalt listen before leaping.* For Lemay, this means finding the individuals and groups that are talking about a specific organization and "listening" to their online conversations to determine needs, issues, concerns, and interests.

2. *Thou shalt use thy profile properly.* Twitter profiles are key to attracting an audience and engaging with followers. To maximize their value, Lemay recommends that public sector organizations include the following in their corporate profiles:

   - Your picture should either be the organization's logo or the picture of a senior, recognizable official.
   - Your profile, while limited to 160 characters, should include a link to the organization's website, a description of its mission, what the account author intends to tweet about, and something personal, if appropriate.
   - Your user name, while limited to 15 characters, should be universal enough that members of the general public can recognize and associate the name with the organization.

3. *Thou shalt have a disclaimer.* To build loyalty and trust with followers, Lemay recommends that Twitter accounts include a disclaimer about how the account will be used, for example, times when tweets will be made (business hours), times when mentions are going to be checked (daily, weekly, etc.), and personnel limitations in terms of being able to respond to inquiries in a timely fashion. Posting a disclaimer on the organization's main website and then linking it to the Twitter bio is an effective way to communicate this.

4. *Thou shalt not bully.* Public organizations assume a certain amount of authority in their tweet content in order to discourage users who intend to mislead the public or disparage the organization's reputation. Lemay recommends taking this position to an extreme, including "reporting or threatening anyone with legal action over coincidental and unintentional similarities with your name, trademark, or other. Nothing will get you on the wrong end of a Twitter storm faster and your organization's reputation can be permanently damaged" (Lemay n.d., 8).

5. *Thou shalt tweet regularly.* Regular activity on Twitter is central to keeping and growing an audience. Lemay says that the easiest way to follow this commandment is to set a daily and weekly schedule, even if only to reply quickly to an interesting post.

6. *Thou shalt integrate thy tweet approval process.* Given the number of approval processes that exist in most public sector communications workflows, Lemay recommends that the Twitter approval process is integrated with regular content approval processes. Some basic principles for an integrated approval process include blanket approval for certain types of basic content that can go into any type of platform, such as news releases, ministerial announcements, and FAQs; clear approval levels for specific kinds of content (e.g., minister's office approval for ministerial photos, or director general or assistant deputy minister approval for program announcements); and clear posting authorities for different individuals (e.g., senior analysts can post tweets on X subject without approval, interns/summer students can only tweet media releases, and John Doe is authorized to tweet at his discretion on select topics during crisis situations).

7. *Thou shalt not register alternate accounts.* Unlike website domain registrations, Twitter forbids users from registering multiple accounts

for the same use or to prevent use by others. According to Twitter: "You may not create serial accounts … with overlapping use cases"; "You may not create accounts for the purpose of preventing others from using those account names"; and "accounts that are inactive for more than 6 months may be removed without notice" (Twitter 2014). Malicious activity is dealt with by having users reporting it to Twitter authorities, who can issue a permanent suspension.

8. *Thou shalt not automate thy tweets.* After bullying, Lemay says that nothing turns Twitter followers off more than automated tweets. Not only is it against Twitter rules (and thus could result in permanent suspension if reported), but automated tweets can also lead to trouble if the original source of the automated content is not reviewed prior to distribution. In Lemay's words, "You may remember recently that some politicians (who shall remain anonymous) recently got a nasty surprise when false tweets began showing up on their accounts. You see, these politicians were tweeting the RSS feeds of a higher up whose site had been hacked. So the false tweets were being spread throughout their network of tweeters. Needless to say, they don't do that anymore!" (n.d., 14). To help maintain "freshness," Lemay recommends that public sector organizations create—and stick to—a schedule to tweet on a regular basis, tweet important information when it is first released and then again for peak viewing times (usually early morning, early afternoon, and after dinner time), and, if an organization's tweet audience is international, plan to tweet the same content three times at 12-hour intervals with additional tweets of different content in between.

9. *Thou shalt tweet in the first person.* Research shows that tweets from an individual have larger followings than tweets from organizations. To "humanize" organizational accounts, Lemay recommends that organizations (1) identify one or two spokesperson(s) to tweet on behalf of the organization, (2) mention the first names of the people who will be doing the tweeting in their profile (e.g., "This is the official Twitter account of the Department of Friendliness. Marc, Lindsey, and Todd will be tweeting with you."), and (3) "brand" an account to a senior executive by including that person's picture and bio

on the profile page and having that individual tweet on behalf of the organization.

10. *Thou shalt not bait and switch.* The most popular Twitter accounts are always the most truthful and transparent. Accordingly, Lemay recommends that organizations find a way to highlight what is interesting about material without exaggerating (e.g., don't say that important changes in a major program will be announced when only minor changes are forthcoming).

11. *Thou shalt not spam.* Lemay recommends that users become familiar with Twitter's acceptable use policy, which defines any violation that can result in permanent suspension as "spam," including posting misleading links; posting duplicate content over multiple accounts or multiple duplicate updates on one account; posting multiple unrelated updates to a topic using #; ending large numbers of duplicate @replies or mentions; sending large numbers of unsolicited @replies or mentions in an attempt to spam a service or link; adding a large number of unrelated users to lists in an attempt to spam a service or link; repeatedly posting other users' tweets as your own; creating or purchasing accounts to gain followers; and using or promoting third-party sites that claim to get you more followers.

12. *Thou shalt be selective of whom to follow.* The interactive nature of Twitter makes it important for account holders to be selective and strategic about whom to follow, as following an account can be considered an endorsement of the individual or organization who owns the account. Lemay suggests that the following kinds of accounts are good to follow: programs/initiatives that exist within the organization that have their own Twitter presence; agencies, board, commissions, or other government departments that share the organization's mandate; international organizations that contribute positively to the industry of which the organization is a part; post-secondary institutions that have programs related to the organization's domain of expertise; and key industry associations.

13. *Thou shalt monitor thy account.* Creating a Twitter account and keeping it "alive" requires constant care and tending. Before even setting up an account, Lemay suggests developing a Twitter "plan" that answers the following questions: Who will monitor the account

for mentions or direct messages (e.g., praise, criticisms, retweets, @ mentions)? How and when will the account holder respond to both positive and negative postings? Who are the key contacts that questions can be referred to? What happens if your account gets hacked? What if someone sends out a tweet by mistake?

14. *Thou shalt contribute to the conversation.* On Twitter, retweeting content can have the same effect as issuing an original tweet, and a potentially greater effect if that content comes from a key stakeholder. As Lemay says, "that is the whole point of using Twitter—circulating important information" (n.d., 21).

15. *Thou shalt measure for success.* Regardless of the medium, good communications practice demands that performance be measured; this applies to Twitter. As a start, Lemay recommends measuring the following:

- *Followers*: Measuring the number of people who follow an account's tweets provides a basic sense of the number of individuals an account has reached. This basic metric can be enhanced by correlating follower numbers with specific topics, timing, events, and so on.

- *Retweets*: Retweet counts allow you to measure the number of people who are forwarding Twitter content from one account to the followers of other accounts.

- *@mentions*: @mentions allows you to measure the number of questions or comments an account receives through Twitter.

- *Quality* of retweets and @mentions: With a bit of research, account owners can assess the quality of retweets and @ mentions. For example, is material being retweeted by influential individuals or groups? Do they have many or few followers, and are they influential in a particular policy network? As Lemay suggests, "If you notice individuals who have taken to retweeting your content, it may be useful to develop a relationship with them. Then, when you have really important content you are going to send out, you can let them know in advance. It will ensure they retweet it and give them a scoop of sorts. Win-win!" (n.d., 22).

9.4 EVALUATION

As discussed in chapter 8, communications activities in any medium need to be evaluated against whether they are successful or not in achieving objectives established on three levels: output, outtake, and outcome. Evaluation of communication outputs focuses on measuring the number of tangible goods or services a specific communications activity produces, for example, X number of tweets, Y number of Facebook page updates, or Z number of blog entries, as well as the intended number of target audience members that a specific communications activity reaches. Evaluation of communication outtakes focuses on measuring the level of awareness, retention, and/or comprehension of core themes and messages that target audience members derive from a specific communications activity, for example, a 5 percent increase in target audience awareness of policy X, 85 percent of the population of region Y that understands the behavioural implications of a new regulation, or 95 percent of city's population that understands new municipal voting procedures one year after their introduction. Evaluation of communication outcomes attempts to measure the extent to which target audiences change their behaviour as a result of the awareness, retention, and/or comprehension they derive from a specific communications activity, for example, decreasing the rate of fatal injuries on construction sites by 2.5 percent as a result of targeting young construction workers with a Web 2.0–based awareness campaign.

Output Evaluation

At a basic level, most of the major Web 2.0 platforms allow users to track how their account postings are being followed. The basic search engine on Twitter, for example, allows users to search for tweets that mention a specific user (enter @ followed by the user name in the basic search box), account, content, or hashtag. The advanced search engine allows users to use Boolean operators to refine searches, as well as filter for specific time periods and URLs.

At a slightly more advanced level, sites such as TweetDeck provide a dashboard service that allows users to manage Twitter and Facebook accounts from a central page, including the ability to both send and receive posts within the dashboard and monitor how posts are being followed.

Application 9.10: Create a TweetDeck Dashboard

Once you have registered on Twitter, log-in to the TweetDeck main page (https://tweetdeck.twitter.com) and add a new column based on the search results using the name of prominent public sector representative or organization. Scan the results. Repeat this process, varying the column type (e.g., by "Notifications," "Followers," or "Activity") until you have three or four streams on your dashboard and can follow updates in real time.

Other sites offer web analytics for specific Web 2.0 platform activity. TweetReach, for example, provides details of who is reading tweets issued from a particular account, when they are being read, and how they are being shared.

Application 9.11: TweetReach Results

Once registered on Twitter, log-in to the TweetReach main page (www. tweetreach.com) and enter the name of a prominent public sector representative or organization in the search window. Scan the results, paying particular attention to "Reach," "Exposure," "Contributors," and "Most Retweeted Tweets." Based on these results, how effective do you think your chosen individual or organization's Twitter activity is?

Conduct another search of a different individual or organization in the same sector (e.g., federal politician, provincial labour department) and compare the results. Does one individual or organization have vastly better results than the other? Why do you think that is the case?

At a more advanced level, HootSuite offers both free and premium fee-for-service dashboard-style tracking services. In HootSuite's free version (see application 9.9 above), users can monitor activity on up to five different accounts at a time (e.g., Facebook, Twitter, LinkedIn, WordPress), including feeds from any saved searches (e.g., a specific hashtag search) or other specifically identified accounts (e.g., accounts a user may be following).

Google Analytics (www.google.com/analytics/) is the most popular currently available service for website tracking (on approximately 55 percent of the 10,000 most popular websites in 2012) (Empson 2012). At a basic level, Google Analytics allows users to track how many people visit a site (including unique visitors, page views, and pages viewed per visit) on a daily, weekly, and monthly basis; average visit duration; percentage of new visits; and "bounce rate," or the percentage of single-page visits in which the visitor left the site from the entrance page. At a more advanced level, Google Analytics provides detailed statistics on a number of output metrics:

- visitor behaviour (new versus returning, frequency, recency, and length of engagement)
- technology (views by browser type, network, mobile device type, etc.)
- traffic origins, including traffic from search engines, referrals from other websites (including specific pages within those sites), referrals from other Web 2.0 platforms, etc.
- content usage, including the pages on which visitors enter and exit the site, how often and how long visitors view individual pages, the extent to which visitors search the site for specific content, and the extent to which visitors interact with features such as slide shows or embedded videos

FIGURE 9.3: GOOGLE ANALYTICS

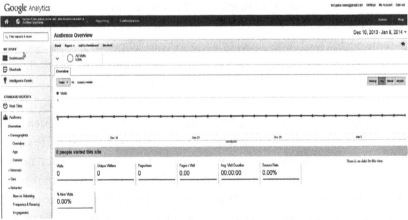

Source: Google Developers. 2014. "Google Analytics: Report Data Calculation." Google.com. https://developers.google.com/analytics/resources/concepts/gaConceptsDataCalculation

Outtake Evaluation

Sentiment is one of the most popular outtake metrics in the Web 2.0 environment. It can be used to gauge how target audience members generally feel about the content of online postings. The advanced search function on Twitter, for example, allows users to filter results by positive or negative sentiment.

Application 9.12: Twitter Sentiment Results

Once registered, log in to Twitter and enter the name of prominent public sector representative or organization into the search window. In the search results page, click on the settings wheel and choose "Advanced Search." In this window, enter the name of your chosen individual or organization one again and check "positive" or "negative" to limit results by sentiment. Based on reported results, what do you think is the source of the positive or negative sentiment in the content of the tweets?

In a similar way, Social Mention also allows users to filter the content of more general Web 2.0 search by sentiment.

Application 9.13: Social Mention Sentiment Results

Go to Social Mention (www.socialmention.com) and enter the name of prominent public sector representative or organization in the search window. Scan the results, paying particular attention to the "sentiment" and "passion" results and try to identify the positive and/or negative words that contribute to that tone.

Outcome Evaluation

Bitly offers users a basic tool to evaluate the impact of a communications output on the behaviour of individuals in the Web 2.0 environment—namely, how many people "click through" a URL posted on Twitter to go to a recommended website (the Twitter click-through rate). Because Twitter messages are limited to 140 characters, a number of sites, such as Bitly, allow users to convert long URLs into shortened ones for the Twitter environment. Once pasted into a tweet, users can return to the Bitly interface and generate four click-through statistics: how many people clicked on a link; how many people clicked on other Bitly links (that point to the same page); the number of referring sites (where your Bitly link was clicked on); and the location (country) of people who clicked through.

Klout (and similar services, such as Kred, PeerIndex, Social Mention, and SocialPointer) gives users the ability to do basic outcome evaluation by measuring how much "influence" a user has as a result of activity on sites such as Facebook, Twitter, Google+, LinkedIn, Foursquare, and Wikipedia. Klout defines influence as "the ability to drive action, such as sharing a picture that triggers comments and likes, or tweeting about a great restaurant and causing your followers to go try it for themselves" (Klout 2012). The Klout search engine "scrapes" data from over 35 usage points on Facebook (likes, comments, and number of friends in the network), Twitter (follower counts, retweets, list memberships, and the number of "influential" people who retweet users' posts), Google+, LinkedIn, Foursquare, and Wikipedia to produce a basic Klout score on a scale of 1 to 100, with 1 being the least influential.

Application 9.14: Klout Assessment

Once you have registered and logged in, Klout will prompt you to connect to networks that you are a member of (e.g., LinkedIn, Google+, Facebook, Twitter). From here, click on the "Dashboard" page and view your overall social media history, breakdown by connected network, and score impact analysis. In the search window, enter the name of prominent public sector representative or organization and wait for Klout to identify their Klout score and Top Moments (social media posts that generate action from people within social media networks).

Klout generates three additional scores to provide deeper insight into the basic score: (1) a True Reach score that reports the actual number of individuals who actively follow and react to online postings; (2) an Amplification score that reflects the "likelihood" that a user's postings will generate action (e.g., retweets, @messages, likes, and comments); (3) a Network score of between 1 and 100 that aims to reflect the degree of influence of a user's engaged audience (those counted in the True Reach score). Klout also identifies the top five sources of a user's influence and the top five sources who are influenced by the user. The result is a basic sense of the impact a user has on Web 2.0 behaviour.

Google Analytics offers a slightly more robust outcome measure, albeit limited to website performance. As part of its analytics suite, users can measure something called "goal conversion," which occurs when a visitor to a site completes a desired action on the site, such as submit a Contact Us form, submit a question, register to receive a newsletter, read an article, or download a report.

As in the output domain, HootSuite offers a comprehensive suite of outtake and outcome evaluation services. As part of its premium service, Hootsuite allows users to integrate over 30 types of analytics into a single dashboard, including popular evaluation tools such as Facebook Insights, Google Analytics, Twitter Profile Stats, and Google+ Pages Analytics.

CONCLUSION

Web 2.0 technologies have fundamentally changed the way communications is conducted in Canada's public sector. As the case of Ontario's new drivers' rules makes clear, it is no longer possible for public authorities to "just ignore legitimate people on social media" (Skeaff 2012). More than that, public authorities have to recognize and develop the expertise to deal with the fact that "all traditional policy actors engaged in policy-making activity have moved online" (McNutt 2012, 321). What do Web 2.0 technologies mean for the conduct of public sector communications in this country? At a minimum, public sector organizations and their communications staff need the capacity to do four things: (1) research the Web 2.0 environment for intelligence on emerging issues and policy networks; (2) analyze the strategic significance of Web 2.0 research results and determine how best to respond; (3) understand the expectations and master the technical requirements of communicating content in the Web 2.0 environment; and (4) evaluate the performance of Web 2.0 communications activities at the output, outtake, and outcome levels.

As much as this chapter tries to put forward a coherent sense of how public sector communications is affected by Web 2.0 technologies and what those working in the sector need to do in order to function effectively with those technologies, at the end of the day most public sector organizations "are still exploring what [they] can do with this new thing called social media. Both in terms of what [they] can do with content on each platform, and how [they] work with it as an organization.... who does what, who's in charge of what, how does this all now fit into our working lives as communicators" (Skeaff 2012). It is critical to understand that all of the Web 2.0 technologies examined in this chapter must ultimately be seen as tools that can either help or hinder the facilitation of and support the basic public sector communications function (1) to transmit and disseminate information about public programs and services to citizens and (2) to listen to citizens and incorporate their needs and views into governing processes. As the Institute for Citizen-Centred Service puts it: "Using [Web 2.0] tools is really not about the tools. The tools are innovative, new, and different from other tools used in the past, but they are still just tools/technologies. The fundamental innovation is in the approach to work—pooling the knowledge, expertise, and skills of employees from across the organization to work jointly on shared goals and objectives and to conduct their business in an open and transparent manner that is subject to the scrutiny of others" (2009). Blaise Hébert sums up this point: "It's not about the tools. The collaboration characteristics that you are looking for are human ones, NOT technical ones (2012).

The last word here goes to Bruce Skeaff:

> Interactive electronic engagement—social engagement—with each other and the organizations with which we live—including our governments—is not going away. It's no flash in the pan. It's the future.... So, do it. Do it right. Do it intelligently. Do it safely. Integrate it into everything you do. Be friendly, personal and personable while you are online. And make sure you are having some fun while doing it. Because if you're not having any fun, you're doing it wrong. (2012)

LEARNING ACTIVITIES
For these activities, identify a public sector organization that you have some affinity with.

Activity 9.1: Research
Use the research tools presented in this chapter to describe your chosen organization's presence in the Web 2.0 environment, that is, how your public sector organization presents itself in terms of its goals, mission, and values on social and professional networking sites, multimedia sharing sites, blogs, and wikis.

Activity 9.2: Analyze
Identify a recent public issue that your chosen public sector organization has been dealing with and describe how it has treated that issue in the Web 2.0

environment. Using your knowledge of strategic communications planning, identify and describe the strategy you think your organization used to deal with the issue in the Web 2.0 environment, especially the output, outtake, and outcome objectives you think it established.

Activity 9.3: Communicate

Identify and describe the specific tactics—including key messages—that you think your chosen organization used to deal with the issue identified above.

Activity 9.4: Evaluate

Use the evaluation tools presented in this chapter to evaluate whether and how your organization was successful in achieving the output, outtake, and outcome objectives you identified in activity 9.2 above.

FURTHER READING

While slightly dated now, Borins and colleagues' 2007 *Digital State at the Leading Edge* provides a wide-ranging assessment of the impact, use, and management of information technology in Canadian government. As the title suggests, Kathleen McNutt's 2014 article "Public Engagement in the Web 2.0 Era" provides a contemporary assessment of how social collaborative technologies have changed e-participation in the 21st century.

ONLINE RESOURCES

Steve Richards provides good insight into social media strategy in "Why You Need a Social Media Strategy, Not a Facebook Strategy" (2010) on his Econsultancy site. The Washington-based Communications Consortium Media Center (www.ccmc.org/node/16229) and Communicate & Howe! (www.communicateandhowe.com/2013/12/16/nonprofit-communicators-toolbox-the-digital-revolution/) both provide excellent digital media "tool boxes" on their respective sites.

QUESTIONS FOR CRITICAL REFLECTION

1. How important is it for public sector organizations to actively maintain a Web 2.0 presence? What are the implications of not doing so?
2. What role can young professionals play in bringing Canadian public sector organizations into the Web 2.0 era? Are young professionals better equipped to play this role than older professionals?

KEY TERMS

blog: Short for web log, blogs are websites published on the Internet in order to disseminate information or provoke conversation.

Internet: The global system of interconnected private, public, academic, business, and government computer networks linked by a broad array of electronic, wireless, and optical networking technologies.

podcasts: Digital media broadcasts consisting of an episodic series of files (audio, video, PDF) that users subscribe to and download through web syndication, or stream online to a computer or mobile device.

RSS (Rich Site Summary): A web service that uses standard web feed formats to publish frequently updated information found in blog entries, news headlines, audio, and video.

sentiment: A popular outtake metric that can be used to gauge how target audience members generally feel about the content of online postings.

Web 1.0: An early stage in the evolution of the Web distinguished by a static, top-down approach to web usage and user interfaces.

Web 2.0: The "Internet-based tools and services [like Facebook, YouTube and Twitter] that allow for participatory multi-way information sharing, dialogue, and user-generated content" (TBS 2011).

World Wide Web: The system of interlinked hypertext documents (text, images, videos, and other multimedia) accessed via the Internet using a web browser.

wikis: Collaborative websites that allow users to add, modify, or delete content via a web browser, usually using a simplified markup language.

Key Web 2.0 Technologies Mentioned in This Chapter

Web 2.0 technologies are the "Internet-based tools and services that allow for participatory multi-way information sharing, dialogue, and user-generated content. This can include social media, which allow participants with distinct social/user profiles to create, share and interact with user-generated content, including text, images, video and audio (e.g., Facebook, Twitter, YouTube, LinkedIn, blogs) as well as collaborative technologies that allow multiple users to collaboratively create content (e.g., wikis, Google Docs)" (Treasury Board of Canada Secretariat 2011). The following list describes the most important Web 2.0 technologies that public sector communications professionals need to know about today—social networking sites (Facebook, Google+), professional networking sites (LinkedIn), multimedia sharing sites (YouTube, Flickr, Instagram, podcasts), blogs (Twitter, Tumblr), and wikis.

BoardReader: A website with a search engine that specializes in finding content posted only on web forums and message boards.

Canadian Blogosphere: A website that allows users to search popular Canadian blogs—including political blogs—and produces results that can be ranked according to popularity, topic, and author.

Facebook: A social networking service that allows registered users to post various kinds of information about themselves, their interests and tastes, and link to others who share similar backgrounds and tastes.

Flickr: An image- and video-hosting website that allows registered users to post and share photographs and videos.

Google+: A social networking and identity service that bills itself as a "social layer" built upon online platforms including Gmail, Google Profiles, Messenger, Circles, Hangouts, and other customizable Google products and services such as news feeds.

Google Analytics: A web analytics service that allows users to track how many people visit a site (including unique visitors, page views, and pages viewed per visit) on a daily, weekly, and monthly basis; average visit duration; percentage of new visits; and "bounce rate," or the percentage of single-page visits in which the visitor left the site from the entrance page. At a more advanced level, Google Analytics provides detailed statistics on a number of output metrics.

Gov.politwitter: A companion website to PoliTwitter that allows users to track the Web 2.0 activity of major Canadian public sector institutions and organizations.

HootSuite: A social media management system used to collaboratively execute search and intelligence campaigns across multiple social networks from one secure, web-based dashboard.

Instagram: A free photo-sharing program and social network that allows users to take a photo, apply a digital filter to it, and share it with other users on Instagram and other social networking platforms.

Klout: A website that allows users to conduct basic outcome evaluation by measuring how much "influence" a user has as a result of activity on sites such as Facebook, Twitter, Google+, LinkedIn, Foursquare, and Wikipedia.

LinkedIn: A social networking website designed primarily for professional networking. It allows registered users to develop a detailed online resume and maintain a list of contact details of people with whom they have some level of relationship.

PoliTwitter: A non-partisan website containing a search engine that allows users to track content posted by members of Parliament on Twitter, Facebook, YouTube, Flickr, and various blogs.

Social Mention: A website with an advanced search engine that allow users to search content concurrently across multiple social media platforms.

Tumblr: A micro-blogging platform and social networking website that allows registered users to post multimedia and other content to a short-form blog.

TweetReach: A website that allows users to search details of who is reading tweets issued from a particular account, when they are being read, and how they are being shared.

Twitter: An online social networking and micro-blogging service that allows registered users to send and read text-based messages of up to 140 characters, known as "tweets," through the Twitter website interface, short message service (SMS), or a range of applications ("apps") for mobile devices.

YouTube: A video-sharing website on which registered users can upload, view, and share a wide variety of video content, including movie and TV clips, and music videos, as well as amateur content such as video blogging, short original videos, and educational videos.

NOTE

1 This section is based on and abridged from Alain Lemay's excellent *15 Commandments for Government Agencies on Twitter.*

WORKS CITED

Air Force Public Affairs Agency. n.d. "Air Force Web Posting Response Assessment." www.afpc.af.mil/shared/media/document/AFD-091210-037.pdf

Antelman, Kristin. 2004. "Do Open-Access Articles Have a Greater Research Impact?" *College & Research Libraries* 65: 372–382.

Baily, Martin N., and Robert Lawrence. 2001. "Do We Have a New E-conomy?" *American Economic Review* 91 (2): 308–312.

BoardReader. n.d. "Overview." www.boardreader.com/info/about.htm

Borins, Sandford. 2011. "Which Digital State Is Now at the Leading Edge? Contrasting Canada and the United States." In *Public Sector Reform Using Information Technologies: Transforming Policy into Practice*, edited by Thanos Papadopoulos and Panagiotis Kanellis, 1–16. Hershey, PA: IGI Global.

Borins, Sandford, Kenneth Kernaghan, David Brown, Nick Bontis, Perri 6, and Fred Thompson. 2007. *Digital State at the Leading Edge*. Toronto: University of Toronto Press.

British Columbia. Office of the Chief Information Officer, Ministry of Citizens' Services. 2009. "Policy Summary No. 33: Use of Social Media in the B.C. Public Service." www.cio.gov.bc.ca/local/cio/informationsecurity/policy/summaries/33_social_media.pdf

Campbell, Rob. 2008. "The Facebook Factor in Canadian Politics." Ezine9.com. http://business.ezine9.com/the-facebook-factor-in-canadian-politics-3a34bbb8b5.html

Eagleton-Pierce, Matthew. 2001. "The Internet and the Seattle WTO Protests." *Peace Review* 13: 331–337.

Empson, Rip. 2012. "Google Biz Chief: Over 10M Websites Now Using Google Analytics." Tech Crunch. April 12. techcrunch.com/2012/04/12/google-analytics-officially-at-10m/

Ferguson, Rob. 2008. "3-year Driver Curb Planned for Youths." *Toronto Star*, November 18. www.thestar.com/news/ontario/article/538684--3-year-driver-curb-planned-for-youths

Google Developers. 2014. "Google Analytics: Report Data Calculation." Google.com. developers.google.com/analytics/resources/concepts/gConceptsDataCalculation

Hajjem, Chawki, Stevan Harnad, and Yves Gingras. 2005. "Ten-year Cross-disciplinary Comparison of the Growth of Open Access and How It Increases Research Citation Impact." *IEEE Data Engineering Bulletin* 28 (4): 39–47.

Hébert, Blaise. 2012. "Winning Over Hearts and Minds." Paper presented at the Public Sector Social Media 2012 Conference, hosted by the Conference Board of Canada, Ottawa, Ontario.

Institute for Citizen-Centred Service. 2009. "Case Study: Social Media Use in the City of Ottawa." www.iccs-isac.org/en/msd/casestudies/msd_socialMedia_Ottawa.htm

Klout. 2012. "What Is Influence?" *Klout*. December 4. http://support.klout.com/customer/portal/articles/679051-what-is-influence-

Lacharite, Jason. 2011. "The Internet and Electronic Democracy in Canada: Reaching the Limits of E-Government and the False Promise of Digital Democracy?" *Canadian Political Science Review* 5 (1): 1–19.

Lemay, Alain. n.d. *15 Commandments for Government Agencies on Twitter*. Ottawa: Focus One Communications. http://api.ning.com/files/CsePX8HSY-

2R5Ealmirobz3-lYcIGOHJWTspOwD9Eh9WtSHl27KWlVTyj9psnPV1M-VB95lHceIxfHE0Ixol2vrQse-VWz4HNm/ThouShaltTweetGuideFinal.pdf

Margetts, Helen. 2009. "The Internet and Public Policy." *Policy & Internet* 1: 1–21.

McNutt, Kathleen. 2012. "From the Outside In: The External Face of e-Government." *Journal of Information Technology and Politics* 9: 319–337.

McNutt, Kathleen. 2014. "Public Engagement in the Web 2.0 Era." *Canadian Public Administration* 57 (2): 49–70.

McNutt, Kathleen, and Meaghan Carey. 2008. *Canadian E-Government: Purpose and Practice*. Regina, SK: Saskatchewan Institute of Public Policy.

McNutt, Kathleen, and Gregory Marchildon. 2009. "Think Tanks and the Web: Measuring Visibility and Influence." *Canadian Public Policy* 35: 219–236.

Ontario. Ministry of Transportation. 2008. "Making Ontario's Roads Safer." News release. November 18. http://news.ontario.ca/mto/en/2008/11/making-ontarios-roads-safer.html

Richards, Steve. 2010. "Why You Need a Social Media Strategy, Not a Facebook Strategy." Econsultancy. August 10. https://econsultancy.com/blog/6406-why-you-need-a-social-media-strategy-not-a-facebook-strategy

Roy, Jeffrey. 2006. *Transformation for the Digital Age: E-Government in Canada*. Ottawa: University of Ottawa Press.

Scott, David Meerman. 2008. "The US Air Force: Armed with Social Media." WebInkNow. December 15. www.webinknow.com/2008/12/the-us-air-force-armed-with-social-media.html

Shachtman, Noah. 2009. "Air Force Releases 'Counter-Blog' Marching Orders." Wired. January 6. www.wired.com/dangerroom/2009/01/usaf-blog-respo/

Skeaff, Bruce. 2012. "The Challenges of Leadership: Overcoming Obstacles on the Path to Social Media Success." Paper presented at the Public Sector Social Media 2012 Conference, hosted by the Conference Board of Canada, Ottawa, Ontario.

Treasury Board of Canada Secretariat (TBS). 2011. "Guideline for External Use of Web 2.0." November 18. www.tbs-sct.gc.ca/pol/doc-eng.aspx?id=24835&section=text

Twitter. 2014. "The Twitter Rules." Twitter.com. https://support.twitter.com/articles/18311#

Waters, Richard D. 2007. "Nonprofit Organizations' Use of the Internet: A Content Analysis of Communication Trends on the Internet Sites of the Philanthropy 400." *Nonprofit Management and Leadership* 18: 59–76.

CHAPTER 10
CONCLUSION

CHAPTER OVERVIEW

This chapter contains a capstone activity learners can use to apply the knowledge and skills covered throughout the book in a single, integrative exercise based on developing a contribution to a fictitious cabinet submission on a major public sector initiative.

LEARNING OBJECTIVE

After completing this chapter, you will be able to apply the knowledge and skills covered throughout the book in a single, integrative exercise.

INTRODUCTION

This book began by defining communications as a core management function that both public and private organizations use to control the flow of information between themselves and their various internal and external audiences to help achieve strategic organizational goals. In the public sector specifically, communications is defined as an information- or knowledge-based resource that is provided or withheld from societal actors to "influence and direct policy actions" in two separate domains (Howlett 2009, 24). In the substantive domain, public sector organizations use communications to effect change in "the type, quantity, price or other characteristics of goods and services being produced in society, either by the public or private sector" (Howlett, Ramesh, and Perl 2009, 35). In the procedural domain, organizations use communications to effect change in how individuals and groups behave in policy processes, particularly the agenda-setting and formulation stages at the front end and the implementation and evaluation stages at the back (Howlett 2009; Howlett, Ramesh, and Perl 2009).

Chapter 1 reports that, in practice, public sector organizations use communications to achieve a blend of substantive and procedural goals, with the specific kind and exact mix of instrumentation used by any one organization determined by that organization's mandate and overall role in the public sector. In organizations such as the federal Privy Council Office and Ontario Cabinet Office that have strong procedural mandates (in this case, to help first ministers and their cabinets set the government's overall strategic directions and legitimize government actions once determined), communications personnel work almost exclusively in areas dedicated to achieving procedural goals. In contrast, in organizations such as Statistics Canada and the Toronto Transit Commission that have strong substantive mandates (focused primarily on the production and delivery of public goods and services), communications personnel focus on producing and disseminating information to support producer and consumer behaviour. Organizations such as Health Canada exist somewhere in between, with roughly half of staff engaged at the front end of the procedural domain, using communications tools to influence the behaviour of actors in various policy stages, and the other half designing and using communications tools to change the behaviour of producers and consumers of goods and services. This distribution of resources across the substantive and procedural continuum at Health Canada reflects its role as industry regulator, fiduciary of public health, and policy-maker and executor.

For the practitioner, this book uses a strategic approach to explain how professional communications is conducted in Canada. It defines the main areas of responsibility in a new professional's communications job according to the key activities involved in strategic public sector communications, and is organized accordingly. From a strategic perspective, the main activities involved in the conduct of professional public sector communications can be defined as follows:

- describing the strategic environment that defines and within which public sector communications takes place
- identifying the individuals and groups that have a stake in how public sector organizations achieve their strategic goals

- defining the objectives that communications initiatives are designed to achieve
- crafting the key messages that organizations use to communicate with targeted audiences
- developing a set of core tactics used to transmit key messages to targeted audiences, namely press releases, backgrounders, FAQs, letters to the editor, speeches, public events, and various Web 2.0 technologies
- evaluating whether and how communications activities achieve stated objectives

Within this framework, chapters 2 through 4 explain the broad, strategic environment in which communications takes place in Canada's public sector. Chapters 5 through 7 describe the main tactics that public sector organizations use to achieve strategic communications objectives, with a particular focus on those tactics with which new professionals are expected to be proficient at the start of their careers. Chapter 8 highlights some of the key research tools that public sector organizations use in communications evaluation to establish baselines and populate indicators at the outtake and outcome levels. Chapter 9 defines what public sector communications professionals need to know about Web 2.0 technologies in order to research, analyze, communicate, and evaluate effectively in the Web 2.0 environment.

LEARNING ACTIVITY

This final, capstone activity is designed to provide learners with an opportunity to apply the knowledge and skills covered throughout the book in a single, integrative exercise. The activity itself requires learners to work in small groups of three or four to develop a communications plan and supporting tactics for a fictitious cabinet submission on a major public sector initiative.

Background: Cabinet Decision Making in Canada

In Canada's Westminster-based parliamentary system, the **cabinet** is the decision-making body led by the first minister (premiers in the provinces, the prime minister federally) and composed of those individuals whom the first minister appoints as ministers with specific governmental responsibilities. Cabinet as a whole is responsible for deciding on the overall direction and key issues of government. It is the central and final forum for reaching a politically authoritative consensus on government issues under the first minister's leadership. The major decisions that cabinets typically make include the creation, elimination, or restructuring of an existing program or service; the introduction of a new policy position or changes to an existing policy position; any proposal that requires the passage of legislation or regulation; a public response to an urgent, strategic, or unanticipated issue; the launch of a high-profile external consultation; and/or to address a significant issue for intergovernmental affairs. Cabinets also make decisions about a variety of other more operational issues, including review and approval of regulations, orders-in-council, and appointments.

Cabinet Structure

In most jurisdictions, **full cabinet** is a largely formalized structure used to confirm the decisions and recommendations made by subsidiary committees of cabinet. Full cabinet membership includes the first minister and all members appointed to cabinet. The most important cabinet committee is the **priorities and policy committee**, a small 8- to 10-member "inner cabinet" chaired by the first minister and composed of his or her most trusted ministers, who are also the chairs of the other policy committees. This body is usually responsible for determining the government's overall medium- to long-term goals and priorities. **Policy committees** give cabinet members the opportunity to review policy proposals from departments in detail, direct revisions where necessary, and make recommendations to full cabinet on how to proceed. **Treasury boards** are cabinet committees that provide oversight of the government's financial management and spending, as well as on human resources issues. In most jurisdictions, the treasury board (or its equivalent) acts as the employer for the public service, and establishes policies and common standards for administrative, personnel, financial, and organizational practices across government. It also controls the allocation of financial resources to departments and programs. **Legislation and regulation committees** ("legs and regs") provide detailed scrutiny of all legislation, regulations, orders-in-council, and petitions to cabinet.

Cabinet Decision-Making Process

The following is a simplified description of how cabinet decision making typically proceeds in Canada:

1. An individual department develops a submission to cabinet (variously called a memorandum to cabinet, cabinet submission, etc.) that describes the nature of the issue or problem for which cabinet direction is being sought; the government's current position on the issue or problem; some kind of justification of why action is needed at this time; options for proceeding, including a full cost and risk analysis; a recommended option; and a communications plan for that option.

2. The minister of the sponsoring department presents the request for cabinet decision to a policy committee of cabinet.

3. The chair of the policy committee reports back to full cabinet with the committee's recommendations.

4. If there are fiscal, legislative, or regulatory proposals, these also need to be vetted by the appropriate subcommittee of cabinet prior to proceeding to full cabinet.

5. Full cabinet reviews the recommendations of subcommittees, makes a decision, and issues specific directions to the departments involved via an official cabinet minute.

6. If legislation or a regulation is required, the department of justice works with legislative staff to draft the statutory instrument prior to introduction.

Decision-Making Documents

In all jurisdictions, cabinets make decisions on the basis of formally submitted decision documents referred to variously as memoranda to cabinet, **cabinet submissions**, or cabinet decision documents. Despite differences in name and content, five components typically make up a document seeking a cabinet decision in Canada: (1) an analysis document, (2) an implementation plan, (3) a legislative strategy, (4) a communications plan, and (5) an overview document. The **analysis document** forms the intellectual "heart" of a cabinet submission—it includes all of the sponsoring department's "due diligence" on the issue. It describes the issue to be discussed at cabinet, the minister's recommended course of action and any funding requirements, the rationale for proceeding, alternative options that could be pursued, and considerations to be taken into account. The **implementation plan** provides details on how the recommended option would be implemented, operated, and terminated over its timeline. In most jurisdictions, information covered in the implementation plan is often a summary of a more detailed implementation submission that would go to the treasury board for approval after the initial submission to cabinet. The **legislative strategy document** contains details for a legislative strategy, particularly if the policy initiative requires the passage of some type of statutory instrument. The **communications plan** sets out the strategy for communicating the substance of cabinet's decision. The **overview document** provides a short, concise, readable overview of the request for a cabinet decision.

The Activity

In groups of three or four, identify a major federal or provincial/territorial initiative that has not been implemented to date. The initiative should have been clearly identified in the governing party's electoral platform, discussed in a recent throne speech, and potentially mentioned in a recent budget speech.

Once you have identified such an initiative, imagine that your group has been tasked with contributing to a fictitious cabinet submission on that initiative by drafting an overview document, a communications plan, and various communications products to support delivery as follows.

Activity 10.1: The Overview Document

The overview document (1,000 words/two pages maximum) should include the following:

- *key issue*: a one-sentence summary of the issue cabinet is being asked to address
- *rationale*: a clear discussion of why the government needs to act on this issue at this time, for example, a recent court ruling, a binding international agreement, an interprovincial agreement, an economic benefit that will be missed, an election commitment
- *recommended course of action*: a discussion of the specific roles and authorities of respective departments in implementing the initiative, any statutory instruments that are likely to be used (legislation, regulation), and a high-level plan for funding the initiative
- *key considerations*: a discussion of possible adverse consequences of proceeding and not proceeding, potential impacts on other

programs and services, potential effects on intergovernmental relations, and potential budgetary concerns

Activity 10.2: The Communications Plan

The communications plan (2,500 words/five pages maximum) should include the following:

- *communications objectives and considerations*: a clear rationale of how the initiative is linked to the government's strategic agenda, three or four objectives that will be achieved through the communications plan, and a detailed discussed of expected results
- *public environment analysis*: an assessment of the public environment that identifies and describes key stakeholders, the state of public opinion on the initiative, federal/provincial/territorial positions on the initiative, and any related media coverage
- *anticipated reaction*: a detailed description of the anticipated reaction from key stakeholders
- *key messages*: a broad overview of the "storyline" for the initiative, as well as three to five key messages for the initiative
- *tactics*: a detailed description, including rationale, of the specific tactics that will be used to deliver the key messages (both traditional and new media tactics)
- *evaluation strategy*: a detailed description of how the communications plan will be measured for effectiveness

Activity 10.3: The Tactics

For your chosen initiative, develop the following:

- one press release for print media (500 words/one page maximum);
- one backgrounder for a website (1,000 words/two pages maximum);
- one FAQ for a website (10 questions and answers/one page maximum);
- one letter to the editor of a local newspaper (250 words maximum);
- one speech to be delivered by a senior organizational spokesperson (a minister or deputy minister) to a public audience at a major initiative launch event (500 words maximum);

- a plan for a major launch event (1,500 words/three pages maximum) that includes
    - event objectives and target audience(s);
    - three possible event locations;
    - a realistic budget for the event (based on primary research);
    - a promotional strategy;
    - a critical path to delivery; and
    - a strategy for communicating in the Web 2.0 environment, including output, outtake, and outcome objectives and recommended Web 2.0 platforms.

Be sure that these tactics are consistent with the key messages you developed as part of activities 10.1 and 10.2 above.

FURTHER READING

Ted Glenn's 2005 chapter "Politics, Personality and History in Ontario's Administrative Style" provides some insight into Ontario's cabinet decision-making machinery and process (in *Executive Styles in Canada: Cabinet Decision-Making Structures and Practices at the Federal and Provincial Levels*).

ONLINE RESOURCES

Theresa McKeown's "How to Write Memoranda to Cabinet" on her Public Sector Writing website provides additional insight into writing cabinet decision-making documents (www.publicsectorwriting.com/?page_id=383). The federal Privy Council Office provides technical guidance to authors of cabinet documents in "A Drafter's Guide to Cabinet Documents" (www.pco-bcp.gc.ca/index.asp?lang=eng&page=information&sub=publications&doc=mc/guide-eng.htm).

For an interesting example of a fictitious memo to the federal cabinet, see "Draft Memorandum to Cabinet: (Suggested) Framework Policies for the Canadian Broadcasting System" on the Friends of Canadian Broadcasting website (www.friends.ca/brief/383).

QUESTIONS FOR CRITICAL REFLECTION

1. How important do you think communications considerations are to cabinet decision making in Canada? What evidence do you have to support your position?

2. How important do you think the communications function is, in general, to the process of governance in Canada? What evidence do you have to support your position?

KEY TERMS

analysis document: Forms the intellectual "heart" of a cabinet submission and includes all of the sponsoring department's "due diligence" on the issue.

cabinet: The decision-making body led by the first minister (premiers in the provinces and the prime minister federally) and composed of those individuals whom the first minister appoints as ministers with specific governmental responsibilities.

cabinet submission: Also known as a memorandum to cabinet or a cabinet decision document, this is a formally submitted decision document that informs and supports cabinet decisions.

communications plan: The part of a cabinet submission that sets out the strategy for communicating the substance of cabinet's decision.

full cabinet: A largely formalized structure used to confirm the decisions and recommendations made by subsidiary committees of cabinet. Full cabinet membership includes the first minister and all members appointed to cabinet.

implementation plan: The part of a cabinet submission that provides details on how the recommended option would be implemented, operated, and terminated over its timeline.

legislation and regulation committees: Also known as "legs and regs" committees, these committees provide detailed scrutiny of all legislation, regulations, orders-in-council, and petitions to cabinet.

legislative strategy document: The part of a cabinet submission that contains details for a legislative strategy, particularly if the policy initiative requires the passage of some type of statutory instrument.

overview document: The part of a cabinet submission that provides a short, concise, readable overview of the request for a cabinet decision.

policy committees: These committees provide cabinet members with the opportunity to review policy proposals from departments in detail, direct revisions where necessary, and make recommendations to full cabinet on how to proceed.

priorities and policy committee: A small 8- to 10-member "inner cabinet" chaired by the first minister and composed of his or her most trusted ministers, who are also the chairs of the other policy committees. This body is usually responsible for determining the government's overall medium- to long-term goals and priorities.

treasury board: A specialized cabinet committee that provides oversight of the government's financial management and spending, as well as human resources issues.

WORKS CITED

Glenn, Ted. 2005. "Politics, Personality and History in Ontario's Administrative Style." In *Executive Styles in Canada: Cabinet Decision-Making Structures and Practices at the Federal and Provincial Levels*, edited by Luc Bernier, Keith Brownsey, and Michael Howlett, 155–170. Toronto: University of Toronto Press.

Howlett, Michael. 2009. "Government Communication as a Policy Tool: A Framework for Analysis." *Canadian Political Science Review* 3 (2): 23–37.

Howlett, Michael, M. Ramesh, and Anthony Perl. 2009. *Studying Public Policy: Policy Cycles & Policy Systems*. Don Mills, ON: Oxford University Press.

APPENDICES

APPENDIX 1.1: WHAT IS CANADA'S PUBLIC SECTOR?

According to Statistics Canada, the **public sector** refers to the collection of organizations involved in the production, ownership, sale, provision, delivery, and allocation of public goods and services (2013). Canada's public sector is composed of four concentric layers of organization: core government departments; agencies, boards, and commissions; public enterprises; and closely aligned organizations.

Core Government Departments

Canada's constitution provides for a system of government called **federalism** in which political power is divided between one federal government and 10 provincial governments. In this system, each level of government has authority to govern in a number of prescribed areas and includes both legislative and executive branches. The legislative branch (the **legislature**) is the body of government in which representatives elected by citizens make decisions about the common good, and issue laws based on those decisions. The **executive branch** is responsible for implementing the decisions made by the legislature. It is composed of a **political executive** (the first minister and his or her chosen ministers, who together exercise authority over the direction of governmental action) and a **permanent executive**, the system of authority, people, offices, and methods—the public administration—that political executives use to achieve defined objectives.

The government departments that make up the permanent executive form the core of Canada's public sector. Government departments are formally established under legislation to produce, deliver, and coordinate public goods and services. Government departments are headed by a cabinet minister, who is responsible for ensuring that the department operates within and achieves the government's overall strategic objectives, and a deputy minister, who oversees program delivery and internal departmental management. Table 1.2 identifies 10 major areas of government activity and provides examples of various Canadian government departments that fall within each area:

TABLE 1.2: CORE GOVERNMENT DEPARTMENT CLUSTER AREAS

Activity area	Examples of Canadian departments	Responsibilities
Community and Social Affairs	• Children and Family Development • Community and Social Services • Family Services and Labour • Francophone Affairs • Housing and Communication Development • Seniors • Social Development • Veterans' Affairs	Social assistance, child welfare, community development
Economic	• Agriculture and Rural Development • Economic Development and Trade • Industry and Economy • Energy, Mines, and Natural Gas • Fisheries and Aquaculture • Jobs, Tourism, and Skills Training	Economic development, trade, various supports to specific industries
Education	• Education • Advanced Education and Literacy • Apprenticeship and Trade Certification • Enterprise and Advanced Education • Training, Colleges, and Universities	Primary and secondary education, post-secondary education, apprenticeships, and labour market training
Environment	• Environment • Environment and Sustainable Resource Development • Natural Resources	Environmental protection, natural resource management and development
Foreign Affairs	• Defence • Foreign Affairs • International and Intergovernmental Relations	Relations with foreign governments
Health	• Health • Health and Long-Term Care • Sport and Recreation	Doctors, nurses, drugs, hospitals, long-term care, and public health
Human Services	• Citizen's Services • Citizenship • Human Services • Immigration and Multiculturalism	Citizenship and immigration
Intergovernmental	• Aboriginal and Northern Affairs • Aboriginal Relations • Intergovernmental Affairs • Municipal Affairs	Relations with the various levels of government in Canada
Justice	• Attorney General • Solicitor General • Justice • Community Safety and Correctional Services	Court administration services, criminal prosecutions, legal aid, policing, correctional facilities, public safety
Transportation and Infrastructure	• Highways and Infrastructure • Transportation and Infrastructure	Roads and highways, transportation planning

Source: Author.

ABCs and Public Enterprises

Agencies, boards, and commissions (ABCs) are the next layer in Canada's public sector and can be defined as a broad category in which organizations have statutory responsibilities to "administer, fix, establish, control, or regulate an economic, cultural, environmental, or social activity by regularized or established means in the public interest and in accordance with general policy guidelines established by the government" (Brown-John 1981, 35). Five main types of ABCs can be discerned here: (1) adjudicative bodies provide established, bias-free processes to settle disputes between individuals and public policies as set out in legislation, regulation, or policies (e.g., Ontario Municipal Board); (2) legislative bodies have authority to prescribe specific regulations within guidelines set out in legislation (e.g., Canadian Radio-television and Telecommunications Commission); (3) research bodies conduct research and contribute to public policy (e.g., National Research Council, Social Sciences and Humanities Research Council); (4) advisory bodies provide advice to governments on key aspects of public policy (e.g., Ontario's Pesticide Advisory Committee); and (5) administrative bodies provide coordination and administrative services (e.g., Council of Ministers of Education, Canada; Intergovernmental Conference Secretariat).

ABCs and Crown corporations have statutory foundations that set out their mandates, authorities, and structures, as well as the roles and responsibilities of key actors (e.g., chair, the board of directors, chief executive officer). And like Crown corporations, ABCs are usually governed by some type of board appointed by the minister and are accountable to the legislature and for the exercise of their powers. Consistent with their quasi-judicial role, adjudicative ABCs are themselves responsible for developing specific rules and procedures and for following them in their decision making. Ministers are ultimately responsible for the operations of ABCs, but like Crown corporations, they must maintain an arm's-length relationship with them—especially adjudicative bodies.

Public enterprises are "companies in the ordinary sense of the term, whose mandate relates to industrial, commercial or financial activities but which also belongs to the state, are owned by the government or the Crown or whose sole shareholder is the government or the Crown" (Barker 2008, 90). Examples of federal Crown corporations include the Canadian Broadcasting Corporation, the Canada Mortgage and Housing Corporation, Canada Post, and the Royal Canadian Mint. Provincial Crown corporations include the Liquor Control Board of Ontario, the Nova Scotia Gaming Corporation, and Manitoba Hydro. Table 1.3 provides a list of federal Crown corporations organized by department:

TABLE 1.3: FEDERAL CROWN CORPORATIONS GROUPED BY PORTFOLIO

Portfolio	Crown Corporation
Agriculture and Agri-Food	Canadian Dairy Commission
	Farm Credit Canada
Atlantic Canada Opportunities Agency	Enterprise Cape Breton Corporation
Canadian Heritage and Official Languages	Canada Council for the Arts
	Canadian Broadcasting Corporation
	Canadian Museum for Human Rights
	Canadian Museum of History
	Canadian Museum of Immigration at Pier 21
	Canadian Museum of Nature
	National Arts Centre Corporation
	National Gallery of Canada
	National Museum of Science and Technology
	Telefilm Canada
Citizenship, Immigration, and Multiculturalism	Canadian Race Relations Foundation
Employment and Social Development	Canada Mortgage and Housing Corporation
Finance	Bank of Canada
	Canada Deposit Insurance Corporation
	Canada Development Investment Corporation
	Canada Pension Plan Investment Board
	PPP Canada Inc.
	Royal Canadian Mint
Fisheries and Oceans	Freshwater Fish Marketing Corporation
Foreign Affairs, Trade, and Development	Canadian Commercial Corporation
	Export Development Canada
	International Development Research Centre
	National Capital Commission
Industry	Business Development Bank of Canada
	Canadian Tourism Commission
	Standards Council of Canada
Natural Resources	Atomic Energy of Canada Limited
Public Works and Government Services	Canada Lands Company Limited
	Defence Construction (1951) Limited
Transport	Atlantic Pilotage Authority
	Blue Water Bridge Authority
	Canada Post Corporation
	Canadian Air Transport Security Authority
	Federal Bridge Corporation Limited
	Great Lakes Pilotage Authority
	Laurentian Pilotage Authority
	Marine Atlantic Inc.
	Pacific Pilotage Authority
	Ridley Terminals Inc.
	VIA Rail Canada Inc.
	Windsor-Detroit Bridge Authority
Treasury Board	Public Sector Pension Investment Board

Source: Treasury Board of Canada Secretariat. 2014. *Corporate Profiles—Crown Corporations.* Ottawa: Treasury Board of Canada Secretariat. www.tbs-sct.gc.ca/reports-rapports/cc-se/corporate-societe/ccp-pse-eng.asp

The government creates Crown corporations to achieve some defined public good that it feels cannot or will not be provided by the private sector, but that needs to be achieved outside of the human resource and administrative policies and procedures found in government. As such, each Crown corporation has its own foundational legislation that outlines its unique policy and operational frameworks, including the responsibilities of its boards of directors and chief executive officers, and the corporation's relationship with the minister responsible and, ultimately, the legislature. Political executives retain ultimate control over the direction of Crown corporations, as ministers are usually responsible for appointing members to the corporation's board of directors, recommending the approval of the corporation's plans and budgets, and tabling its annual reports and summaries of its approved plans and budgets in Parliament. The board of directors is responsible for the overall management of the businesses, activities, and other affairs of the corporation; the CEO is responsible for the day-to-day management of the corporation on behalf of the board of directors.

Closely Aligned Organizations

The fourth layer of Canada's public sector involves **closely aligned organizations**, which are legally autonomous organizations with financial and administrative relationships with government that are sufficiently close as to make them, for all intents and purposes, government-directed organizations. Most of these organizations exist at the provincial/territorial and municipal levels in two primary areas—health and social services, and education. The former include hospitals and children's aid societies and the latter include universities, colleges, vocational and trade institutions, and elementary/secondary schools.

Municipal Government

Municipal government makes up a third—but constitutionally unrecognized—level of government in Canada. According to the Constitution, provincial governments have exclusive authority over the creation and organization of municipal governments in Canada. **Municipal governments** are local governments, which are often assigned powers over areas such as local transportation systems, land use planning and development, waste management, public utilities, and parks and recreation.

Like their federal and provincial counterparts, the public sector at the municipal level has a core made up of departments, an array of agencies, boards, commissions, and public enterprises that are accountable to municipal councils, and closely aligned organizations that are largely reliant on municipal governments for funding. Table 1.4 illustrates the scope and range of organizations that exist within the City of Toronto's broader public sector:

TABLE 1.4: ORGANIZATIONS WITHIN THE CITY OF TORONTO'S BROADER PUBLIC SECTOR

| Agencies | | | Corporations | |
Service agencies	Quasi-judicial and adjudicative boards	Partnered agency	City corporations	Partnered corporation
• Board of Health • Exhibition Place • Heritage Toronto • Police Services Board • Public Library Board • Sony Centre for the Performing Arts • St. Lawrence Centre for the Arts • Toronto Atmospheric Fund • Toronto Centre for the Arts • Toronto Parking Authority • Toronto Transit Commission • Toronto Zoo • Yonge-Dundas Square	• Committee of Adjustment • Committee of Revision • Compliance Audit Committee • Property Standards Committee/Fence Viewers • Rooming House Licensing Commissioner • Sign Variance Committee • Toronto Licensing Tribunal	• Toronto and Region Conservation Authority	• Build Toronto Inc. • Casa Loma Corporation • MasterCard Centre • Toronto Community Housing Corporation • Toronto Hydro Corporation • Toronto Port Lands Company	• Waterfront Toronto

Source: City of Toronto. 2014. *City of Toronto Agencies and Corporations.* www.toronto.ca/abcc/pdf/chart-abcc.pdf

Public Sector Employment

Employment statistics provide a good indication of the relative size of Canada's public sector. The public sector employed just over one-fifth (3.6 million people) of Canada's total workforce of 17.4 million people in 2011, with health, social service, and education organizations representing just over half of all public sector workers (1.9 million people). Core government departments and their agencies, boards, and commissions at the federal, provincial, and local levels accounted for 40 percent of all public sector workers (1.4 million), with the remaining 10 percent (300,000 people) of public sector workers employed in public enterprises.

TABLE 1.5: EMPLOYMENT BY SELECTED INDUSTRY, 2011

Selected industry	Number of individuals employed
Canada total	17,354,000
Public sector	3,631,837
Government	3,313,320
Federal general government	427,093
Provincial and territorial general governments	356,709
Health and social service institutions	859,350
Universities, colleges, vocational and trade institutions	382,245
Local general government	608,094
Local school boards	679,828
Government business enterprises	318,519
Federal government business enterprises	102,319
Provincial and territorial business enterprises	147,914
Local government business enterprises	68,286

Source: Statistics Canada. 2013. *Public Sector Employment, Wages and Salaries (Employees)*. CANSIM, Table 183-0002. www.statcan.gc.ca/tables-tableaux/sum-som/l01/cst01/govt54a-eng.htm

KEY TERMS

agencies, boards, and commissions (ABCs): A broad category of public sector organizations that have statutory responsibilities to "administer, fix, establish, control, or regulate an economic, cultural, environmental, or social activity by regularized or established means in the public interest and in accordance with general policy guidelines established by the government" (Brown-John 1981, 35).

closely aligned organizations: Legally autonomous organizations that have sufficiently close financial and administrative relationships with government as to make them, for all intents and purposes, government-directed organizations.

executive branch: The branch of government responsible for implementing the decisions made by the legislature. In Canada, the executive branch is composed of a political executive and a permanent executive.

federalism: A system of government in which political power is divided between one national central government (the federal government in Canada) and multiple subnational governments (provincial/territorial governments in Canada).

legislature: The branch of government wherein representatives elected by citizens make decisions about the common good, and issue laws based on those decisions.

municipal government: A local level of government assigned powers over areas such as local transportation systems, land use planning and development, waste management, public utilities, and parks and recreation. In Canada, provincial governments have exclusive authority over the creation and organization of municipal governments.

permanent executive: The system of authority, people, offices, and methods—the public administration—that political executives use to achieve defined objectives.

political executive: The first minister and his or her chosen ministers who together exercise authority over the direction of governmental action.

public enterprise: A company in the ordinary sense of the term, with a mandate related to industrial, commercial, or financial activities, but which also belongs to the state; a public enterprise is owned by the government or the Crown or its sole shareholder is the government or the Crown.

public sector: The collection of organizations involved in the production, ownership, sale, provision, delivery, and allocation of public goods and services. Canada's public sector is composed of four concentric layers of organization: core government departments; agencies, boards, and commissions; public enterprises; and closely aligned organizations.

WORKS CITED

Barker, Paul. 2008. *Public Administration in Canada*. Toronto: Thomson Nelson.

Brown-John, C. Lloyd. 1981. *Canadian Regulatory Agencies*. Toronto: Butterworths.

City of Toronto. 2014. *City of Toronto Agencies and Corporations*. www.toronto.ca/abcc/pdf/chart-abcc.pdf

Statistics Canada. 2013. *Public Sector Employment, Wages and Salaries (Employees)*. CANSIM, Table 183-0002. www.statcan.gc.ca/tables-tableaux/sum-som/l01/cst01/govt54a-eng.htm

Treasury Board of Canada Secretariat. 2014. *Corporate Profiles—Crown Corporations*. Ottawa: Treasury Board of Canada Secretariat. www.tbs-sct.gc.ca/reports-rapports/cc-se/corporate-societe/ccp-pse-eng.asp

APPENDIX 5.1: SOCIAL MEDIA IN THE PUBLIC SECTOR SPEECH
Remarks by the Deputy Head and Librarian and Archivist of Canada

Good afternoon.

To begin, I would like to thank the Conference Board of Canada for giving me the opportunity to share my thoughts with you today.

As the Deputy Head and Librarian and Archivist of Canada, I have the privilege to look at what is happening in Canadian society from a unique perspective.

More than any other organization, Library and Archives Canada must be extremely careful when it comes to dealing with information resources because they are our raw material. We exist for them. This is our raison d'être. We must ensure that Canadians of today and tomorrow will have access to the information they need to function as a society.

It is not just a matter of providing the required evidence for the administration of the country and its court system, it is also for scientific purposes and for providing Canadians with material that will help them be creative, to continue to construct their identities and support their democracy.

The explosive development of social networking and its effects on the creation of information within both the public sector and Canadian society is fascinating for us. But, as you can imagine, it poses monumental challenges, since the habits and traditional ways of creating information, and the nature and attributes of it, are also changing rapidly. And this has consequences on our traditional ways of functioning as a society, as institutions, organizations, and individuals.

Because Library and Archives Canada is one of the main organizations that has the mandate to manage these information resources for the long term, you will understand that my enthusiasm for social media carries with it some big questions: What is this? What is going on here? What is happening to our traditional ways of operating? Where is my stuff that used to come from publishers? Where is it coming from now? The Web? Who creates it? Is it reliable? Authentic? And so on. It raises a whole new series of questions.

Today, I would like to discuss three of them with you.

First, what is really changing here? We are and have been in the digital era for some time, so what does this mean?

Social media is one aspect of it—an important aspect that is very tangible. But there is more happening out there, which may not always be so tangible but will be quite important for all of us.

Second, I would like to discuss the resulting social transformation. Social media presents a challenge for our society because it means a change in the way we function. But it also represents a wonderful opportunity to become better citizens—to be more informed and engaged, to create better organizations that are more transparent and responsive, and to be more effective as a society, to be better off altogether with a greater knowledge of the beliefs and preferences of each other. In my view, social media can therefore be a great enabler for modern societies.

Third and finally, I would like to give you a brief overview of how Library and Archives Canada is adapting to social media and, more generally, the digital era and how we are reinventing ourselves to respond to this revolution. This will serve as an illustration of how government can rethink its approaches to take advantage of social media.

Let's now turn our attention to the first point and look at how the rise of the digital culture is affecting our society's evolution.

Let me begin from my perspective as Librarian and Archivist of Canada: social media is more than just a communication tool or a space for chit-chat. It is, in many instances and increasingly so, the place where we circulate authentic authoritative information, the place where decisions are being influenced and made, the place where the information needed by jurists, historians and others who are "information dependent" will be found to nurture their processes and continue to make society functional. It is a key component of our modern environment. We cannot ignore that fact.

The interactivity of the Internet, allowing millions of users to communicate directly through blogs, and platforms like YouTube, Facebook, and Twitter has challenged the domination of our traditional media. Behind this great leap in communications technology, there is also a great social and human transformation. This is not the first time we have seen such a change.

And today, the passage from the analogue age to the digital age puts into question the nature of our communications systems, in particular the nature of our writing system. Simply put, we can ask how social media is altering how we create, authenticate, preserve, and access information now and how we will do so in the future?

This is crucial because fundamentally, the manner in which information is encoded and communicated affects the social conventions and power relations within a society. Information is not neutral; neither is the way it is transmitted. For instance, as humanity moved from an oral culture to a literate society, it moved from different social structures and created different sets of complexity.

Oral systems were under the influence of storytellers, orators, public speakers. Writing systems have been under the influence of the literates, the writers, and the publishers.

This means that, over the years, the population at large has functioned within sets of conventions determined by those who made those systems work. In practice, what does it mean?

It means that, in order for scientific, literary, political, or economic ideas and findings to exist and circulate, they had to fall within that triage exercise and filtering system. This was our guarantee of quality, authenticity, and authority.

We used to rely on it to function. It was the convention, the key trust of our social system. This is still true today but it is somehow crumbling.

With the rise of communication in digital format simply "mediated" by the Internet via social media, we reintroduce an element of the oral culture into societal discourse. What is the impact of that change?

Something is being transformed here and it is profound. And this brings me to my second main point.

The ephemeral quality of digital information is more like the ephemeral nature of the spoken word than the enduring presence of the written word captured in clay, parchment, or paper. This written word was challenged, annotated, verified, reviewed, revisited, built upon, etc.

Our relationships and traditional beliefs vis-à-vis information, are changing. Our expectations vis-à-vis content are different. We do not read the way we used to. This is because what we have in front of us has different attributes, and doesn't come from the same origins. The reputed analyst is no longer significantly different from the blogger. Is it not fair to ask, in today's environment, what is, if any, the difference between an analysis and an opinion?

Today, conventional practices that characterize written communication are being transformed by new behaviours made possible by the expansion of digital communication and social media.

For instance, in government, the notions of transparency and access to information are changing with the recent inclusion of electronic conversations conveyed by email and text messaging.

And placing restraints on the flow of information by assigning secret or sensitive status to some of the information is more and more difficult than it was in the realm of paper.

As well, our notions of privacy are also evolving.

These days, you can find pictures of yourself on the Internet in photos of your first grade class, a university party or those taken randomly on the street. We can be filmed at any time without our consent and this can be uploaded to the Internet.

Given the popularity of Facebook and how people are using it to express themselves, to share their deepest concerns, beliefs, and motivations, it was only a matter of time before the courts were called upon to rule on whether what was posted on our Facebook—the private section—could be seized during litigation if it helped to render justice.

Similarly, our conception of copyright is changing rapidly.

We can also see that at the individual level, the rise of the digital landscape affects the way we read and write.

Certainly with the arrival of social media, people have learned to compress their messages into shorter units of discourse, often less than 144 characters. This has also brought about changes in how we communicate. It stands to reason that traditional forms of grammar and spelling have been transformed in this environment.

In a similar vein, we tend to read less from a single authoritative voice in a book and much more from extended conversations carried on by multiple (quote unquote) "speakers."

Overall, maybe we should think of this type of communication as a new system of human expression that brings us not only new ways to capture and represent information but turns it into new social conventions as well. For that, we must always keep in mind that "digitized" does not equal "digital." Digitized is essentially a digital surrogate of a physical information resource. Digital affects our relationship with the moment and context of creation, the dissemination, the format, the context of reading, the preservation, and the access to information resources.

Social media is more than just a new buzz. It has fundamental effects on the way we are organized and how we function as a society. There is a changing notion of authenticity and authority with regard to digital-borne information. Now information can easily be modified and repurposed, often leading to a situation where a later remixed version gains more importance than the original.

This, of course, has broad implications for the society in which we live and our bureaucracies that seek to administer government policy.

In order for our democracy to function effectively, we must, among other things, have reliable records that document why and how government decisions are made, what resources are allocated, and what are the results obtained.

This brings us closer to our own challenges.

The Government of Canada now uses social media and websites to conduct its business. It is fair to say that it is taking a measured and sensible approach to adopting these new platforms as part of its communication practices.

Why? Because of the unpredictable nature of technological innovation.

Government of Canada institutions have to provide Canadians with timely, accurate, and complete information about federal programs and services.

This is necessary in our democratic process.

It is also the key to safeguard Canadians' trust in public institutions.

We must therefore be prudent in the use of new communication platforms to assure continued confidence in these public institutions.

Charged with the responsibility of spending taxpayer dollars wisely, those of us who oversee budgetary expenditures cannot trade off fiscal responsibility for the desire to embrace the latest trend in communications technology just to appear "cool."

How are these communication technologies, such as social media and interactive websites, changing how public institutions conduct their business? Is the change profound or are we just replicating the use of traditional media on new platforms?

The impact and consequences of this shift are probably profound, but these communication technologies still rely on platforms that enable us as public institutions to exchange information with Canadians.

They rely on the basic notion of literacy, which is not necessarily about reading, or writing, or arithmetic, but rather about the capacity and competency of processing information resources differently.

This is the new social literacy of the 21st century.

How does the digital era translate in the day-to-day life of an organization? How can we respond to it? This will be my third point for today.

For Library and Archives Canada, it raises several important questions. And for each of you, it will raise different questions. But the point I am making here is that it is important to identify those questions within each of our own contexts. The main question we should all ask ourselves is how social media can truly support the mandates of our organizations. Social media potentially offers endless opportunities. But how can it truly improve our work or improve government?

Given that more and more communication that might have national significance is migrating to social media, how are we, at Library and Archives Canada, going to make sure that it becomes part of the documentary heritage that we preserve for future generations?

How are we going to separate what is significant from what constitutes noise?

How can we describe important information so that it can be discovered easily?

What measures will be put in place to ensure that the information is preserved?

Certainly, to face these challenges we will have to move beyond the methods of the past and develop new approaches, policies, and techniques.

And we shouldn't lose sight of the fact that the new communication applications create new opportunities to widen the scope of the meaningful participation afforded to citizens in regard to governance.

How do we capture outside experts on policy matters?

What should not be overlooked is that, when used intelligently, wikis and blogs can be used to tap into the "wisdom of crowds."

This will allow citizens to participate at the critical juncture of policy formation: when essential questions are being asked and when potential solutions are beginning to take shape at the table.

Essentially, Library and Archives Canada makes use of crowdsourcing to complete its own description activities, thereby enabling individuals to participate directly in the description and enrichment of Canada's documentary heritage.

For example, we have digitized approximately 200,000 photographs taken by the official photographers of the Department of National Defence between 1939 and 1945 in an online research tool entitled Faces of War.

This unique collection of images allows Canadians to interact and collaborate with Library and Archives Canada by adding comments to any of the photographs found in the Faces of War database. This is but one aspect of what we refer to as "crowdsourcing."

This has proven highly useful, not just for individual Canadians, but also for military historians reflecting on facts found in the photographs.

It also enables us as a nation to remember the people in these photographs, along with our veterans who experienced the hardships of war and military conflict.

In a similar vein, we have been working with the indigenous peoples of Canada's northern territories in a collaborative effort called Project Naming to provide biographical information to enrich the descriptions of photographs taken of Canada's north.

Again, we notice that the exercise has shown positive social benefits in that younger generations of First Nation peoples are reconnecting with their Elders and becoming more appreciative of their heritage.

We are also on Twitter, Facebook, and YouTube. We have a blog and we publish podcasts.

For Library and Archives Canada, social media brings two challenges. How can we use these new tools to make our collections more discoverable and accessible? How can we be more efficient and better serve Canadians using these tools? At the same time, we know that the right documents might be created outside of government circles and that getting them at the right time could also mean finding them in non-governmental sources. We need to ask ourselves how we can capture the right information to ensure that we properly document Canadian society and the country's heritage.

As a result, the task of providing Canadians with timely access to their authentic and authoritative documentary heritage is far more challenging today than before the arrival of the Internet.

Our most daunting task is to sort through the sea of noise represented by all the social media activity and identify the communication that has national significance. Conceptually, to move us forward on this front, we are in the process of developing what we call the whole-of-society approach. This is the answer to this challenge.

What we are doing is developing the tools that will help us observe any targeted area of Canadian society and analyze the social context in which the communication takes place.

This approach gives us the means to cast our net much wider and will allow us to capture the significant portions of social media activity as it relates to the communication occurring in more traditional sources.

To make this more concrete, imagine 50 years from now being able to call up on your screen not only the electoral results, newspaper articles, and television excerpts pertaining to the next federal election, but also representative samples of what was happening in the blogosphere, on Facebook, Twitter, and YouTube.

As you can imagine, to achieve this level of documentary capacity is a major challenge.

Nevertheless, it is well worth the effort as we will obtain a much better representation of Canadian society for documentary heritage purposes.

In closing, I would like to suggest that the rise of social media for government and non-governmental organizations represents both a rupture and continuity with our past.

The element of rupture arises when we try to apply traditional practices, which originated as the means of communication appropriate for the era of the printed written word, to the emerging digital environment.

What worked previously may no longer be transferable to the new order, so we must always be open to the possibility of change.

That being said, we cannot simply implement new methods for the sake of change.

The element of continuity must be within our guiding visions, the raison d'être of our organizations, to ensure that whatever adaptations we choose to undertake, they will be done to advance the core missions of our organizations.

Thank you.

Source: Library and Archives Canada. "Social Media in the Public Sector, 2012. Remarks by the Deputy Head and Librarian and Archivist of Canada." www.bac-lac.gc.ca/eng/news/speeches/Pages/social-media-in-the-public-sector-2012.aspx

APPENDIX 5.2: MANAGING OUR CITY'S GROWTH RESPONSIBLY SPEECH

Introduction
Good evening Ladies and Gentlemen. I am honoured and pleased to introduce the Operations Budget for 2013—totalling $65 million in services for Whitehorse Citizens.

This is the first Operations Budget for this Council and follows on the heels of the 2013–2016 Capital Budget approved by Council on Monday, January 29. I would like to thank Council and our administration for assembling Operations Budget 2013.

Context

Before I get into the details of the budget and on what basis it was developed, allow me to set the context. It is clear to me that our community continues to grow. According to the Bureau of Statistics, the population of Whitehorse has increased again this year and now stands at 27,323 people. I don't think it will be much longer before we surpass the 30,000 mark.

We note that construction in our city continues at a significant rate. A trip through the city's neighbourhoods leaves one with the impression that new builds, whether we're talking about detached, semi-detached, condominiums, or multi-family units, continues at an extraordinary pace.

New developments mean an increase to the city's tax base but also require municipal services and infrastructure in the form of roads, inspections, water and sewer, etc. I believe this Council has delivered an Operations Budget which responds to the city's growth and manages the challenges that accompany development of this nature.

Services for Citizens

Operations Budget 2013 is about services for citizens. These services include things like

- planning future land development opportunities;
- maintaining bridges, roads, and sewer mains;
- programs such as swimming lessons, sport development, and wellness programs at our recreation facilities, serving everyone from preschoolers to seniors;
- removing snow from our streets; and
- fire prevention and firefighting.

Budget Highlights

Operations Budget 2013 is also about new services.

Transit services: During the last six months, we have heard from residents and people involved in the education and private sectors about expanding the City's transit services. This budget responds to these interests by offering evening hours so that our residents who work or attend class past 7:00 pm will have a safe and inexpensive mode of transportation to get them safely to and from work or class. In addition, we intend to collaborate with Yukon College and our commercial partners to explore possibilities for employee and student bus passes.

Building inspections: We will invest in the City's building inspection capacity. During the last five years, building inspection activities have increased a fair amount. I believe this is yet more evidence of our community's growth. In 2013, the City will hire a building inspector, bringing the number of inspectors to five. We think this is an important investment at a critical time given the tragic event of January 2012 and the efforts of both the City and Government of Yukon to make oil-fired appliances safer in our communities.

Volunteer firefighters: Operations Budget 2013 rewards our hardworking volunteer firefighters who have not received an increase to the remuneration paid by the City for their services for well over five years. These are the people who work side-by-side with our firefighters to put fires out and help staff the fire hall when our regular members are responding to emergencies. We will recognize the dedication of these volunteers with an increase to their remuneration.

Balanced Budget

I am pleased to announce that this Council is tabling a balanced budget. We understand the importance of living within our means and controlling spending so that actions of this Council don't burden future Councils.

How did we achieve a balanced budget? By adopting a measured approach, involving both property tax increases and cost-cutting measures, so that at the end of 2013 the City's revenues will equal its expenditures.

Your Tax Dollars

To achieve a balanced budget, the City will

- increase residential and commercial property tax by 3.83%;
- increase curb-side garbage and compost collection fees from $8 to $9; and

- increase user fees for recreational facilities, as the City does each year, by 1.5%.

Utility rates for water and sewer will remain fixed at 2011 levels.

We recognize the importance of tax dollars the City receives from our residents and the business sector. These revenues among other sources provide the City with the resources it needs to deliver municipal services. When the City raises taxes, taxpayers expect a justification for this increase.

Let me make the case now:

Inflation: Each year we are faced with inflationary pressures. Whether it is food, gas, shelter, or electricity, costs increase each year. This year is no different, with inflation reaching nearly 2% in Whitehorse or 1.1% higher than the national rate.

Salary pressures: Salaries and benefits make up nearly half the operations budget. We have negotiated collective agreements with our employees that allow us to remain competitive in terms of making the City an employer of choice in what is also a competitive labour market. To attract employees who are capable and dedicated, we need to offer competitive salary and benefit packages.

City's reorganization: Recently the City completed a reorganization—prepared by an independent third party—focusing on how we are structured to deliver municipal services. The reorganization is a positive step forward as it ensures that we are properly aligned to meet expanding needs and greater responsibilities. This, however, requires financial support.

I think it is important to note that our tax rate, when compared to other cities in Canada, is competitive. Property tax for an average home in Whitehorse remains below the rates in cities such as St. John's, Medicine Hat, Toronto, Victoria, Halifax and Lethbridge to name but a few.

In addition, utility rates, or the rates residents pay for compost and garbage pickup and water and sewer, are on par with the rates charged in other Canadian cities.

Expenditure Reduction Plan

The Operations Budget, however, isn't solely about tax increases. We understand the importance of taking a responsible and balanced approach to managing the City's finances, especially when we are asking residents to contribute more.

This is why the City is implementing an expenditure reduction plan consisting of cost-cutting measures today and the potential for future reductions based on a service review exercise.

We have worked closely with administration to identify a number of measures to reduce and eliminate expenditures. We anticipate that this plan will save the City approximately $600,000. Put another way, we are avoiding an additional 2% tax increase that would result if we do not implement these reductions.

This will not be a painless exercise. Certain positions will be eliminated and employees may be transferred to jobs with a higher priority. Fortunately, services for the most part will not be affected by this reduction and, of course, the safety and welfare of our citizens is paramount.

Citizens may, however, encounter slightly longer lineups at City Hall.

In addition, we will close the Canada Games Centre for four additional statutory holidays, bringing the number of days the Centre is closed due to holidays to six. This will reduce staff costs and is consistent with the hours of operation for recreation facilities in other jurisdictions.

We also intend to reduce snow removal services in Whistle Bend until that neighbourhood is more developed and the tax base has increased.

Council and I want to mitigate any inconvenience these reductions may have on the citizens of Whitehorse. We also want to see service improvements for our residents by focusing on how we do things at the City.

Council and I have, therefore, directed Mr. Westby, our City Manager, to commence a full review of all City services. Mr. Westby has been given a tall order—examine the services offered by the City to determine how we can save the City money and improve services to meet the needs of our citizens and the City. This is a Council priority.

Affordable and Diverse Housing

Another priority of this Council has to do with the city's housing supply. In the last number of years, housing has been a preoccupation at all levels of government and for good reason.

We intend to continue working with our industry partners, the Government of Yukon, and the Whitehorse Chamber of Commerce—which I note is doing an admirable job of keeping this important issue on everyone's agenda.

As I noted previously, residential development in our city's neighbourhoods continues with new construction going up throughout the city. These include both private and public developments like: Brookside 34 units, Central Park

25 units, and Crocus Glen 35 units. There is also Whistle Bend with 3,500 units. Our hope is that these developments will begin to soften housing prices in Whitehorse, making it easier for people to enter the housing market.

The City, however, should not, indeed cannot, afford to be complacent. We readily acknowledge that our economic future is tied to the natural resource extraction sector, which will likely drive the territory forward for the foreseeable future. If the City is to do its part to ensure we are positioned to reap the full benefits of natural resource extraction, we must begin planning for this eventuality now.

This means examining areas in our city, such as the city's south or the Tank Farm, which could be suitable locations for the next Copper Ridge or Whistle Bend. It also means proactively working with the Government of Yukon and the First Nation governments of the Kwänlin Dun and Ta'an Kwäch'än, governments with land in strategic locations throughout the city, to identify the next area for land development.

In addition, we will be looking to new technologies, such as district heating sources, for future subdivisions as a way of reducing the city's carbon footprint and to relieve pressure on the Yukon power grid.

Improving Waste Management
Not all aspects of our city's growth have been favourable.

Here I am talking primarily about the waste generated by construction but also the choices that people make at the checkout. Between 2000 and 2011, the waste generated by the city's residents has increased by 85%. During this same period, the amount of waste diverted from the waste management facility has failed to keep pace.

In other words, we continue to produce more and more waste but we are not significantly increasing the amount of waste we divert from the waste management facility. The increase in waste puts direct pressure on the life of the landfill.

This has costs. A recent independent assessment of the city's waste management facility concluded that it has 41 years as opposed to 78 years left before it becomes completely full.

What this means for the City and its residents is that we have much less time to prepare for the decommissioning of the waste management facility. This has a projected cost of $13.5 million in today's dollars.

The assessment also recommended that the City change how it records its costs based on the expansion of the diversion services the City offers.

To a certain extent, general revenues are presently being used to offset part of the City's waste management costs—contrary to Council policy—which are meant to be addressed entirely on a cost-recovery basis.

We are, therefore, adopting two measures to address this priority area:

1. First, we will increase user fees for garbage, compost, and recycling to reflect the true cost of municipal waste management services, and we will prepare for decommissioning of the waste management facility by increasing the annual contributions to the capital reserve.
2. Second, we will introduce a Solid Waste Action Plan in the near future. The goal of this plan will be to maximize waste diversion and minimize waste generation as we move forward on the path toward zero waste. Council will be seeking public feedback during the development of this plan.

Conclusion

To summarize, Council is seeking to establish an operations budget which will manage taxpayer contributions in a responsible manner, consisting of

- modest tax increases, combined with targeted strategic increases in services, most important of which is transit;
- spending reductions, with a minimal reduction in services.

We are also looking to implement our strategic priorities by

- taking action to improve services for citizens,
- improving our waste management services through enhanced activity reporting and the implementation of a waste diversion strategy, and
- taking action to contribute to the conditions necessary for diverse and affordable housing to emerge.

I believe we are on the way to accomplishing these objectives with Operations Budget 2013.

Thank you.

Source: City of Whitehorse. 2013. "Mayor's Speech—Operations Budget 2013: Managing Our City's Growth Responsibly." www.city.whitehorse.yk.ca/modules/showdocument.aspx?documentid=3044

APPENDIX 6.1: EVENT BUDGET TEMPLATE

Show name:				
Show dates:				
Show location:				
	Estimate	**Cost**	**Variance**	**Comments**
Space rental				
Space				
Deposit				
Other				
Subtotal				
Exhibit				
Design				
Fabrication/purchase				
Exhibit refurbishing				
Graphics design				
Graphics production				
Refurbishing				
Rental				
Shipping preparations				
Storage (pro-rated)				
Insurance (pro-rated)				
Other				
Subtotal				
Shipping				
To show				
From show				
Show to show				
Customs broker				
Other				
Subtotal				
Personnel expenses				
Salaries				
Staff training				
Staff incentives				
Pre-show dinner				
Staff attire				
Transportation				
Hotel				
Food/entertainment				
Temps				
Other				
Subtotal				

Promotion				
Advertising				
Client hospitality				
Direct mail				
Giveaways				
Literature				
Mailing list rental				
Press conference				
Press kits				
Sponsorships				
Translation				
Website				
Other				
Subtotal				
Conference/seminars				
Audiovisual production				
Printing				
Speaker fees				
Speechwriter				
Other				
Subtotal				
Lead gathering				
Labour				
Lead forms—printing and design				
Card readers—rental				
Postage				
Telephone follow-up				
Other				
Subtotal				
On-site services				
Audiovisual production				
Carpet rental				
Cleaning				
Computer equipment rental				
Custom signage				
Drayage				
Electrical service				
Floral/plant rental				
Furniture rental				
Internet services				
Photography				
Riggers				
Security				
Telephone				
Set-up/dismantle labour				
Other				
Subtotal				

Follow-up and evaluation				
Mailings				
Lead follow-up				
Post event report				
Surveys				
Subtotal				
Miscellaneous				
GRAND TOTAL				

Source: Adapted from event management training materials developed by the Canada School of Public Service.

APPENDIX 6.2: EVENT CRITICAL PATH TEMPLATE

Event:					
Location:					
Dates:					
Date	**Task**	**Person responsible**	**Date to be completed**	**Comments**	**Complete**
12 months prior to event	• set objectives for participating in event • select space: study floor plans, traffic patterns, services, and audience makeup • read contract carefully; understand terms, show rules, payment schedule, and space assignment method (by product category, seniority, membership, etc.) • negotiate speaking, sponsorship, and exhibiting opportunities • send in space application and first payment • prepare budget • engage stakeholders				
6 months prior to event	• determine exhibit goals • select primary vendors (exhibit house, transportation company, installation/dismantle supplier) • decide if new exhibit is needed. If so, begin design process. (If using a portable, the design process may not require this much lead time.) • plan show advertising				
4 months prior to event	• select staff • make airline, hotel, and car reservations • determine exhibit needs (if using existing properties): refurbishments, additions, and changes • select display products • plan inquiry processing procedures • communicate with primary vendors (exhibit house, shipping, installation/dismantle) regarding services needed and dates • develop floor plan for exhibit • finalize new exhibit design • execute show-related advertising				
Date	**Task**	**Person responsible**	**Date to be completed**	**Comments**	**Complete**
3 months prior to event	• carefully read and review exhibitor manual • select portable exhibit supplier • review exhibit floor plan and note target dates and restrictions				

Date	Task	Person responsible	Date to be completed	Comments	Complete
	• plan any in-booth presentations/demonstrations • create list of required services, noting deadlines for "early bird" discounts • distribute event plan to staff • reserve any additional meeting rooms (for hospitality events, press conferences, etc.) • select catering menus (for hospitality events, press events, etc.) • meet deadlines for free publicity in the exhibitor guide preview • submit authorization form if you are using an exhibitor-appointed contractor • plan pre-show meeting				
2 months prior to event	• preview new custom exhibit • finalize graphics art/copy • plan and arrange any temporary staffing needs • order staff badges • send information to other branches or partners exhibiting in booth • create and order lead forms; finalize inquiry processing procedures • prepare orders for shipping, electrical, cleaning, floral, etc. Take advantage of any pre-pay discounts • if using suppliers other than official show contractors, send notification and proof of insurance to show management • follow up on all promotions, making sure everything is ready to ship by target date • prepare press kits • check/update budget • develop VIP treatment/tours, etc. • check with staff on airline and hotel reservations and travel dates; make needed changes • develop briefing packet for booth staff • schedule training for booth staff at show • send reminder to upper management about briefing meetings (in office and at show); include agenda				
Date	**Task**	**Person responsible**	**Date to be completed**	**Comments**	**Complete**
1 month prior to event	• follow up on shipping orders • follow up on installation/dismantle schedule; get an estimate on costs • call to reconfirm airline, hotel, and car reservations; make needed changes • follow up on target dates with all vendors • confirm availability of display products/literature • preview new portable display • send all needed materials by target shipping date to avoid express mail shipments • distribute briefing packet, including training materials, to all booth staffers • set up and hold pre-show briefing meeting in office • set up in-booth conference room schedule for prearranged meetings at show • send follow-up reminder to upper management about briefing meeting; include agenda • determine date and time for exhibit; review agenda, purpose of show, demonstrations, rehearsals, show specials, etc. • ensure that you have the following items before leaving for the show: traveller's cheques, credit cards, copies of all orders and cheques for services paid in advance, phone numbers and addresses of all vendors, engineering certificate for exhibit, shipping manifest, return shipping labels, and additional badge forms				

Upon arrival	• check on freight arrival • check with hotel about reservations for staff, as well as any meeting rooms and catering orders • find service area; meet electrical and confirm date and time for electrical installation • supervise booth set-up • hold pre-show briefing and training for staff the day before the show				
During event	• reserve next year's space • conduct daily meetings with staff • confirm arrangements for booth dismantling and shipping • arrange for lead forms to be shipped back to office daily for processing				
After event	• supervise booth dismantle • handle leads • debrief staff • send thank you notes				

APPENDIX 7.1: SAMPLE BRIEFING NOTE FORMATS

Sample Information Note Format

Title: Snapshot of issue, as well as who requested the briefing note

Purpose of note: One sentence describing why this briefing note was requested

Issue: Concise summary of the circumstances that prompted the request for the briefing note— should include the problem being addressed, how the problem arose, and why it is important

Background: Bullet point list of relevant facts that led up to the situation requiring a briefing note

Current situation: Concise description of where the issue stands, focused on what is happening now and who is involved

Key considerations: Brief examination of important facts, considerations, and developments related to the issue

Key messages (if requested or required): Three or four most important things the organization should say about this issue, written in active, tight language

Author: Writer's name and phone number

Approved by: Who has approved the final version of the briefing note

Date: Date final approved briefing note was delivered

Sample House Note Format

Title: Snapshot of issue, as well as who requested the briefing note; title can include the purpose (e.g., "For Question Period")

Issue: One or two lines about the issue and why it has come up in question period

Anticipated questions: Compilation of questions most likely to be asked of the briefing note recipient by the media or the provincial or federal legislature. These questions can be broad-based and related to policy, or can be specific to a situation or issue. A good approach to building this list of questions is to use the traditional journalistic five *w*'s approach. For example:

- Who will be affected, both positively and negatively?
- What is being proposed or has happened, and what is being done about it?
- When will it happen, or come into effect?
- Where does government stand on this issue, and where will the effect be greatest?
- Why did government act/not act?
- How is this going to work, or be paid for?

Key messages: The most important things your organization has to say on the issue at hand, in order of importance; if there is a lot to say on the issue, consider organizing as primary and secondary key messages

Background: Background information for a House note should be limited to what is required to ensure the minister's understanding of the issue

Author: Writer's name and phone number

Approved by: Who has approved the final version of the briefing note

Date: Date final approved briefing note was delivered

Sample Decision Note Format

Title: Snapshot of issue, as well as who requested the briefing note

Purpose of note: One sentence describing why this briefing note was requested

Issue: Concise summary of the circumstances that prompted the request for the briefing note—should include the problem being addressed, how the problem arose, and why it is important

Background: Bullet point list of relevant facts that led up to the situation requiring a briefing note

Current situation: Concise description of where the issue stands, focused on what is happening now and who is involved

Key considerations: Brief examination of important facts, considerations, and developments related to the issue

Options/recommendations: Flowing from the analysis and using political acumen, brief list of options or a single recommendation—with risks and benefits identified—of the best next step for the organization

Key messages (if requested or required): Three or four most important things the organization should say about this issue, written in active, tight language

Author: Writer's name and phone number

Approved by: Who has approved the final version of the briefing note

Date: Date final approved briefing note was delivered

APPENDIX 7.2: SAMPLE ISSUE NOTE

Auditor General's Report Criticizes PRESTO Costs

Issue

The Auditor General of Ontario's report shows the PRESTO fare-card system and several other projects within Metrolinx's Regional Transportation Plan have experienced significant cost increases over their initial assessments.

Suggested Response

Implementing a responsible, world-class, integrated transportation system for the Greater Toronto and Hamilton Area (GTHA) is very important to Metrolinx and that is why we developed the PRESTO Next Generation.

Since we launched PRESTO six years ago, technology has advanced and the Toronto Transit Commission (TTC) and OC Transpo (Ottawa) have joined the partnership. This new, expanded system allows us to serve more riders, relieve costly road congestion, and offer convenient public transportation throughout the GTHA during the Pan Am Games in 2015.

To ensure the fiscal responsibility of such projects, Metrolinx is working closely with our government partners, managing many procurement functions in-house, and utilizing partnerships with the private sector, which will help keep the wheels moving forward.

Background

Auditor General of Ontario 2012 Annual Report

On December 12, 2012, the Office of the Auditor General of Ontario released its annual report, which includes a section about Metrolinx. The objective of the Metrolinx section was to assess whether the organization had adequate systems and procedures in place to cost-effectively implement the early stages of the Regional Transportation Plan and regularly report on progress toward achieving its goals. After reviewing several major priority transit projects contemplated within the Regional Plan's first 15 years and speaking to municipal partners and transit agencies, the report notes that Metrolinx has encountered challenges in successfully implementing some best practices. Auditor General Jim McCarter's report uses information up to March 31, 2012.[1]

PRESTO Next Generation

The City of Ottawa and the TTC had not agreed to implement the PRESTO fare card when it was initially developed. To meet the requirements to service both cities after they conditionally agreed to the partnership, PRESTO Next Generation was developed at an anticipated cost of $498 million, according to the report. In total, the overall cost of developing the original and new PRESTO systems could total more than $700 million, making it one of the more expensive fare-card systems in the world. However, increased server and system capacity is required to manage the increased volume and business requirements of the partnership with the TTC, which has over 80 percent of the GTHA's transit ridership.

A December 12, 2012, *Toronto Star* article by transportation reporter Tess Kalinowski says Metrolinx has signed an agreement giving it intellectual property rights to the PRESTO system and that the agency is managing more procurement in-house to contain costs. The Province originally contracted private provider, Accenture, to build the fare card and operate the system for 10 years for about $250 million. Instead of using Accenture to procure the 10,000 card readers needed on the TTC, Metrolinx is doing that job itself and expects to save $20 million.[2]

Serving More Riders

The number of riders using PRESTO has grown significantly since the audit period in March 2012, Metrolinx CEO Bruce McCuaig says in the *Toronto Star* article. The report indicates that only 6 percent of regional transit users, or 18 percent once GO Transit was included, had signed on to PRESTO at the time. By September, those numbers had more than doubled, to 13 percent of local riders and 60 percent of GO riders, according to McCuaig.

While overall provincial population growth has slowed, this is not consistent across the region. About 100,000 new residents are coming to the region each year after decades of under-investment and strained transit systems. Increased employment opportunities outside of downtown areas, workers pursuing specialized jobs further from their homes, and soaring oil prices are creating higher demand for convenient regional public transportation.[3]

Expanding PRESTO throughout the TTC is a bold project that will replace traditional tokens, tickets, and passes to join other world-class transit systems. The TTC estimated that once the PRESTO system is fully operational, fare collection costs could be reduced by $10 million annually from current levels. The capital investment for the TTC project will be up to $255 million and will serve 1.6 million daily customers.[4]

Costs of Congestion
The report entitled *Costs of Road Congestion in the Greater Toronto and Hamilton Area* assesses the economic impact traffic congestion has on the region. In 2006, the annual cost of congestion to commuters in the two areas was $3.3 billion, which comes from travel delays, increased impact on the environment, increased vehicle costs from travel delays, and increased chance of vehicle collisions. Additional costs to the economy as a result of commuters having less time to be productive (in the form of gross domestic product) is about $2.7 billion.[5]

The report estimates that these costs to local commuters and the economy will increase to $7.8 billion and $7.2 billion by 2031. The Big Move is a regional transportation plan that aims to vastly improve the 2031 outlook by relieving congestion, shortening travel times, reducing impact on the environment, and improving productivity. The major infrastructure construction program will also create thousands of jobs.

Air Rail Link—Pan/Parapan American Games
The Union Pearson Express (Air Rail Link) will operate on a 25-kilometre rail route and the total trip between Toronto Pearson International Airport and downtown will take 25 minutes. Trains will depart Union Station in Toronto and the airport every 15 minutes, making stops at Bloor and Weston stations.

The auditor general's report also indicates that Metrolinx's initial assumptions about projected annual ridership on the Air Rail Link between Union Station and Pearson International Airport are overly optimistic. The report estimates that the cost of a one-way ticket on the Air Rail Link could well be $28 if the aim is to break even in its first year, which will negatively affect the projected ridership capture rate. While current estimates for ridership on the Air Rail Link range from 1.2 million to 1.8 million passengers in the first year of operation, ridership is dependent on a number of variables. Metrolinx continues to evolve the model for ridership forecasting using technical analysis and expert opinion. It anticipates ridership growth over the first three years of operation.

The target completion date for this project is spring 2015, in time for the Pan/Parapan American Games to be held in the Greater Golden Horseshoe Region during summer 2015. The overall budget for the Toronto 2015 Games is $1.44 billion; the Games will bring more than 10,000 athletes and officials to the region. The Games will involve more than 17,000 volunteers, and will create economic and sport infrastructure legacies for future generations.[6]

NOTES

1 Office of the Auditor General of Ontario, "Chapter 3: Metrolinx—Regional Transportation Planning," in *Office of the Auditor General of Ontario 2012 Annual Report,* 205. www.auditor.on.ca/en/reports_en/en12/309en12.pdf

2 Tess Kalinowski. "Auditor General Says Presto Smart Card Cost Has Ballooned to $700 Million," *Toronto Star,* December 12, 2012. www.thestar.com/news/city_hall/2012/12/12/auditor_general_says_presto_smart_card_cost_has_ballooned_to_700_million.html

3 Metrolinx, "Metrolinx Five Year Strategy 2012–2017," June 2012. www.metrolinx.com/en/aboutus/publications/StrategicPlanJun2012_FINAL-EN.pdf

4 Metrolinx, "PRESTO Projects." www.metrolinx.com/en/projectsandprograms/presto/presto_projects.aspx

5 Metrolinx, "Costs of Congestion," www.metrolinx.com/en/regionalplanning/costsofcongestion/costs_congestion.aspx

6 Toronto 2015: PanAm/ParapanAm, "FAQs," www.toronto2015.org/lang/en/the-games/faq1.html

APPENDIX 8.1: QUESTION TYPES

Question type	Example
OPEN-ENDED	
Highly open-ended (virtually no restrictions)	Tell me about yourself.
	What is photography like?
	How is life in Brazil?
Moderately open-ended (restrict interviewees to a narrower response and greater focus)	Tell me about your first internship at a radio station.
	What led you to leave your career in advertising and return to school to pursue your interest in photography?
	What are the main ways that life in Brazil is different from life in the United States?
CLOSED	
Highly closed (interviewees select answers from specified choices)	How would you describe the performance of your new car? excellent, good, fair, poor
Bipolar (a special type of closed question that has only two answer options that are at opposite ends of a continuum)	Have you finished your assignment?
	Is the electricity on or off?
	Do you like or dislike your new computer?
	How old are you?
Moderately closed (ask for specific information)	In what languages are you fluent?
	When did you move to Chile?
Primary (introduce topics or new areas within a topic; can stand alone out of context and make sense)	Describe your ideal job.
	How do others describe the gardens you design?
	How did you first get interested in surfing?
Secondary (attempt to elicit more fully information asked for in a primary question or previous secondary question; may be open or closed)	Most people are uncomfortable with silence, so will try to "fill" it by talking; as the interviewer, resist the inclination to talk; instead, wait for the interviewee to continue, prompting him or her by saying, "I see," "Go on," or "Tell me more."
Nudging probes ("questions" that encourage interviewees to keep talking, but don't suggest a particular direction)	Is there anything else you would like to add?
	Are there any questions I should have asked, but didn't?
	Was there anything more you wanted to cover?
Clearinghouse probes (a check to be sure you have elicited all the information an interviewee wants to provide on a topic or in the interview)	What happened after you found your old guitar in the attic?
	Tell me more about your experiences as a bicycle messenger in New York.

Probes to increase depth of content (encourage interviewees to provide greater information about a particular topic)	Explain the process for reinstalling computer software in greater detail.
Probes to increase clarity (focus on clarifying particular words interviewees have used)	How are you defining "excellent"? What do you mean when you say the website's design is "drab"? I'm not sure I understand what you mean by "incompetent."
Probes to identify feelings (the interviewer attempts to have the interviewee explore the feelings underlying particular statements)	Why do you think you feel that way? What led to your happiness when you were a child? What were you feeling at the time?
Probes to get the other back on track (used when the interviewee veers far from the topic or doesn't answer the question the interviewer asked)	So how did that affect you? Let's return to your years as a newspaper editor. You began by talking about the first short story you wrote.
Mirror or summary questions (summarize series of answers to ensure understanding)	I'll review what you've covered... I want to be sure that my notes are accurate. First... Let me check to see if I understand your points...
Reflective questions (restate the answer to check that the interviewer has heard the interviewee correctly)	Did you say the article was old or bold? Your sister's name is Irene or Joleen? Was that in 1988 or 1998?
Hypothetical probes (pose a hypothetical situation and ask interviewees to respond)	Suppose you could live anywhere in the world. Where would that be? Imagine that you could go back in time. Who is the one person you'd like to meet? Say you've just won the lottery—$50 million. What would you do with the money?
Reactive probes (test an interviewee's reactions to a controversial statement; these should be used with care as interviewees may become offended and abruptly end the interview)	A recent newspaper article characterized your work as "unimaginative, void of any feeling, and tragically over-priced." What is your response? The university you attended has a reputation as a party school. What do you think about that? Most of the students in your classes receive As or Bs. How do you explain that?
Leading (expected answer is implied or stated in question)	Wouldn't you agree that older homes have more charm than modern ones? Don't you think essay exams are easier than multiple choice? Aren't you a big fan of the Indigo Girls?

Loaded (imply both the answer and some negative belief, behaviour, etc. on the part of the respondent; provides a strong, direct, virtual demand for a particular answer; often include emotionally charged language, name-calling, entrapment)	Are you still as boring as you were 10 years ago? How can you rot your brain by watching that idiotic television show? So you're going to take that worthless idea of yours to the boss?
Tag (inserted at end of answer; often weaken impact of answer)	You agree with my assessment, right? I feel that's a good idea, don't you? You don't have to answer that question, okay?
Multiple (two or more questions asked at the same time; also called double-barrelled questions)	How did you like your trip to Hollywood? What was the most interesting part? Meeting the star of the movie, getting to walk around the movie lot, being mistaken for a star? Name your three favourite authors, the books you like best by each author, and why you like those books. Tell me about the first house you remodelled. Where was it located? Why did you choose that house?

Source: Adapted from Stephanie J. Coopman. 2006. "Conducting the Information Interview." Rogue Communication. www.roguecom.com/interview/index.html

APPENDIX 8.2: COMMUNICATIONS EVALUATION TOOLS SUMMARY

Method	Description	When to use
Surveys	Using simple and inexpensive technology, a basic survey can consist primarily of multiple-choice questions that can be administered online or in person with results available within days. Tactics for selecting survey participants include: pre-determined population (e.g., a group of 10 policy-makers); a sample from the general public (e.g., random users who enter your website); snowball sampling, where you survey one person, ask if he or she knows someone else to survey; and intercept survey, where you "intercept" members of your audience at a particular location appropriate to your communication activities and survey them on the spot.	Most appropriate in the planning stages and during implementation. Surveys are useful for categorizing and comparing data at a given point in time, as well as over a period of time. For this reason, they can be very helpful in establishing baselines and for monitoring progress.
Interviews	Interviewing consists of selecting a handful of individuals who represent the base of your audience and asking targeted yet open-ended questions. This will allow you to receive better insight into how people are responding to your communication activities.	Appropriate at any stage of planning or implementation. For example, you are about to draft a new institutional communication plan, but you first want to know how your key stakeholders and audiences view your organization and its leadership, contributions, successes, and failures. Interviews with representative constituents will give you insight into these areas.
Focus groups	You may want to bring together a group of people from your audience to test new messages, or to have a directed group discussion about your communication activities. Unlike interviews, focus groups are moderated by a facilitator and allow people to bounce ideas off one another, building a richer set of data. There are professionals who specialize in conducting focus groups who can help you design one or more sessions tailored to your needs, as well as to analyze the results.	Appropriate during planning and early implementation, or when you are ready to advance to a new phase of your communication efforts. Focus groups are also especially useful when you want to test a specific message, tactic, or approach. For instance, you are planning a three-year campaign to generate support for medical treatment for children living with HIV/AIDS. You have come up with two different creative approaches and are not sure which one would better speak to your audience.
Observation	You may want to observe individuals or groups to see how they are responding to certain messages. This is particularly useful with communication initiatives that involve participatory discussions, public forums, and debates.	Appropriate during implementation. For instance, your organization offers a training program on environmental issues for high school students. After the training, the students are expected to return to their schools and conduct their own awareness campaigns. You are interested in learning more about how the students are doing back at school, and whether the messages they are using are effectively reaching their peers. A trained observer could visit a sample of schools and witness how the students organize their peers to take action on Earth Day.

Quantitative data collection	Websites, blogs, and other social networks allow you to collect useful data. For instance, on a website, you can track the number of daily or monthly visitors and page views. For blogs and social networks, you can track the number of subscribers and number of comments left by visitors. Additionally, you can refer to online services that rank blogs' popularity and use these ratings to compare your blog to others in the field.	Appropriate at any stage of planning or implementation. You want to know if your readership is growing and whether the number of comments is rising.
Quantitative data analysis	While it may sound daunting, you can use the data collected from web-tracking or media-monitoring services to conduct statistical analysis of the possible relationships between your communication activities and external changes.	Appropriate during planning and at any stage of implementation. For example, six months after launching your blog, you want to test whether there is a connection between increase in comments and the ranking of your blog. Does the number of weekly posts relate to the frequency with which others reference your blog? Statistical analysis can explore these relationships.
Content analysis	To assess the quality and tone of your media coverage, or to review the content of specific programming that reaches your audience, this technique can provide powerful insights. However, the process is often time-consuming and the people carrying out the analysis need to be well trained in the technique to ensure objectivity and consistency.	Appropriate during early stages and throughout implementation. For example, media coverage of your issue has increased, but you sense that negative coverage is dominating the air and radio waves. To find out if this is the case, so you turn to content analysis.

Source: Adapted from Communications Consortium Media Center. 2004. *Guidelines for Evaluating Nonprofit Communications Efforts.* Washington, DC: Communications Consortium Media Center. www.innonet.org/resources/files/Eval_comm_efforts.pdf

COPYRIGHT ACKNOWLEDGEMENTS

Feature 2.1: Letter, Rob Morris Mandate, by Brad Wall, Premier of Saskatchewan, 2007. Reprinted with permission.

Feature 5.2: "Yukon Government Gives Mining Exploration Program a Boost," Yukon Government, January 29, 2013. Reprinted with permission.

Feature 5.3: "Saskatchewan Remains On Track for Balanced Budget," Government of Saskatchewan, February 15, 2013. Reprinted with permission.

Feature 5.4: "Department of Human Resources: Report on the Staff Retention Policy Year Ending March 31, 2011," Northwest Territories, Department of Human Resources, 2011. Reprinted with permission.

Feature 5.5: "Submission of the New Brunswick Department of Agriculture, Aquaculture and Fisheries to the External Review on Northern Shrimp," New Brunswick Department of Agriculture, Aquaculture and Fisheries, 2012.

Feature 5.6: "E-Money," Bank of Canada, 2014. Reprinted with permission.

Feature 5.7: "City Hall Wall of Windows—FAQs," City of Calgary. Reprinted with permission.

Feature 5.8: "2009 Organic Products Regulations: Questions and Answers," Canadian Food Inspection Agency, 2009. Reprinted with permission.

Feature 5.9: "Provincial Public Safety Telecommunications Network (PPSTN): Questions and Answers," Ministry of Government Relations, Saskatchewan, 2010.

Feature 5.10: "Dear NDP: CIDA Does Not Need Your Economic Advice," Julian Fantino, in *Huffington Post*, December 21, 2012.

Feature 5.11: "Letter: Kelowna's Last Public Post Office Moving Closer to Its Demise," Dawn Klappe, in *Kelowna Capital News*, July 4, 2013. Reprinted with permission.

Feature 5.12: "Councillor Explains," Nando Iannicci, in *Mississauga News*, March 28, 2013. Reprinted with permission.

Feature 5.13: "Speech Given by Mayor Al McDonald Ground Breaking Ceremony Airport Industrial Business Park," City of North Bay. November 18, 2011. Reprinted with permission.

Feature 5.14: "JFK, Berlin, 1963: The Right Time. The Right Place. The Right Message," Andrew Cohen, in *The Globe and Mail*, June 25, 2013. Reprinted with permission.

Features 7.1, 7.2, 7.4, 7.5, 7.8, 7.9: "Example of a Briefing Note," Theresa McKeown, in Public Sector Writing. Reprinted with permission.

Features 7.3, 7.6, 7.7: "Memo Warned Toews of Risks in Dropping Gun Show Rules," David McKie, in *CBC News*, November 13, 2012. Reprinted with permission of David McKie.

Feature 9.1: "Policy Summary No. 33: Use of Social Media in the BC Public Service." Copyright © Province of British Columbia. All rights reserved. Reproduced with permission of the Province of British Columbia.

Figure 9.2: "Ontario Ministry of Labour Posting Response Chart" from Bruce Skeaff, *The Challenges of Leadership: Overcoming Obstacles on the Path to Social Media Success*, paper presented at the Public Sector Social Media, 2012 Conference. © Queen's Printer for Ontario, 2012. Reproduced with Permission.

Appendix 5.1: "Social Media in the Public Sector," Remarks by the Deputy Head and Librarian and Archivist of Canada, Library and Archives Canada, 2012. © Government of Canada. Reproduced with the permission of Library and Archives Canada (2014).

Appendix 5.2: "Mayor's Speech—Operations Budget 2013: Managing Our City's Growth Responsibly," City of Whitehorse, 2013.